RANDOM THOUGHTS
The Humanity of Teaching

BY LOUIS SCHMIER

MAGNA PUBLICATIONS, INC.
Madison, Wisconsin

RANDOM THOUGHTS:
THE HUMANITY OF TEACHING
by Louis Schmier
Professor of History
Valdosta State University

Magna Publications, Inc.
Madison, Wisconsin

Magna Publications, Inc.
2718 Dryden Drive
Madison, WI 53704-3086
608/246-3580

Design by Tamara L. Cook

Library of Congress Cataloging–in–Publication Data
Schmier, Louis, 1940 –
       Random thoughts: the humanity of teaching/by Louis Schmier.
          p.   cm.
       ISBN 0-912150-43-2
       1. Teachers — United States.   2. Teaching — United States.
       I. Title.
       LB1775.2.S35   1995
       371.1'02'0973—dc20

                                                        95-24081
                                                           CIP

To my son, Robby,
who entered our lives as a precious gift,
who has made me grow,
who has forged my moral core,
who has made me think and feel and learn anew,
and when I stumble has taught me
humility and compassion.

CONTENTS

INTRODUCTION

by Richard Garlikov

*C*an someone be teaching if no one is learning, or even if only a few students are learning, or if students are learning a very minimal amount? Of course, we *call* people teachers who have the appropriate training and contract, and who collect a paycheck for showing up at a school every day and making presentations to students — even when those students don't learn much, if anything, from those presentations. Even students will call someone a teacher when they have not learned anything from him or her, as when a student says something like, "Mr. Barnes is such a terrible geometry teacher. The only thing he has taught me all year is to hate going to his class and to hate geometry." Unless Mr. Barnes just comes in and talks about the weather or politics, students will still call him a geometry teacher — even if he does not teach *them* any geometry.

Perhaps it is time to rethink what we *should* call teaching. Just as it sounds odd for a student who fails Mr. Barnes' course to say, "Mr. Barnes taught me geometry," it should sound just as odd to say, "These students don't learn geometry, though Mr. Barnes teaches it to them." Making a presentation is not the same as teaching if that presentation has no result in learning, and if it has no chance of having a result.

Now it may be that no one could reasonably be expected to get certain students to learn in a class, or any students to learn much in a class. So we may simply want to call "teaching" any attempt to teach material to students, as long as some learn some of it, or as long as "better" students would have learned it with the same teaching methods. Better teachers, then, might be those who make more entertaining, witty, erudite, or interesting attempts to teach, regardless of how much more, if any, might be learned by students. The best teachers would, in this interpretation of teaching, simply be the best presenters.

But there are some of us who believe that this is a mistaken way to view what teaching is about or ought to be about, particularly as a greater percentage of the population is being encouraged to get more and more formal education. The effort by high schools and colleges should not be just to weed out those who cannot learn by certain supposedly traditional methods, but to find more and more methods by which all those who can learn will. This is not just what *good* teaching is about, but what *teaching*, if it is to be called teaching at all, is about. If there are methods available to teach geometry to Mr. Barnes' class so that all, or at least many more, students learn it — and if Mr. Barnes does not successfully seek or use any of those methods — then it doesn't matter how much geometry Mr. Barnes teaches a few students, or could have taught some other students, using the techniques and presentations that he uses. Mr. Barnes has *not* taught this class of students geometry.

The question is whether there are such methods, and that is a difficult question to answer sometimes. But the question should not be whether a teacher has to use, or seek to use, a method that is likely to work in order to be called a teacher. The answer to that should be a resounding "Yes!" If presenters present information that has no meaning for students — and if those presenters do not even care that it has no meaning — then they should not be considered teachers, at least not for the particular students in their classrooms. They are not just bad teachers; they are not teachers at all.

To those who narrowly view teaching as a job or even a career, this idea of what it is to be a teacher is often repugnant. They merely want to know their material and to present it in whatever way will allow the "good" or "average" students to get it, at least for the tests and exams. What happens to those who don't get it, or what happens to the students' "knowledge" after the course is over, is of no concern to them. They want to present material or assign material, and if students don't learn it, that is the students' problem, not theirs. They don't want to be "teaching kindergarten" or having to be "nursemaids."

As you will see, quickly and consistently as you read this book, Louis Schmier is not someone who believes that teaching is merely showing up, presenting relevant material, testing it, giving grades, collecting a paycheck, and getting promoted. For him, it is a constant struggle — often an agonizing struggle — to reach students and to figure out ways to reach more, to reach all; to reach them in order to teach them. It is not his intention to water down his course content, but to make rigorous content accessible to all the students he can. You will see that he views his role to be not only teaching those competent and confident students who will work at learning and who already know how to learn, but getting all students to be competent, confident, curious, and inspired lifelong students, who learn as much as they can, who can extract meaning from what they learn, and who can meaningfully apply it, not simply recite it. That is not an easy task in today's world, particularly with students who have not previously had the most meaningful, beneficial, stimulating, challenging, and successful learning experiences or lived in environments conducive to encouraging study and reflection.

I first came across Louis' "Random Thoughts" as he shared them with the many thousands of us who use the Internet, the electronic "Information Highway." There are many groups of people, frequently teachers and students, who regularly communicate with each other by computer on the Internet, posting messages for all members or for specific individual members of a group to read. Louis posts his Random Thoughts to a number of these "discussion groups," and the responses are almost as interesting as the messages themselves. One person wrote that Louis' messages were the best part of her week or month when they arrived, and that they always gave her hope and encouragement to be the kind of teacher she wants to be — encouragement she does not get in the school district where she works. I myself always save Louis' messages until I am done reading all of my other electronic mail for that day, so that I can savor them in unhurried reflection. He expresses ideas about teaching that I share, and says them in ways I often have not conceived of or considered. I find them always a treat.

Yet there are those other "teachers" who view Louis as — in the words of one professor I hope my children never have — "that human computer virus" who afflicts their screens with unwanted ideas, and who perhaps torments whatever consciences they have about teaching ineffectively year after year without trying to change how they do it and without even caring whether they reach more students or not, because they think it is the students' fault that they do not learn. They would rather place blame on others than do the work that alters the circumstances in order to make blame unnecessary.

Louis calls his Internet postings Random Thoughts because they occur to him randomly as he reflects on the day's particular student joys and triumphs, or upon the anguish of his own difficulties and perceived failures in reaching students or helping them learn. And he calls them Random Thoughts because he has no preconceived, systematic pattern to their content and sees none in them. But I do not consider them random, because Louis is always thinking about his students and his teaching. He may have his more worthy ideas randomly, but he does not just reflect randomly on his teaching.

I believe there are clear, consistent themes in his reflections and his writing. They are all about nurturing the blossoming of human beings whose lives touch his. He is interested in getting through to all his students and in finding out what is required to do that. He believes all of them can be successful if they are reached and if they can be inspired and nurtured in ways he is certain must exist and in ways that are within his own reach to provide when necessary. He is intent on finding out what the students' needs are and on finding out what is needed by him, and within him, to meet those needs.

And though he teaches college-level history, what he is really teaching, and modeling, is what we can learn from history and from each other about what it is to be the best kind of human being — one who continually tries to do better; one who is competent to recognize and do good; one who has integrity, conscience, and commitment; one who cares about others and can work with others in cooperation, courage, encouragement, enjoyment, harmony, mutual growth, and mutual fulfillment as far as the human condition permits.

What follows in **Random Thoughts** is an eloquent expression of the reflections Louis Schmier has had so far about teaching and the actions he has taken to pursue and fulfill those thoughts. He would be the first to say that there are effective teachers who teach differently from him, who ask different things of their students, and who do different things in their classrooms. His is not meant to be the only possible teaching model. But I believe that there can be no effective teachers who do not have the same concerns and the same passions about teaching and about their students' learning and blossoming as Louis does.

In that sense, this book is a guide to teaching for anyone who wants to be not only a good teacher, but a teacher, worthy of the title at all.

Richard Garlikov
Birmingham, Alabama

PART ONE

Wednesday, 13 July 1994

A SEARCH FOR MYSELF

*T*he pre-dawn moments, when I power-walk in the streets — where each Random Thought originates — are precious to me. I have come to look forward to that little less than an hour it takes me to complete one of my six-mile routes. For me, an early riser, that wee hour of the coming day has become a time to watch and feel things beginning to move forward. I feel beautiful and fresh and good. After all, I haven't done anything yet; I haven't ruined anything, said anything wrong, made any mistakes, or done anything rotten.

I walk to feel alive, not just to live. Walking is my spiritual aerobics. I exercise as much to keep my soul in youthful shape as to keep my aging 53-year-old body trim. It is my quiet time, my reflection time — what I call my "just to …" time. I think everyone should have their own "just to …" time and scenery. For me, it's a cleansing, creative, and nurturing time to reflect on the unknown adventures of the coming day and the lingerings of yesterday. I lose myself in a moving capsule of silence, to be alone with myself, to continue a never-ending inward journey in search of myself that I started three years ago, and, if I'm both courageous and lucky, to discover a bit more of my true self and about the mission of my craft. Those moments on the street are my time to float free, to drift with the currents of my spirit and emotions, unfettered by the cluttering flotsam of noise, movement, people, sights, or schedules. I just leave the tap to my spirit open, walk, and let whatever is in the pipelines spontaneously and honestly flow out.

So, here I am, with the first introductory Random Thought shortly after dawn, just off the streets of graying Valdosta, Georgia, after a walk — at home, sitting in front of the computer in my sweat-soaked grubbies, sipping a cup of freshly made coffee and letting my fingertips do their own walking on the keyboard as they translate into electronic bites the words and feelings that poured out while I was walking.

It was a warm 79 degrees and a drenching 72 percent humidity this morning. A tepid, light, steamy fog hung in the air. Everything looked muted in the faint, soft, early-dawn glow. Swarms of annoying gnats and clouds of attacking mosquitoes, bred by incessant afternoon storms, billowed along my route. A person doesn't just walk, but wades and swats and whiffs along this asphalt swamp. "Comfortable" and "weather" are not words used together during the summer months down here in south Georgia.

This sultry morning, early in my route, I was thinking. "How the hell did I get myself into this?" I asked myself in an almost castigating tone. "Here I am almost three years after I started withdrawing from the devouring publish-or-perish rat race to devote everything I had to teaching — struggling to write introductory Random Thoughts to a collection of reflections that I never had any intention of publishing." It was just then that I stumbled. As I walked on, it occurred to me that I had tripped over a branch that I had not caused to fall from the tree above, that at my age I still had sufficient reflexes and agility not to have fallen flat on my face, and that I continued walking along a route I had laid out on streets others had designed and built. I started thinking about how strange and twisting my life's route has been, how chance and karma and maybe destiny, as well as the thoughts and actions of other people, interplay with my inner self, with my strengths and weaknesses, with my talents and inabilities, with my determination and doubt, with my courage and timidity, and with my loves and dislikes, to lead me through a little bit of comedy, a little bit of satire, a little bit of tragedy, a little bit of high adventure, and a little bit of drama.

As I look back on the slightly more than five decades of my life, and browse through its chapters, they seem to have closed and opened without my permission and without any conceivable plan. The words "unexpected," "unintentional," and "unforeseen" seem to have played prominent roles in almost all of them. Many were the times that I asked, as if someone were listening, "What if I hadn't done this?" or, "What would have happened if I hadn't gone here?" or, "Where would I be if I hadn't known so-and-so?" I sometimes almost get the feeling that someone is telling me to get my hands off my life, that it's none of my damn business. I can't plan it or control it to make the "right" personal and career moves — those self-serving, easy, safe, and comfortable decisions — and still reach my full potential. I should just get out of the way, go with the flow, and get on with this wondrous, unnerving, mysterious trip. It's almost as if someone moves in on me every now and then at will, shouts "Boo!" in my face, and startles the hell out of me just as I am comfortably and safely settling in. It's like being told to get onto a bus and to say to the driver, "Take me wherever you're going," and just sitting back and going for an adventurous ride to that somewhere called destiny or potential. Now, as I go back over my life's table of contents, I think that maybe the paths I walked were far less haphazard than they ostensibly look. Maybe everything was laid out to arrive at this particular chapter in my life when I take great pride in being told by a student named Barbara, "You're not a professor, you're a teacher."

That gets me thinking about a portion of a letter written to me eight months ago by Barbara, whom you'll meet later in the book in a Random Thought entitled "Barbara." The letter is pinned to the bulletin board in my office. I've read those words so often that I've memorized them:

I want to be a teacher, and I want to try to teach like you.
I want to know, how did you become a professor? When did
you change and become a teacher? And I've learned that there is
a heck of a difference between a professor and a teacher. And I'd
like to know about why you teach the way you do. I think most
of what you do is because of who *YOU* (her emphasis) are.
But who are *YOU*? I'd like to really know more about who *YOU*
really are.

"But who are *YOU*?" It's an uncomfortable question, a releasing question,
a challenging question. I have been struggling to write these introductory
comments for some time. I now realize why writing this part of the book is
as comfortable as walking in the south Georgia summer weather. It is far
more difficult than I thought it would be, because it is putting unexpected
demands on my sense of self, testing my identity, and challenging my
integrity. It reminds me that the lease on comfort is short. It is easy, and
humbling, to forget how quickly you become nervous when you are
unsure whether others will share your passions, understand your insights,
accept your beliefs, and consider your teaching techniques.

But I realize this morning that this introductory part of the book isn't the
problem — it's *me*. It's not the external pressures I feel, but the internal
ones. I've been subconsciously trying to write defensively, in case I was
offensive, by separating myself from this writing, to distance it from *me*,
to hide *me*, to protect *me*. I've felt threatened by *me* because I'm afraid of
disappointing myself. I've been trying not to be *me*. I see now how that
undertow for approval and acceptance apparently has been getting
dangerous. I have been letting myself get too sensitive about the currents
of possible response to my words. Of course, by *my words*, I really mean
me. I have been unwittingly threatened with getting stuck in the quicksand
of caution, ego, and image. But my conscience won't let me do it.

So I've decided that I have to write more *from me* and less *for you*. Unless
I take you on an honest, and uncomfortable, journey inside my being,
where my personal and professional spirit — and the Random Thoughts
— originate, these introductory words will be hollow, spiritless, and meaningless. So it is not about style, content, intent, or even about the Random
Thoughts themselves that I now want to write. It is *me* about whom I want
to talk. Because whatever the Random Thoughts are, as Barbara so astutely
observed, I carry them inside of *me* every hour of every day, inside and
outside class, on and off campus. They flow out from the depths of *me*.
They are *me*.

The Random Thoughts were unexpectedly born out of personal trauma and
family crisis that exploded into a spiritual and emotional nova of liberating

self-reflection, self-examination, and spiritual revelation that ultimately was to shake me out of personal and professional stagnation. It occurred on a fateful October day in 1991, during a challenge session at The Family Learning Center at Hyde School in Bath, Maine. It forced — and continually forces — me to think about how I label myself, how that labeling affects how I perceive myself, how I expect myself to behave, how I label others, and how that labeling affects my attitudes toward others.

The path that led to Hyde was not a delightful stroll down the yellow brick road. From the fall of 1990 through the summer of 1991, everything in my life seemed to be coming apart. My wife was still wrestling with the recent death of her father after a decade-long struggle with cancer. She had gone back to school and was struggling to change the direction and meaning of her life. She was barely coping with a new job as a legal assistant to a leading lawyer. She was traumatized by the unexpected death of her younger sister during routine gall bladder surgery. She was worried about her mother, who was having an almost impossible time dealing with the compressed succession of tragic loss. My older son, Michael, was experiencing a serious personal anxiety crisis while away at the University of North Carolina-Chapel Hill.

I was buckling mentally, emotionally, and physically under the weight of having to be the family's tower of strength. My scholarly and teaching activities were becoming less satisfying, less fulfilling, and less meaningful, and I didn't know why. And finally, the eight-year, daily, consuming struggle my wife and I had fought over our then 14-year-old son, Robby, was reaching a climax.

Robby has a condition called Attention Deficit Hyperactivity Disorder. It was not suspected until he was six years old. His condition, however, continued to be improperly diagnosed, improperly treated, improperly addressed, improperly understood, ignored, and/or denied. We watched and listened helplessly as so many professionals fumbled about. There were so many offices, so many experts, so many tests, so many quick cures, so many regimens, so much medication, so much counseling, so much advice, so many promises, so much desperation to believe, so many hopes, so many disappointments.

We watched and listened helplessly as this highly intelligent, compassionate, sensitive, and vulnerable human being was stripped of his dignity, swept up, and thrown away like a broken branch by so many middle-school and high-school educational groundskeepers who were merely interested in maintaining the neatness of their manicured institutional landscape. We had to contend with so many teachers and administrators who were more concerned with weeding out than nurturing, more concerned with discipline and order in their classes than with his human growth, more concerned with their instruction than his learning, more concerned with their comfort and convenience than his struggle and hurt, more concerned with their control than his empowerment, more concerned with their pay stubs than the cost to his psyche, more concerned with their feelings than with his spirit.

In countless and fruitless meetings with teachers and administrators, we requested, pleaded, demanded, and confronted. We had to helplessly hear them tell us or whisper in his ear or publicly proclaim aloud in class or gossip to each other that he "needs better parents," "needs more of the paddle than his pills," that he was a loser destined to fail, wasn't worthy of their concern, had no right to achieve, had few prospects for achievement, should have little expectation for success, was someone no one could do anything with, and would likely wind up in the gutter.

He was shunned by the "better" students, made into a leprous outcast by so many teachers, shunted into meaningless "study management" classes, frequently hidden away in ISS (in-school suspension) cells, at times exiled from the campus, and always thrown into depressing isolation and loneliness. Those words, gestures, and actions were poisoned spears that were mortal blows to his spirit.

When he was bled white of all self-worth, and he said that he believed that his biggest mistake was being born, my wife and I cried uncontrollably.

These were the dark, struggling years during which Robby lost all self-esteem, trust in others, trust in himself, focus, meaning, purpose, direction, fight, dignity, and pride; when he just plain gave up on himself; when the grimaces and growls of resentment, frustration, and anger replaced the childhood smiles; when the melancholy of resignation eclipsed all joy; when the sorrow of hurt, shame, and despair dulled the sparkle of laughter; when he slipped from enrichment classes, bounced down class levels, landed in some remedial classes, cut classes, flunked course after course, and failed an entire grade; when he got in with a bad crowd, became a "head-banger," costumed himself in long hair and leather jacket and motorcycle boots, challenged all authority, had trouble with the law, got into drinking and smoking and sex, and roamed the streets late at night.

Everything was crashing down around us. There were no reassuring voices, and there was no understanding and comforting presence, no rescuing guidance, no saving vision. We were at each other's throats and blaming each other. I have never felt such fear, pain, confusion, frustration, helplessness, and anxiety in my life. I couldn't get away from it; I couldn't make it go away. Nothing was able to satisfy me, to fulfill me, to make me happy.

7

But I couldn't show it. I had no one with whom I could share the heavy burden of my feelings, and I felt so alone. My wife could not take on any more; my son Michael was away at UNC and had more than enough to handle; my friends could not and did not understand. I was expected to be the family's Olympian, able and willing to take the load off others. It was a role I tragically, and willingly, played. After all, I was a Ph.D., a scholar with a national reputation in my field of research, a leader on the campus, a crackerjack teacher. I could answer questions, solve problems, bear loads. I could handle the tears, pain, and sorrow. It was expected of me; I demanded it of myself. Ph.D., frailty, and confusion are not synonymous terms. And, though I didn't know it at the time, it made me feel needed and important.

I don't want to say that we were individually and collectively dysfunction al. I don't think you can get the full understanding of what we were experiencing with the word "dysfunctional." Dysfunctional sounds so cold, so detached, so clinical, so sterile. It's a euphemism that avoids the humanity, emotion, and pain of the experience. Life was truly hard to bear.

There were the endless nights of uneasy sleep, wondering why, listening for the slightest sound of Robby leaving the house, waiting for the sound of him returning, or waiting for the police to telephone and ask us to pick him up. The days were blighted by darkness. Many were the times I beat my fists on the walls, cried in my office, and cursed God at the top of my voice in the backyard for tormenting this innocent child. The pain had a psychic intensity that frightened me. There was such grief and fear that I covered my eyes and plugged my ears and wrapped myself in padding so that I would not see or hear or feel the agony. I didn't want to think, to feel, to touch at all. There were times I thought I was among the walking dead because I had so shut down.

Then, by the merest of chance, after a long search we found a very special school — Hyde School in Bath, Maine — with teachers who were even more special human beings — caring, compassionate, understanding, and dedicated, but tough and demanding. Hurt, desperate, and nearly broken, we had lost all belief in miracles, and almost all hope. Nevertheless, seeing Robby once again in handcuffs and being told that he had flunked the entire ninth grade, we knew time had run out. To save our son, to rescue him from what seemed to be dismal prospects of either prison or a grave, to give him one last chance at the future, we took a chance and sacrificed our future. We cashed in our retirement nest egg and enrolled him in Hyde.

It didn't take long to discover that Hyde School isn't just any ordinary private prep school for troubled children. It's not a place where parents send their children to "get fixed" by someone else. Parents do not just "dump" their troubled children at Hyde's door and then drive off into the vacationing sunset. They must "enroll" at Hyde themselves. They sign on for a difficult, continuing, and intensive program of family seminars and challenge groups in which they and their children struggle to face and truly get to know themselves and each other. The program consists of daily journal writing, fall and spring family weekends at Hyde, annual visits to Hyde's Family Learning Center, participation in monthly regional meetings of Hyde parents, and annual regional retreats.

That's how I came to be sitting in my first challenge session at the Hyde Family Learning Center. I have to admit that I was sitting there "just for Robby," smugly going through the motions. I was just putting in the time, winging it, and faking it.

Then it happened.

I was leaning back nonchalantly in my chair, listening to other parents, thinking, "What 'touchy-feely' bullshit. All these people with problems with divorce, alcohol, drugs, and/or abuse, spilling their guts about their parents and childhood. Susie and I are lucky we don't have any of that."

Suddenly, without warning, someone or something screamed "BOO!" so loud that my ears hurt and my soul reverberated. It was what my son Michael would call "one of those sudden, Hollywood-type moments" when I instantly saw and recognized my basic, tragic flaw. It happened almost as an overwhelming, sudden, unexpected, uncontrollable, painful volcanic eruption of honesty about myself that I couldn't stop from occurring. I don't know what triggered it at that moment. Maybe all those years in the fires of emotional, spiritual, and mental hell had unknowingly "softened" me up, as a metallurgist works his metal in the furnace before reshaping it.

I lurched forward in my chair. As tears poured from my eyes, I heard myself releasing an anger and resentment at being treated as if I had committed some crime for having exited the womb as the second son. I could hear the sounds of me blurting out long-buried frustration, hurt, and sadness at being the second son — "dismissed," "ignored," "forgotten," and "taken for granted." I stunned myself by openly admitting, for the first time, to deep-seated feelings as a child of having been "home alone" in my home, of feeling unloved by my parents, of feeling unworthy of their love, of being increasingly shunned by my older brother — who increasingly saw me as a challenge, as he was increasingly unable to live up to his top billing as the First Born — and consequently of having a strong need to be important, needed, seen, and loved. Something had taken control. It was as if another person, the *real* me, imprisoned and hidden inside me all these decades, had broken free and had stepped outside, without my permission, to expose himself.

It was a painful moment. I saw all so clearly how the dead hands of the past were controlling me in the present. I saw how I carried all the feelings of insecurity, self-doubt, and diminished self-worth wherever I went — how all the needs to be important, needed, seen, and loved, which I had been denying and hiding all these decades behind masks of humor, degrees and résumés, and a position of authority, influenced everything that I believed and did, both personally and professionally.

Someone or something had started performing spiritual surgery. It opened personal issues and the unresolved resentment — long suppressed, denied, or ignored — that were crucial in shaping who I was and what I did, and were crucial to face if I was to reshape both myself and what I do.

For the next few days at Hyde, I felt myself being stripped to my core spiritually. The regional wilderness retreat in the mountains of north Georgia a week later — which you will read about in two Random Thoughts entitled "The Climb" and "Blueberries" — continued this deep, painful, and honest ongoing conversation with myself. I started a never-ending challenge of my values, a review of my priorities, a ripping away of my masks, a questioning of my identity, an examination of my purposes, a review of my life's personal and professional goals, an identification of my weaknesses, and a discovery of my strengths.

This isn't something that I enjoy admitting, but I'm not embarrassed by it. It was and still is part of me. From that moment on, as a colleague wrote about me, there was and is what a jazz musician might call a personal, professional, and curricular "back beat" of words that keep challenging me, keep me growing and learning: Who am I? Why am I doing what I am doing? How do I feel about what I and others are doing? Why do I teach? What is meaningful about what I do? What are things I need to do, should do, and can do if I am to have the chance of being a truer person as well as a truer teacher?

I consider this breakthrough one of the most important personal and professional moments of my life. On that day at Hyde, I started hammering away at and tearing down the walls, and I started to throw the locks and keys away. It was a time to find the strength and courage to admit that I needed to face up to and start letting go of the old illusions and fears, for overwhelming and new possibilities and potentials. As Pink Floyd's lyrics from "Coming Back to Life" say, "I knew the moment had arrived for killing the past and coming back to life." While I knew that not everything could be changed immediately or even completely, however I faced it, nothing could be changed until and unless I faced it and continue to face it.

Enough for now. I'm drained. More sometime later when the spirit strikes me.

Tuesday, 26 July 1994

FROM PROFESSOR TO TEACHER

I haven't been thinking about much else except Barbara's questions: "How did you become a professor?" "When did you change and become a teacher?" They are tough questions. The answers are tougher. To answer them, I have to bare some more of my soul. It was a mentally and emotionally rough walk this morning, and the incessant early-morning heat, humidity, and bugs had little to do with it.

I have to admit that I did not go into academia like some intellectual Sir Galahad in quest of the Holy Grail of wisdom. I became a history major while attending Adelphi College in Garden City, New York, only because I screwed up my pre-med program and any chances of going to medical school. I was a World War II military history buff as a teenager, nothing else interested me, and my sophomore advisor said I had to major in something. I backed into academia on the rebound, then, for want of something else to do. I didn't want to go into the military because I had heard something about a place called Indochina; I was afraid I didn't have what it took to survive and succeed in the sordid world of business; I didn't know what I wanted to do with my life; and I discovered the ivory tower was a safe haven from the stress of life.

I did not get a Ph.D. because I thought I could be a superb scholar and a modern-day Herodotus or Pliny. It was all Dr. Birdsall Viault's fault. He was a young history professor at Adelphi in whose class I had accidentally enrolled. He took me under his wing. He was impressed with my exam essays, research papers, and class performance. He said I was a good researcher, critical thinker, and writer. He told me that I would make a good historian. He strongly suggested that I go on for my master's degree after I graduated from Adelphi. So I went to St. John's University, only because it was inexpensive and it was closest to where I worked to earn my tuition. And when I completed my master's a year later, and went to Dr. Viault and asked, "Now what?" he replied, "Go south, young man." So I went into the unknown wilds of what I thought was the "uncivilized" South to an idyllic place called the University of North Carolina, which I knew nothing about, to get another advanced degree that meant little to me and with which I did not know what I would do.

I did not go into the classroom on a mission or with a sense of calling to instill the awe and wonder of learning in the coming generation. Like most graduates, I was being groomed as a research scholar. I was dumped, untrained, into a classroom — first at nearby North Carolina State University and then at UNC — to teach a freshman survey Western civilization history course that few students, professors, or graduate students took seriously. We learned on the job, without guidance, by the seat of our pants, more often than not by aping our lecturing professors.

Once inside the classroom, however, I stayed there because I could hide from both others and myself. I could be something I had always dreamed of being. I never had the dedication or discipline or self-confidence to cut an academic swath. I was at best a mediocre athlete. To gain attention in high school, I had resorted to humor and had become the class clown, a punster, and a prankster of such repute that they talked of my antics long after I graduated. Being voted by my high school teachers as one of the college-bound students least likely to succeed didn't help shore up my weakened sense of self-worth any more than did my lackluster performance in college. At UNC, one of the top universities in the country, I had this deep-seated fear that, being surrounded by smart people, it would be just a matter of time before I would be detected. I discovered, however, that the door to the classroom was locked tighter than the door to the bedroom. Even my professors didn't dare invade the inner sanctum of *my* classroom.

The classroom became the one place where I could compensate, feed my ego, and fill a void. I was important in there; it was the one place where I felt important. I could be a leader and students would follow. In the classroom, I was the sage on stage, at the head of the class. I was needed, looked up to, seen, wanted. I could be smart and look smart, and no one would challenge me; I could exhibit self-confidence and no one would be the wiser. So, contrary to the advice of my professors, I decided that I would concentrate on my teaching rather than on research.

Nevertheless, in the process I desecrated myself. All around me were the subtle signs that I was a failure, for everywhere I turned I continued to be haunted by the image of being a second son. I did not see the Ph.D. so much as a membership card in an exclusive intellectual club as a second-class degree for cerebral second sons, compared with the more prestigious and lucrative M.D. so wished for me — and them — by my parents. The classroom had little glitter of prestige. By all of society's standards, it was a place for life's second sons. There was the pervasive attitude that when a person couldn't do anything else, he or she could always teach. In academia — whose priorities dwelled on the length of the scholarly résumé of awards, grants, consultancies, conference papers, and publications — the teacher was treated as the second son. Moreover, my discipline was often academia's second son, at the low end of both the social totem pole and the salary scale. The imagery of being the second son came to me every time I heard the demeaning statements about the uselessness of history and people's dislike for what one student described as a "boring memorization of a bunch of stupid dates, places, and names." It was a discipline that always had to fight for recognition in a society that demanded practical application.

Where I landed carried with it the image of the second son, not the fabled fame, fortune, and prestige that I thought I needed to bring me attention, happiness, peace, well-being, and love. I wished for things I could not have; I tried to become something I was not; I dreamed and fantasized of doing things I could not; and I failed to appreciate fully my own untapped inner strengths: my energy, creativity, imagination, individuality, self-reliance, and sensitivity. My barreled definition of success and my shallow appreciation of myself left me with a sense of humiliation at ending up as a teacher at a small, out-of-the-way college in a region of the country and a state known more for *Tobacco Road* and *Gone with the Wind* than its intellectual accomplishments. Later, as a published scholar, national reputation notwithstanding, I found myself once again as the second son in an area of history that more than one fellow historian denigrated as "an insignificant country side show to the big tent of this sub-field of American history."

My son Robby was a profound gift who forced me to open my heart and eyes. I mean it finally dawned on me. What the hell did reputation, publication, awards and grants, and promotion have to do with real success and fulfillment?

The truth is that, for the first time, when I was faced with the very real possibility of losing my son, whom I loved more than my life, everything else seemed so inconsequential, so small, so transitory, so superficial. And I asked questions that forced me to evaluate myself and my life for the first time and decide who I had been, who I was, and who I wanted to be. *I* forced *me* to acknowledge that I was pretending to be satisfied with both me and my life.

Lord, that truth deeply hurt. I started to see that, as I had walked through the chapters of my life, I had strayed from the truth of myself, blinded and shackled by thoughts, feelings, ideas, and dreams that so often had been created by decisions influenced by others in my family, in academia, and in society. Surviving my experience taught me things that I probably would not have learned any other way. It was a hell of a learning tool. I'm not sure I would recommend using it.

At the same time, I think we learn and grow most from those experiences that are hard and painful — at least challenging — rather than from the ones that are easy. Like any pain, however, mine was a gift fraught with opportunity — but only if I had the courage to open it. I discovered that such an effort is, as someone once said, seldom a convenient scheduling of an appointment; a polite tap on the shoulder; a quiet, almost unnoticed whisper of a "may I?"; a protective "excuse me"; a safe stay at home; a comfortable repose in an easy chair; a pleasurable stroll in the garden; or a leisurely weekend canoe ride down a meandering river. It's an arduous and dangerous trek over treacherous terrain, a lonely exposure of strengths and weaknesses, a stark rejoinder, and maybe even a howling reprimand.

I have discovered over these past three years, however, that as I walked the hard road and asked myself the hard questions about myself and what I do, and did not rest until I started getting the honest and painful answers, I began entering into another world. I found something no one could give me. I found something I did not think I possessed. I acquired the knowledge that I am stronger and worthier and more talented inside than I ever thought I was.

Slowly and painfully, I have learned that I had been running after things I thought would bring me inner contentment — things like getting parental approval, degrees, reputation, tenure, and prestige. I have to admit that all they got me were heightened anxiety, a greater disturbance of my inner sense of peace, a deepening prejudice against myself, greater limits on my sense of self, and a subtle disdain for students, who were a constant reminder of my shortcomings, who were a barrier to achieving recognition, and who were, as a colleague said, a "nuisance necessary to pay the bills." I started to discover that I needed things and approval only to the extent that I was not inwardly defined, only to the extent that I thought I needed something from others, only to the extent that I did not accept who I was.

I started looking around at the "system." I started asking myself, "Why is this business of being a college teacher such a struggle for me? Why is it such a thankless task?" It is because to be a teacher is to challenge the legitimacy of all the accepted material criteria for success. It is because to be a teacher requires an almost unimaginable strength of character to reject those priorities. It takes a lot of courage to spend the enormous amounts of energy and time required to teach — energy and time that cannot be spent on advancing a professional career. Teaching demands an almost heroic sacrifice of personal and professional advancement in a system that does not give great attention to teaching and the well-being of the student. It is so much easier and safer and more secure to accept those priorities and tilt yourself toward yourself in the name of the survival of both you and your family, leaving the students "home alone."

I used to bemoan so often how I had to sacrifice the classroom for the archive because of the demands that the system imposed upon me. Now I see that I had acquiesced to the system only because it was in my interest to do so and because I did not have the strength to do anything to the contrary.

In 1976, for example, my colleagues on the Promotion and Tenure Committee judged all nine years of my teaching efforts and campus activities as "non-professional": the establishment of the Faculty Scholarship Program for needy students, the creation of the Week of Seminars program that became legendary, experimentation with interdisciplinary and topic courses, introduction of a costumed lecture series, development of the honors program, initiation of administrative reforms to ensure quality education. The committee refused to approve my promotion to full professor. These were both my colleagues and my friends, many of whom had worked with me on these projects. We were faculty at a college that bragged about being a "teaching institution" but was selling out to the pressures of reputation, power, and money that lay in research and publication.

Instead of fighting the system, in a self-righteous pout I resigned from all campus activity, stopped experimenting with teaching techniques, and went elsewhere to be seen, recognized, appreciated, and important. Whatever recognition I had from the students wasn't enough, because they were not my equals and no one really listened to students. I "played the game," increasingly sharing the classroom with the archive, and went on a 15-year research and publication binge that resulted in the acquisition of a national reputation.

Now, I have to admit that when I say "they" or "it" made me do it, I was deluding myself and shirking responsibility for my own actions and thoughts and words. *I* forced myself into the publish-or-perish rat race. In this particular and critical instance, I already had tenure. The promotion was inconsequential since it carried no additional salary increase. But my ego — the need to be recognized — required that I be promoted. I thought a promotion, and later a few publications, would somehow change my inner life and I could go back to teaching. But there was always "just one more." The more renowned I became, the more renowned I wanted to be. The more books and articles I published, the more books and articles I wanted to publish. The more conference papers I presented, the more conference papers I wanted to present. The more grants I received, the more grants I applied for.

To achieve all of this, I became more sensitive to what others thought, and thus lost a measure of the independence I so valued. I used to say agonizingly that I couldn't do what was needed both to publish and to properly teach, but I never made the hard choice in the interest of the students. The lure of reputation was too great. I felt I had done my moral duty merely by recognizing my dilemma. I used to say that it was a "vicious devouring monster" that I couldn't stop, when all I had to do was say a simple and firm "No." By gesture or deed or word, in one way or another, for a variety of reasons, regardless of cost, I, like so many of us, submitted, got with it, became a particular type of team player, and "played" the game because it was safe and easy and self-serving.

I see now the power I can impose on the "system." I am not apart from the "system." I am part of it. No, I *am* the system. I bought into it to satisfy my needs and thereby helped to fashion, reinforce, and defend what it is, because it was in my interest to do so. And I must therefore assume ownership for all to which I have submitted and which I have promoted. I see now that I cannot change a system that I am a part of by pointing the finger at someone or something else, by conforming, by submitting, or by rationalizing its actions. I know I cannot start on that tough, long road of changing myself as long as I acquiesce to the system. I think it was Carl Jung who once said something to the effect that if parents want to change a child, they should first look at themselves. If I wanted to change the hold the system had on me, I first would have to look at myself, assume ownership for my decisions and actions, then struggle to change myself and my beliefs.

Don't think that the years following the explosive experience at Hyde have been a picnic. Instant self-realization did not automatically translate into instant self-reflection and self-actualization. There was doubt, hesitancy, denial, fear, hedging, rationalization, stumbling, weakening. Knowing deep down that I had to examine my value system was one thing; to actually examine it and admit that it had to be changed was quite another, more difficult thing; and to start changing it was still another more threatening thing. This process wasn't some instant miracle in a revival tent where Brother Dan touched my head and said, "Heal," and I threw off the crutches and freely walked off stage, arms outstretched, screaming, "Praise the Lord." This was a long, arduous, painful program of spiritual, mental, and emotional rehabilitation of my beliefs.

My beliefs! Everything is a component of my personal beliefs. I believed in who I was; I believed in the effectiveness of what I did; I believed in the importance of what I did; I believed in the sincerity of what I did. I had to ask myself to honestly address all of those belief systems, to go to the very fiber of my being. I was on a terrifying journey into the unknown that I did not always like making.

I had prided myself on being a good teacher. My students felt I was a good teacher. Others felt I was a good teacher. And I have to admit that there was a lot of fun, laughter, and camaraderie with the students, especially during those heydays of the late 1960s and early 1970s, and with those who were most like me.

Yet I was humbled as I realized that, starting in the mid-1970s, I had acquired a pattern of behavior similar to those teachers who had so brutally thrown Robby away and whom I had berated. As I had inflated myself, I had inadvertently diminished myself. Whereas I thought that I was always on the move, I was often just running in place. No matter what I did, with the exception of being involved actively in the civil rights movement and maybe protesting the war in Vietnam, I had to accept the fact that I was motivated as much out of *selfishness* as *selflessness*, as much out of feeling and looking important as doing something important, as much out of fear and compulsion as a joy of learning or persuasion. I saw that I was more concerned with my teaching than students' learning; I saw how, when they ignored my "best" efforts, in self-defense I generally blamed them. I had to accept that I was not being a real person and treating others as real people, that while I talked of respect for students, I kept so many at a distance.

It was a hard pill to swallow. I had prided myself on being thoroughly taken with the students and discovered that I was far more taken with myself. I gloried in being a caring teacher and discovered that I cared far more for my needs than for theirs. I thought I varied myself to accommodate differ- ent students and saw that I was far more the same with everyone and less sensitive to the human diversity. I had to face up to the truth. I needed a greater understanding and appreciation of my "inner" strengths. I needed to learn how best to apply them to my "outer" works. And I worried whether I had the courage to remodel or abandon my past attitudes and behaviors.

When I was forced to look deep inside myself, and when I forced myself to continue looking inside, I wasn't "cured." I learned so much about life and so much about myself through constant prodding, provoking, probing, soothing, laughing, yelling, and consoling, by myself and other people.

With their help, I started writing a "windows" program for my spirit. I constructed a box, if you will, into which I placed all of my hurts, resentments, fears, doubts, and worries. In another box, I placed all of my hopes and optimism, as well as a catalog of my "inner" strengths, energy, creativity, imagination, sensitivity, and individuality. Over the last few years, I have obtained a picture and a vision of how I want to feel, the type of freedom I want to have, the experiences I want to initiate, the person and professional I want honestly to be. Slowly but surely, that second box has expanded to become my life and profession.

Nevertheless, however the grip of the dark hand of the past is loosened and its weight is lessened and confined to that first box, it remains always there to be contended with. You never get over it; you never leave it behind. It's always there. But I struggle to use that contention as something productive and positive, as a reminder that there always will be more of the mountains for me to climb, replete with the slips and scratches and even falls — and that each attempt to reach higher will get me closer to the summit, that each experience will make me stronger at the breaking points. There always will be so much more room for self-improvement, so much area for self-development. No, I am not "cured." I have just acquired another set of problems, questions, and issues to live with.

Robby simply offered me an experience to explore who I am and to get in touch with strengths and abilities I didn't know I had, to see them differently, to use them differently, to see myself differently, and to become someone different. I found myself moving from old personal and professional patterns that no longer fit comfortably to a new way that felt intensely authentic and beneficial. I realized that I had ended up running after things like degrees and publications when, in fact, I ran past the students who could give me an inner sense of peace and contentment. I came to realize that the old values and things — salary, promotion, tenure, reputation, approval, recognition, etc. — that I thought were important no longer were important. I came to realize that students who were not as important were all that was important.

Once that occurred — once the quest for material success and approval that had acted as a weight on my psyche started lifting — I no longer felt stuck running in the rat race on the endless treadmill. The personal, social, and academic systems, as people call them, lost their heavy, tight grip on me. I was truly amazed at how easily I could re-enter the classroom and close the door behind me on publications, conference papers, projects, grants, and consultancies.

I had repressed myself in personal expectation as well as in social, personal, and academic convention. I now slowly and painfully seized the intensive opportunity to explore what has emerged as a new authenticity. I slipped out from the public eye on my terms. I decided to stop playing the destructive publish-or-perish game, because while I was publishing, I was perishing.

To be sure, I would not be seen as the authority in my field, as the pathfinder in my area of research. But that's OK. It's now far less important for me to be cheered on or to be recognized for "great things." I am coming to terms with the need to be needed, loved, seen, wanted. I am far less driven by whether the world knows about me or not. Curiously, there is not as much of an undertow of regret as I feared there would be.

I redefined my perception of being important. It no longer means always being loudly and obviously in front of everyone. It now means following what's true in my own heart and having the strength, courage, and conviction to face myself, to always question myself, and to be responsible for myself. It didn't take the pressure away. But the fear has certainly lessened. As that fear has weakened, I've started feeling such freedom.

I feel more empowered to deal with whatever I need to deal with and find meaning in whatever I honestly find important, so that what I do counts for something more than selfishly feeding my ego, adding to my résumé, increasing my renown, and guaranteeing an income.

Isn't it strange? Susie and I sent Robby to Hyde School to find himself — but I found that *I* was unexpectedly starting to find *myself*. By some quirk of fate, I got the opportunity to find a different place for success and inner peace in my life at the same place.

Tuesday, 16 August 1994

THREE TEACHING PRINCIPLES

I went walking a bit later than usual this morning because it was drizzling when I got out of bed. When I left the house, the air was relatively cool and bug-free. It seemed that this particular Dog Day was whimpering. The sun was on the horizon and the partly cloudy sky was awash with the colors of dawn.

As I enjoyed what we call a very rare "soft" August morning, I was thinking about Barbara's last question, "Why do you teach the way you do?" I turned a corner near the school yard, stopped, and gazed admiringly down the street at a distant, single cloud painted in blues, reds, and oranges. Golden rays fanned out from its top edges like visual trumpets heralding the coming of a new day as they raced through a dazzlingly rainbowed corona. It was a magnificent sight that gave me the answer to Barbara's question.

"Every student should have a chance to shine like this," I thought as I remembered my Emerson. "Every student should have a person who wants to help him or her become the person he or she is capable of becoming, and I'll be damned if I am ever going to let one human being fall through the cracks in my classes without a fight." Over the last three years, this has emerged as my first principle of teaching.

As I began to change the image of myself, I began to change my image of my profession. I began to expand my parochial view of what it meant to be a teacher and put aside my demeaning evaluation of it. I saw more than ever that the classroom is not a dead end; it's the exit from a dark cave. I slowly began to see teaching as a calling rather than just a job. The students became my profession. I became far more interested in the well-being of the student than chasing the golden fleece of "subject mastery."

As a teacher, I started to see that my purpose is to create an environment in which the students address themselves honestly, and to help students develop the attitudes that will allow them to get to know themselves and start becoming who they truly are and are capable of becoming. I wanted to bring something wonderfully magical and mysterious into an otherwise grueling and torturous experience. I became interested in endowing students with a lifelong love of learning, opening their minds with the power of reasoning, opening their hearts with the power of humility, creating a self-reliance, helping them learn how to learn, giving them a glimpse at the awe and wonder of learning, and giving them a glimpse at the awe and wonder of their potential.

As I changed my life, I began to see once again — but far more clearly — that teaching is much more and far more difficult than just showing up for a classroom presentation. Expectations are how we imagine ourselves and others. They are themselves predictions. As I began to realize my own value, I began to appreciate the value of the students. As I learned to appreciate my own untapped potential, I learned to appreciate theirs. As I started to hold myself sacred, I began to see the often desecrated and self-denigrated students as human beings who also were sacred, who had something worthy and beautiful about them. Like myself, I started to see them not only as they were, but began appreciating them for what they were yet to be and were capable of becoming.

Lately, there have been times when I've walked into class feeling as if I were coming out of a dark age into an age of human dignity. I've come into the room, hesitated, scanned the room, looked at each student with a respect far deeper than I ever had before, and wanted to proclaim, like Miranda in the *The Tempest*: "O, wonder! How many goodly creatures are there here! How beauteous mankind is! O brave new world, that has such people in 't!"

I have decided that real learning involves a change of attitude and behavior no less than does real teaching. I have come to believe that teaching is more of a calling forth of wholeness to be a better person than just a jamming in of information, that it must deal with the entire person, not just the mind. Teaching should make students and teachers aware of their sacredness, give them high expectations of themselves, and change their lives.

That brings me to my second principle of teaching. I believe that there are emotional and spiritual components to education, as there are to everything, that are inseparable from its intellectual aspects. I am a member of a profession, however, that so often wants to treat both students and professors as if they are emotionally sterilized, that feels far more comfortable dealing with only the intellect rather than the "touchy-feely stuff" of the whole person. But there is a fascinating marriage between emotion and intellect, between what people think, feel, know, say, and do. A metaphor exercise that I use at the beginning of my classes — which you will read about in two Random Thoughts — gives me greater understanding of and sensitivity to how so many students find it so difficult to perform when they are treated as half-adults and half-children; when they have been denied the opportunity to become emotionally and intellectually independent; when they have seldom been trusted to seize the chance to educate themselves; when they have been told, in so many words, that they aren't worth the effort; when they see and hear so much that only reinforces their feelings of insecurity, self-doubt, and diminished self-worth.

It seems to me, then, that the need to value effort as well as ability and to develop attitude as well as talent is obvious. I think it is important to know historical facts, to be able to deal with chemical formulae, to operate a computer, and to understand Shakespeare. I think it is important to have critical thinking, problem-perceiving, problem-solving, communication, and social skills. I think it is essential to apply those skills and utilize formulae, axioms, and facts in a subject area. The emotional aspects, however, of deep hurt, self-denigration, and emptiness hinder sincere and honest effort and ultimately impact on performance, just as self-confidence, self-worth, pride, integrity, pursuit of excellence, and humility bring out the willingness to work hard and accept challenge and develop the student's innate ability.

When students are not performing, I understand how the messages from past experiences are loud and interfering static, drowning out the voice trying to be heard. So I ask myself very quickly what's going on with their attitudes. I want to know what they bring to the table. I want to know what kind of persons they are and what messages they are hearing, so that I can help them dial into themselves. That is why the introductory "stuff," weekly student self-evaluations, daily journaling, and just the plain small talk that I discuss in my class syllabus are integral parts of my classes.

I believe that it is equally important for students to acquire the character necessary to utilize their intellectual skills: to have the courage to apply those skills, to be honest with themselves and others when they are facing challenges and the going gets tough, to be sufficiently humble to help fellow students along the way and to ask for help, to be confident enough to risk failure, to have sufficient pride to give it their best shot, to be modest enough to know that their best can always be better, to have the daring to venture into new worlds, to find the sense of independence to do what they think should be done, and to have the integrity to achieve the honest way.

But each student stands at a different point on both the emotional and intellectual growth continuum. Each student brings into the classroom different amounts of knowledge, information, and skill, and different degrees of what I call "Learning Dependency." Furthermore, each student has a particular learning style. I struggle to find ways to treat each student in each class in each quarter as a unique individual with unique attributes and potentials, who can't be judged by a single standardized, subjective set of criteria.

Slowly, I've seen that my purpose is not to weed out, unintentionally or otherwise, students who cannot learn by the one method that I once rationalized was comfortable for me, or to inadvertently punish those who have higher barriers to overcome. My purpose is to nurture. In an effort to reach all students, I have to use a diversity of teaching methods that will accommodate their diverse needs and at the same time challenge the students to stretch themselves. The trick is to teach in a variety of ways that fit the different learning styles of different students and allow the students multiple forms of expression. And since I must give a grade, I allow myself a tremendous amount of flexibility, so that I can recognize and acknowledge where each student has been and how far each has struggled to come, and consider not just what they have done but what it took for them to do it.

My third principle is that teaching and learning are acts of human relationships that must eliminate the cold, distancing, destructive, adversarial "we vs. them" mentality that so often pervades the campus. I do not believe that there is anything more powerful in the classroom than a bond of trust, an honest interaction among everyone in that classroom.

The trust issue is very important. Students are stressed because the classroom so often lacks a support system, leaving them with a feeling of isolation. I see students worry themselves sick over the simple acts of studying and coming to class. I hear them express it all the time in a variety of ways: "What do you want?" "What grade will I get?" "Will this be good enough for you?" "What will they think of me?" "Will this be on the test?"

"Is this important?" "Do I have to know this?" The more uncomfortable or scared students are in class, the less effective my teaching and their learning will be. An electronic mail colleague of mine once said, in a play on words, "Students should feel *sacred*, not *scared*."

There's a comfort zone and a trust level created, however, when someone cares enough to be willing to listen, when there is a mutually supportive relationship, and when students find that they are not alone. I have concocted a home remedy for alleviating the stress pangs brought on by panic, helplessness, fear, denigration, and isolation: four pinches of smiles, two dashes of laughter, a cup of trust, four ounces of empowerment, three heaping tablespoons of caring, two teaspoons of respect, a clove of dignity, a leaf of encouragement, and a stalk of love.

The bond is partly forged by sharing myself and the truth of my life. It is a pronouncement that I am not different from the students or above them or better than them.

I remember during a discussion last spring how a student commented with frustration and disgust to a statement I had made: "Damn, Dr. Schmier, we'll never be able to do what you can." It struck me that I had yet to cut completely through the opaque curtain separating us. That afternoon, I rushed home, scrambled up to the attic, opened an old suitcase, grabbed a faded piece of paper, brought it into class the next day, and threw it up on an overhead projector.

Hiding the name at the top of the paper, I told the class, "We're not going to talk about the chapter right off. I have a problem, and I need your guidance. I've been asked to write a recommendation for this student. He's a great guy, but his grades ... well ... what would you do?" They looked at the display of the D's, F's, and C's generously sprinkled through the occasional B's and A's.

Among their comments: "Pretty mediocre," "messed around," "just average," "screwed up big-time," "looks like my transcript," "inconsistent," "doesn't look like he's going far." They finally agreed that I should write an honest letter, but not make it too glowing, and if "you know about him like you do us," talk more about the student's potential than what the transcript shows.

Finally, I uncovered the name on the transcript. It was mine. Their mouths were agape.

At that moment, we bridged the gap. By that action, and others, I announced that, although I stand at a different place on life's road, I was once where they are, and like them I have warts, and that I have been shaped by the same wounds that have shaped them, and that, nevertheless, there is an essence and a uniqueness, a beauty, and a potential in each of us.

All this helps remind us that both I and the students are human beings with the same joys and sorrows, dreams and nightmares, strengths and weaknesses, and complexities, and that we can find supportive and mutually responsible community as struggling, frail human beings.

The bond is also partly forged by actively connecting and engaging the students, myself, and the knowledge of my discipline in a way that allows us to be fellow travelers who teach and learn from each other. I think active learning is far more effective than passive note-taking and memorization. I think active teaching is far more effective than passive presentation. I have found that, if given the chance, most students will be passionate and committed to their own learning if they can see that the subject is within them, useful to them, and applicable to their lives. The more a student is involved in the experience, the less that student will be an unthinking, "going through the motions," robotic copier, memorizer, test-passer, and grade-getter. The more the student shares in control of the classroom and actively helps structure it, the greater the opportunity the student has to be focused and aware, to engage in the subject in a personally meaningful way that makes sense of the experience and facilitates insight and discovery.

In this respect, the most potentially effective teaching technique that I have at my disposal is *me*, the teacher and human being. I find that as I think of *myself* as my most potentially effective teaching technique, I teach better. The more I know about my students, the more I know about myself, the more wisely I will teach. The essence of my teaching is to recognize myself and to understand myself in my teaching. My power to teach, then, flows not just from my mastery of the subject, or from my use of technology, or from the power I have over the students, but from my own self-mastery.

Certainly my responsibility is to ensure that I make available the knowledge of my discipline. But above that, it is my responsibility to care about the students, to treat them with dignity and respect, and to affirm their spirit. It's a kind of love. I have to bare my soul, to be open and honest. I have to be a learner, trying new ideas, reflecting on my experiences, willing to grow and develop throughout my life. I have to be creative, willing to risk the introduction of new and untested concepts and techniques. I have to believe that anything worth doing is worth risk and failure, and that the will to succeed requires the courage to fail. I have to find ways to take an error and turn it into a "magnificent opportunity." I have to have faith and trust in the students and grant them both freedom and responsibility while holding them to high expectations. I have to have a vision that never lets me "get by." I have to be driven by excellence and always stretch myself. I have to throw myself into the classes.

I think that when I teach with joy, students find it easier to learn. Yet I have to practice what I call "tough love." I think there are critical responsibilities the students have — to themselves and to their fellow students, maybe even to me. If we are all to be sensitive to each other's individual differences, if we are all dedicated to enhancing those traits that are unique and positive in each other and challenging each other to stretch beyond our inclinations, if we are to serve as agents of personal and intellectual growth, and if we each are to be responsible for each other's learning, then every student has to be responsible for his or her own learning as well.

Students have to realize that learning is not fun and games, that from nothing comes nothing — that, as I say in my syllabus, "You won't learn how to climb mountains by practicing on ant hills." They have to accept that mastering a skill, or a body of knowledge, or themselves, is time-consuming, hard work. They each have to be aware that discarding old habits and unlearning what they think they know is sometimes tougher than learning new skills, styles, and subject matter. They have to actively give it their best, challenge themselves, understand that if they want to learn, they can learn, and that they should be prepared to do whatever it takes to learn. This is the essence of their growth; it assists the growth of their fellow students and it contributes to my own personal and professional growth.

I see teaching as an art form. It now touches me in a way that is exhilarating and fulfilling. If I can relate to each student in a sort of artistic way — a way that considers who they are and what they are about — I'm sure I'll be a better teacher — for both them and myself. It's that mixture of the technical expertise, the art of teaching, and my passion that gives me the best chance of helping the student be educated.

I've found, however, that it is not enough to experience this spiritual renewal. Teaching, like Thomas Edison said of invention, is "1 percent inspiration and 99 percent perspiration." Nothing is so useless as principles that go unapplied.

The real importance of what I have learned about myself, then, is to convert that experience into *something practical*, to take what I have learned — and am still learning — and put it into everyday language and action. If I have looked at the yesterdays of my life to understand myself, it is to live and work today and for the tomorrows. I have begun to understand that self-evaluation or inward reflection serves no purpose unless I, like the shaman of old, can convert it into an outward sharing, a reaching out, and a giving back.

I want my teaching to speak to the students, to foster a conversation between me and them, among all of us, and between them and themselves. I want to go beyond the mechanics of the classroom — beyond merely having a body of information, organizing a class, writing lectures, being prepared, making up quizzes and exams, grading performance, being prompt, and so on. If all I do is transfer my information to the students' notes and then they transfer it back to the quiz or exam without any interplay in the mind, heart, and spirit — if I do not add to the stature of either myself or the students as thinking, feeling, contemplating people — I have not done very much. No, as a teacher, I have to somehow understand the spirit of each student and touch that spirit. History is my tool for doing that.

Friday, 26 August 1994

YOU'VE GOT TO BE THERE

*A*s I was wandering the dark, clammy streets of Valdosta this morning, I was thinking about skeletons and spirit. Actually, I was wondering how to give you a practical classroom reference point for my Random Thoughts. I thought I'd first give you a thumbnail sketch of how one of my classes is structured and how it operates.

As I see it, the way I structure the class and the techniques I use are a skeleton for applying in the classroom my way of thinking and feeling about the craft of teaching, as well as my way of perceiving myself and the students. Believe me when I say those changes were not the result of a convenient surgical strike of a technique here and there nor of a whimsical and superficial quick-fix approach. Every day since that first challenge session at Hyde, I have gone into class and gone through some hard soul-searching. It has been a continuous process of altering the very soul of the class. I've looked at and asked the "whys" of everything I've done: lectures, grades, quizzes, exams, finals, attendance, reading assignments, using the textbook, office hours, and how I behaved. It has led to an even more painful decision to *totally* overhaul *all* of my educational beliefs and *all* of my teaching techniques that I had picked up by copying my professors — the ones I had practiced for almost 30 years. I wanted to try something very different. Acting on my gut and inspired by Hyde School's approach to education, I wanted to implement my version of a character-based curriculum.

Fundamentally, I decided that I wanted the classroom to be an intimate, caring, and nurturing environment in which the student could feel happy, secure, and creative, but one that was sufficiently challenging so that it wouldn't necessarily be completely comfortable. I decided that I wanted to create a learning community that would afford the students the opportunity to engage in a robust and supportive relationship with me and each other, that would allow them to cope with the challenge to grow and learn, that would emphasize self-awareness, self-development, and self-expression, and that would allow me to be truly a part of the class rather than apart from it. I wanted to scrap formal lecturing, depreciate the value of grades, and emphasize process rather than performance. I wanted to hand over control of the class to the students by giving them reasonable decision powers over their learning and the operation of the class. I wanted to transform myself from the proverbial sage on stage to the guide on the side. I wanted to reduce the impersonality in the class by introducing a spirit of family, by giving the students an identity as part of the class learning community, by moving chairs around and breaking out of the tyranny of classroom chair arrangement so that students could look at each other's faces, and by having students work cooperatively. I wanted to help the students develop skills in studying, problem-perceiving, problem-solving, critical thinking, communication, and socialization. I wanted to introduce daily journaling, weekly self-evaluations, open class evaluations, and bonding "stuff."

But I hesitated because I knew I would be alone out there. I wasn't sure how the administration, my colleagues, and the students would respond to such a revolutionary approach. I wasn't sure my ideas would work.

It was in October 1992. I was talking with Robby on the telephone about my intentions and hesitations. "Dad," he said. "Go for it. You tell me that I have to believe in myself and have the courage to fail if I'm going to try to get anywhere. Now it's your turn to follow your own advice."

Heeding his rebuke and picking up his challenge, I took a deep breath and, in the winter quarter of 1992-93, I went for it.

The structural cornerstone of my method is a clustering of three students into what I call the triad. I chose three because I decided it was a good number: coupling two students can lead to split decisions; four can also result in tie votes; five is too many and allows some students to either get lost, hide, or disappear. With three, the students have to reach a decision one way or another. I decide who shall be in each triad. My selection is a bit random. I don't look at high school or college transcripts. I don't test for hemisphericity or learning orientation or personality traits. I don't balance talkers with shy students and I do not "salt" a triad with at least one "better student." No one does that in the "real world," and I see no reason to try to create a perfectly fitting fantasyland that would be easier to live in for both me and the students. I have only two or three criteria for creating the triad. To give students as real a social experience in the classroom as they face on campus and will face off campus, I insist that each triad be gender-mixed and racially mixed and, if possible, contain at least one non-traditional student. No friends, roommates, lovers, relatives, sorority sisters, or fraternity brothers in the same triads. I don't want the possibility of two ganging up on the third or leaving one out in the cold.

In simple terms, the triads have several purposes: peer teaching, peer support, development of communication skills, development of cooperative skills, and elimination of the sense of competition. The goal is to get each student to recognize the value of being honest with himself or herself about strengths and weaknesses, to establish and sustain a trusting relationship with others in the triad and the class, and to begin an honest sharing of strengths, weaknesses, visions, and experiences. The triads are the place where the students begin to address their personal and social biases and their inhibitions about themselves.

So the triads are more than collaborative seating and study groups. The students in each triad work as if they were one person: they take the weekly quiz together for a single grade, they take exams together for a single grade, and they hand in single sets of written assignments for the same grade. The members of the triads are responsible for each other's success. They act individually only during the daily class discussions.

The triads also offer the students an opportunity to exercise their power as learners. They decide how to prepare the chapter commentaries, what readings to select for the "tidbits" assignment and how to prepare them for class, whether to take one or both or none of the exams, and in what manner they will respond to which questions using what medium. When they come to me with the traditional, "What do you want?" I answer, "Whatever you honestly feel proud about having done, whatever you honestly feel should be done. Take the risk. There isn't going to be a professor 'out there' to hold your hand, lead you down a path, and tell you what to do when you leave campus."

The triads police themselves. If one student proves to be a "problem," the other two members of the triad have to decide how to work with and help that student.

If students come to me saying, "We've got a problem with so-and-so. He just won't carry his load," my usual response is, "What can you do to solve it? Find a way to include him rather than taking the easy way of excluding him. You are going to deal with and work with different kinds of people when you graduate. Better start learning how to do that here." One complaining student said that she was a management major, to which

I responded, "Good. Now start using some of that material in your books and learn how to be a manager." In that sense, the student becomes the teacher as well as the learner. A student who continues to shirk responsibility might find the others voting to remove his or her name from an assignment or, in a rare worst-case scenario, even to flunk him or her for the entire course. It has happened, and I have stood behind the students. Except in the rarest of occasions, however, things work out.

Meanwhile, I keep my eyes and ears open and take the pulse of each student. I am intensely seeing and hearing each student every day as I roam about the classroom; I am reading and commenting on the weekly self-evaluations; I am reading the weekly journals; I am reaching out here, exploring there, talking, commenting by written and spoken word, encouraging, cajoling, comforting, admonishing, conversing, urging, supporting, being tough, being understanding, being flexible, being demanding, and being considerate.

My classroom itself has a physically unique look. There are no neat rows. There is no front or back or side. There is no place to impress, no place to hide, no place to get lost. There is no lectern at the head of the class to which I am chained and the students' eyes are glued. The students are looking all around, straining their necks as I move, as they look at and talk with each other.

The classroom also has a different feel. It is never quiet. I enter class with my boombox playing music and the students leave class to the rhythm of music. During classtime, there is constant movement. I walk. I gesture. They talk. They move. I'm a mover, roaming in and about the triad clusters, whispering in ears, chatting, climbing over empty desks, yelling across the room, tapping on heads and shoulders. I'm all over the place, always sucking on a Tootsie Pop. I'm emotional. The students are emotional. They are talking to each other in their own triads and to students in others. They are moving from triad to triad.

There are no strangers in my classes. I know each of them by their first names. They know each other by their first names. Neither physical nor academic nor emotional structure is the name of the class game. I love spontaneity. I can't stand things that are set. It feels too controlling, too dominating, and not sufficiently stimulating.

As a teacher, I am always looking for motivation, a class that is alive with people dealing with challenge, risk, change, and growth. I'm usually surprised by what happens. That's OK. It tells me that the students are taking control, taking risks, rising to challenges, and learning more than I am teaching.

But I've been stymied on how to catch that spirit for you. That's important, because my classes are not structure; they are spirit.

Well, I hit upon an idea toward the end of my walk today. I decided to create a composite of journal comments made by the students who have been in my classes during the last five quarters and who have given me permission to use them. I'll let them give you a feel for the class in their own words:

> "When I walked into class I thought, 'What have I gotten myself into?' "

> "I thought you were out there. This is wild! You were there sucking on your Tootsie Pop, sitting cross-legged on top of a desk kidding around with a student, dressed in jeans, no socks, playing Red Hot Chili Peppers on your boombox, and I said to myself, 'This man is crazy.' "

> "I first guessed that you were some kind of a nut escaped from the loony bin. But you set the tone for the class by saying without words, 'Here I am, prepared and ready to go.' "

> "You almost acted like an excited cheerleader. You always made us feel good about what we did."

> "I don't like pushy teachers because I want to do what I am used to."

> "Lots of times I forgot you were the prof and thought of you as one of us in class. Heck, you were part of the class."

> "There is nothing that is traditional about this class except that it's called a history class."

> "You really broke the mold, not only about the class but what history is all about. We even used the textbook different. Heck, we actually used it."

> "Those first few days that 'stuff' we did was something else."

> "The biographical interviews allowed us to look at each other in the face instead of at the hairs on the back of each other's neck."

> "I got to know everyone's name."

"The metaphor exercise let us know what each of us was thinking. So did the exercise about what was on our mind. This class is awesome."

"The singing really broke the ice and opened us up as a class. I can't believe we did it, standing up and singing alone with all eyes on each of us. I mean it was like unless we had some heavy chips on our shoulders, and some did, we couldn't possibly be anymore (sic) afraid of looking dumb than getting up and singing alone in front of a bunch of people you've never seen before."

"It really stripped down my defenses and excuses. I think it made it easier for us later to talk in class and be honest with each other."

"That 'stuff' with the chair was out of sight. Forty-six ways to sit on a chair and still counting when class time ran out."

"Seeing how many different ways we could sit on the chair or move it helped me to see things from so many different perspectives."

"That SQ3R and the rooster words really help a lot of us. I always remember the chair and rooster words and learned how to study more and read words less. I read the meaning behind the words more. I learned the reasons not just memorized facts."

"I was impressed with the creativity and imagination of every-one's triad project of the shields. We were relaxed laying on the floor, laughing, and kidding and talking personal stuff with each other as we drew the emblem."

"It was great. We got closer and mingled like in no other class. 'We're getting somewhere,' I said. 'We're starting to become one as a triad and as a class family.' And you did a neat shield yourself."

"I really respected that you didn't hide behind your title like you were better than us."

"You did everything with us. You did 'stuff' with us. You fell off the desk into our arms and trusted us enough to allow yourself to be led around blindfolded. On the biographical introductory stuff you were straightforward with us. I really got a kick when you answered that you thought a great evening would be, without blinking an eye, cooking an exotic dish at home on your wok, sitting down at a romantic dinner in a candlelit room to soft music with your wife, and finishing off the evening with passionate love-making. I have to admit I was startled."

"When someone asked why you teach the way you do, you didn't even hesitate. When you shared with us a very personal story about your son and how his problems helped you to become a better teacher, I was amazed to hear a professor sharing an emotional experience with his students. That made you human in many of our eyes. A lot of us talked about that lots of times. We were amazed that a professor would so respect us that he'd be so straight with students, and a lot of us knew from that moment on that we would be nothing less than up front with you and felt we had to shoot from our hips with you and each other."

"The class has been a wonderful experience. Most of us interacted and learned together."

"Friendships were made and maybe some enemies. We shared thoughts, opinions, passions, fears, and hopes."

"We became one family with unique members."

"We supported each other."

"It brought strangers with different races, ethnicities, genders, and thinking patterns very close together."

"I have grown to be more accepting and I try harder to understand more and judge less."

"If any of us saw another somewhere else, we'd say a 'Hi' and maybe talk a few minutes."

"It was fun, exciting and even a little scary at times. We didn't just work together. My triad took time out to spend time with each other to get to know one another. Sometimes we met with other triads."

"At first, I was uncomfortable because I was the only black, but they showed me it didn't matter. They showed me love and a wanting to share themselves with me."

"We learned a lot more history together than we would have apart. He (one triad partner) had to deal with his male macho stuff. She (the other) came down off her girlie pedestal. I learned I could work with blacks."

"I realize now that not all whites have sheets. Screw that Oreo stuff."

"This place was hopping most of the time."

"Things were original and alive. This wasn't a place for the dead or to be passive and glassy-eyed."

"We were moving chairs around and talking to each other from the second we came into the class."

"It was almost impossible to sit like a wax figure like we do in most other classes."

"I actually enjoyed coming to class."

"The class seemed at times like working on a hobby and not like being forced by your parents to practice the piano when you wanted to go out and play ball."

"I learned so much about history without the drudgery of notes and lectures and naps in class."

"This history class was about people, real people who once lived, and how they connected with us."

"I enjoyed coming to a class that had absolutely nothing boring about it. We never cared about the 'whats' of dates and names. We always talked and thought about the 'whys.' "

"It made us think, really think. I once thought what we did and believed had always been like that."

"I never knew what to expect. I wanted to come to class to see what crazy things we would do."

"I mean one day we did brainstorming with everyone screaming bits and pieces while the Doc scribbled it on the board in his scribble. Another day we did role-playing and I was a slave owner defending slavery or someone else was a Spanish explorer telling us why God approved of everything he did. Still another day we talked about whether Andrew Carnegie was a moral man or if radicals were so dangerous how come we admire a radical like Thomas Jefferson or whether the supporters of the Vietnam War and the protesting draft dodgers who went to Canada were both patriotic."

"We'd do weird things like line drawings to express what we learned."

"We'd have debates on individual rights and capital punishment or on the development of women's rights or a whole bunch of issues."

"We had a few real big fights over racial issues."

"I can't believe when we wanted to talk about free love in the Oneida community, the Doc let us run with it and we wound up talking about our sexual practices and compared them with people a hundred or two hundred years ago and saw how they've changed or haven't changed."

"History seems more real and alive to me now instead of being just a bunch of names and dates. And on still another day we could be doing more bonding stuff that brought us closer together as a triad or the class."

"I never heard a negative in the class. No one was made to look stupid. None of that 'you're wrong,' 'what's wrong with you,' 'you don't belong here,' 'you'll never pass' that we get in other classes."

"No one was ever torn down. We tried to build everyone up. I saw more friendship, support, concern, protection, and progress than ever existed in any class."

"We see so-called mistakes as ways to help us see or to let others show us how to study, understand and think better."

"There is an atmosphere of encouragement into success rather than an intimidation into defeat."

"I'm not comfortable with this class because I'm a better listener than a speaker."

"I learned it was OK to speak up even if my ideas are different and I am more secure in my ability to speak publicly."

"The class discussions were alive with thought-provoking, humorous, emotional, passionate and creative exchange."

"The class is an open forum where there is honesty and freedom to speak."

"I think some get too personal sometimes."

"Some days there is harmony; some days there is division; some days there was argument; some days there is even anger. But, always there was respect."

"I don't like to be controversial in my ideas."

"Dr. Schmier will not tolerate any kind of intolerance of other people's viewpoints. We'd only ask, 'Why do you think that way?'"

"Everyone is free to ask questions, express opinions, discuss real and personal issues, and voice concerns."

"I am fascinated by the counterplay and conversation. Sometimes things get a bit personal, but that's our choice."

"We got into the history of things and saw how history has gotten into us."

"We are participants in the class's (sic) learning process, in our own learning."

"Sometimes, I think we're the teacher."

"We took charge and ran with it. You trusted us and respected us enough to let us control so much of our own learning. I was stunned that you let us change the syllabus, to discuss a chapter longer than scheduled, to let triads work together on the final exam projects."

"We were respected and trusted enough to let us decide what WE thought should be done on the finals."

"I have learned not to be as embarrassed of myself and afraid of failing. My triad helped with that. They would never take a 'no.' They felt responsible for my passing."

"I grew as a student and as a person."

"I'm better at listening to lectures, writing notes, and taking written tests."

"This class taught me a great deal about life. I guess that is what college is all about, right?"

"I learned to take risks, how to take chances, and not be average like everyone else."

"I wasn't going to open doors like most of the others in the class."

"I started to voice my opinion in the discussions, and it felt real good."

"It was awesome, terrific, superb, stupendous at how we were able to establish so much trust among our classmates and feel responsible for each other's success and learn so much history."

"It was a demanding class. You were always in our faces. I even dreamed about this class, but it was filled with understanding, challenge, innovation, and fun."

"It never lost its interest. The unexpected is typical in this class."

"The triads were formed and I was nervous at something so new and different."

"I was skeptical."

"I was scared."

"I don't like relying on someone else for a grade."

"I don't want to be responsible for anyone but me. It's a dog-eat-dog world out there."

"At first, no one cared what anyone else in the class was doing. The more each group got to know one another, the more work was done together. Some hit it off right away. Many did not come together immediately. They struggled. Some reached out for help. Some reached out to try to help one another. With a little bit of talking and understanding most of us worked through things."

"Taking the quizzes together at first seemed like cheating, but it taught me the confidence of my studying and to stick to my guns if I felt an answer was right and how to argue my case."

"I couldn't believe it. The place was abuzz. We were bouncing all over the room, talking, yelling, debating. In a normal class, the room is like a morgue during quizzes. But, there's nothing normal about Dr. Schmier or this class."

"It was a madhouse. If anyone disagreed, someone would scream out 'How did you get the answer?' and we'd be off in a discussion. No wonder a 15-minute quiz took all period, and Dr. Schmier let it go. Every now and then, I'd see a slight smile of approval and satisfaction on his face as we discussed and debated each question within and among the triads."

"I had to argue my case, and we got into heated debates over a question worth only four points on one of the 10 weekly quizzes, but I'll never forget that question or the answer."

"I felt I had to be prepared to answer a 'Why did I get that answer?' thrown in my face."

"I learned more from debating and arguing the answer to quiz questions than I did studying."

"The quizzes were far more of a learning experience that allowed us to tell you how much we had learned than how much we didn't know."

"I learned a lot more how to work with people, not under or above them."

"I really appreciate the fact that the prof also worked with us and even under us, but never over us."

"All of us can be a success. We all can just go about achieving it in different ways. Some of us talk, some of us write, some of us draw, some of us sing."

"I think it really is neat that we could express what we learned in the way we can and want to rather than doing it just the prof's way."

"This was really OUR class! That freedom of the final exam was a tremendous experience. I was impressed with the creativity and imagination on the finals. I didn't think I or anyone else had it in them."

"I was amazed at the cooperation and assistance among the group. It created a sense of pulling together, of a common goal."

"It was sometimes a slow, hard learning process."

"I started getting a concern for everyone else in the class as I started believing that I could do it, and I so wanted each one to do well that I stopped concentrating on myself."

"I helped students in every group in one way or another. And I know I helped myself by doing it."

"Some stragglers remained separated from the others in their triads. In the end, most of the class came together as a family. Some never did get it, but it wasn't because a lot of other people, including Dr. Schmier, didn't try. They didn't understand or want to understand that the triad is not so much a way to organize the class as it is an attitude. They were so scared or arrogant or lazy or selfish. They just wanted a grade and didn't want to learn and didn't want to be bothered. There just wasn't enough time to get through to them. They don't know how much they lost, and they will suffer for it. Thankfully it was only a few."

In the end, most of the students echo what one recently wrote in his evaluation:

By the time the quarter was over, we were like a better informed family. Most of us ended up with a much better understanding of ourselves whether we liked that or not, a deeper understanding and respect for the others in the class, and lots more knowledge of history and how it's in us than we had when we started.

What more could I and the students ask of each other and ourselves for a class?

Wednesday, 31 August 1994

ON RANDOM THOUGHTS

*N*ow that I think about it, my sense of vulnerability, heightened by my struggle to write this introduction, has driven me during these past few months to reflect more deeply on the meaning and purpose of the Random Thoughts. I did not write these reflections as a "pedagogical advisor" to tell you how to teach. I am not the expert proclaiming, "Do it my way because it is the one and only sure way." Random Thoughts were never meant to be and are not a traditional utilitarian "how-to do," a handyman's "fix-it manual," a wizard's magical "bag of tricks," or a chef's "cookbook" of tried-and-true classroom recipes.

I suppose the Random Thoughts were written something like the tales of a shaman. If I remember my college anthropology, the shamans of old were the afflicted healers. They were people who had experienced suffering, illness, and pain themselves and had survived. It was in that recovery that they found their mission of helping others. They assumed a need to show the path to others — to help people who wished to find their own way through life's labyrinth — and shared what they had learned from their experiences. Like the shaman, it's my desire to share what I have learned. I do that with my students in the classroom; I do it with you in Random Thoughts — on the Internet, and now in this book.

Each Random Thought is a description of an unforeseen and unexpected rite of passage. They all flowed spontaneously without any prescribed cadence, chronological sequence, topical order, or ensnaring pedagogical dogma. Because they were not written as a collection or even meant to be read collectively, I have decided that to edit and reorganize them and strip them of their particular emotion and unique character, so that they are uniform and conforming chapters in a book, would be an injustice to their individual spirit. They are a collection of separate and occasional "personal letters" of collegial sharing written to the academic community and shared on the Internet.

They are a recounting of personal and professional experiences, an examination of my beliefs about education, a commemoration of student learning and achievement, a proclamation of faith in students, and a celebration of teaching. They are written more as personal poetry of my heart and soul than as impersonal analytical prose of my conscious mind. I want them to be enjoyed as well as studied, to be experienced as well as read. I want to pump more life and greater meaning into the educational process than does the usual bookish scholarship using bland educationese and lifeless jargon. I want to give education that too often lacking but needed *human* dimension, intimately fleshing out the dynamics of the teaching experience to proclaim that education is a human activity involving intriguing and complex real people with real names, who have real hopes and dreams and strengths and fears and frailties.

The collection is a series of separate reflections about how I struggle to practice my craft and carry on my mission. It is a collection of sharings, discussing why I came to believe the way I do, what I believe, why I teach the way I do, and how I now teach. It's a group of conversations about the human struggle in teaching and learning that brings into focus my own struggles and those of students. In a whimsical moment, I thought of following a colleague's advice and subtitling *Random Thoughts*: *One Professor's Struggle to Help Himself and His Students Become Real Human Beings.*

I also wrote the Random Thoughts for me. They remind me to stop being satisfied with who I was and with who I am, and to explore who I have the potential to be. They remind me not to be arrogant about who I am, but to be humble about who I might become. They remind me that I don't have to run away to get to someplace else. They remind me that the more I question something, the more I develop it; so the more I question, the more I develop. And finally, they remind me, as the opening and closing words of Stanley Kunitz' poem, *The Layers*, say: "I have walked through many lives ... I am not done with my changes."

Have a good one.

Louis Schmier
Valdosta, Georgia

PART TWO

Random Thoughts

Wednesday, 21 April 1993

CHARACTER-BASED EDUCATION

*I*t's 5:30 a.m. I just came in from a rejuvenating four-mile power walk. While traveling the streets, I was thinking about leaving tonight to attend Parents Weekend at my younger son's school in Maine. It's called Hyde School. It's quite a place. He owes his life to it; we owe our lives to it. I'd like to read you a statement about Hyde School:

> ... at Hyde School, we believe in the questions. Who am I? What am I capable of? What's holding me back? How do I get where I want to go? These questions, though sometimes painful, are signposts on a profound and personal journey, a journey to uncover and realize our unique potential. The way may be rocky, but it's a path that none of us can take alone. Without the help of family, friends, and teachers, some of us can get trapped in the questions, with no real skills for making sense of our demons and dreams. ...

Why do I bring this up? Well, while I was walking I was thinking about a conversation I had with a colleague. We were talking about the character-based curriculum I have been developing in my classes. I mentioned to him that at the beginning of the quarter, I had asked four questions of the 140 students in my three introductory history classes. The first question was: "How many of you think you're good, first-class students?" A total of 15 students sheepishly responded. Next I asked: "How many of you consider yourselves as mediocre or average students?" A total of 104 responded positively. Then I asked: "How many of you believe you're capable of being good, first-class students?" A stunning total of 96 raised their hands. And finally, I asked: "What's wrong? Why aren't you trying to reach what you believe you're capable of becoming?" The answer was silence and hesitant mumbles of "I don't know."

"So what's your point?" my colleague asked.

I told him that most of these students are not incompetent. They have great potential, but they are holding themselves back. For a whole bunch of reasons, they don't believe in themselves or are afraid of taking the risk of finding out about themselves. If only, I continued, we, as teachers, could help them find the way to change their attitudes and values, they would unswervingly strive to develop whoever it is they are.

"You're crazy. You and I are professors, not social workers!" was his rebuff.

Aren't we? Or, shouldn't we be? I asked myself these questions as I cut through the darkness. As a personal answer, I think being an effective and meaningful teacher, of any kind or at any educational level, means more than just being a master of a subject, being able to organize and emphasize information, being capable of clarifying ideas and pointing out relationships. If that is the sum of my teaching, then a tape recording, computer program, and/or a book can easily replace me.

No, if I am to deal, as I think teachers must, with the questions posed by the Hyde statement, I must be concerned with more than the subject matter and developing only the student's intellect. I think that any definition of teaching must include both a desire and an ability to motivate students to motivate themselves. Shouldn't the primary concern of the teacher be with developing those attitudes and emotions that energize the intellect to perform? I have reflected long and hard, and I have decided that for me to be an effective and meaningful teacher, I must be driven by a desire to help students tap their unrecognized potential by assisting them to find the hidden elements of their character. By "character" I mean responsibility, honesty, integrity, humility, "hard work," pursuit of excellence, pride, and willingness to help others. I cannot be the teacher I want to be unless I struggle to be a truly reasonable, open, caring, concerned, involved, and imaginative human being.

In short, being a teacher means not just asking students to ask the questions raised at Hyde School, but helping them struggle to find the answers for themselves and use those answers to develop their potential. And if all of that demands that a teacher be a counselor or a confessor or a social worker in addition to being a professor, so be it. That is what makes teaching a calling rather than just a profession or a job.

Have a good one.

Wednesday, 5 May 1993

A "HAPPENING" IN CLASS

*W*ell, it's early in the morning again and I have just come in, dripping wet, from a vigorous power walk. I love roaming the darkened, quiet streets. The air is clean and my thoughts are clear. This morning I was thinking about all that has happened in my classes during the 10 days since I returned from my son's school in Maine. It's really blown my mind and I'd like to share one great event with you this morning.

I found the courage to take the risk to place my students on their honor and trust them to do the right thing. I told them that I was going to let them administer their own weekly quiz. No department monitors. I appointed a student in each of my three freshman history classes to pick up the quiz from the department secretary, hand it out to the triads, use the answer key to have the triads grade their own quizzes, collect the quizzes, and hand them back to the department secretary. I left for Maine nervously thinking about whether I really wanted to know if I had any impact on them after only four weeks of class, and whether my concepts and techniques were working. When I returned, I asked each class how things went. In one class, which consisted of 13 triads, one of the quieter students said, with a noticeably annoyed tone, "Fine, but were we allowed to use the book?"

"Damn," I thought, disappointed. And then I asked the students, "What happened?" Those were the last words I said as the students spontaneously took over for the rest of the class. The conversation went something like this (thankfully, I feverishly but quietly took notes of the discussion):

> "There was cheating in some of the triads. You used the book to look up the answers. I am mad. We didn't cheat."

> "We let Dr. Schmier down. He trusted us."

> "Hell, we let ourselves down!"

> "Why didn't you say something Friday when it really counted? Maybe we could have talked then."

> "I wanted to, but I was scared that everyone would think I was a brown-nosing do-gooder."

> "It's easy to do it now that Dr. Schmier is here to 'protect us.'"

> "I would have backed you up. But I didn't have the guts to say, 'This isn't right. It ain't worth it.' I'm just as guilty letting it happen as those who cheated."

> "Bull! Who are you to accuse others?"

> "I'm mad because we didn't cheat and they're going to get just as good a grade."

"Is that all you're concerned about, the grade? How about doing it just because it's the right thing to do? But I didn't want to get involved either."

"I felt it was none of my business. If they could get away with it … I was sort of envious that I didn't have the nerve."

"Those who cheated, speak up. We know who you are. Do you have the guts to open up right here and now?"

"Dr. Schmier, our triad cheated. I've been feeling shitty about it all weekend. I rationalized that we were only checking three answers, but that's no different since we would have changed them all if they were wrong."

"It's no big deal. We changed only three questions. As I figure, that's about 3/25th of 1 percent of the final grade."

"You sell your honesty cheap."

"I don't see where it's worth it. Something's wrong if a lousy small grade means that much."

"What will you do if some big thing came down, when you people showed no backbone over something this small?"

"We cheated, too. … But I don't think we ought to get punished real hard since we admitted it and some others still haven't."

"You want a reward? Hell, you cheat, you pay. Just because you admitted what we all know doesn't mean you get a medal. What you ought to do is look at yourself and learn. I say, Dr. Schmier, that those that cheated should get 0's!"

"I'll take it."

"There are others. At least go into his office and own up. You screwed us all."

"Wait a minute. I've been listening. We screwed ourselves, me included, by letting it happen when it happened. We all lose his trust. So let's stop feeling so righteous."

> "I think we all ought to leave here and do some heavy thinking
> about just how upstanding people we are. Let's see who has
> the guts to do something about it. How can he trust us again?
> Why should he?"

"Damn," I jubilantly thought to myself. I was so excited. I thought that that
was the end of it, but there was to be more. Students from three other triads
who cheated came to my office and quietly turned themselves in.

> "We figured if others were doing it, it was all right. But that's
> crap. It was wrong and there are no two ways about it. You
> took a risk to trust us and we didn't take the same risk to trust
> ourselves. The truth is that some of us just didn't study and
> this was the easy way out, and the rest of us went along. We
> talked and we decided we want the 0's. We're going to study
> our asses off from now on."

Now that's what I call a value-forming, character-shaping experience.

Understand that I don't teach character. I don't believe I can. I do not
have any curriculum units that say "this is character," or "do this or that"
or "you get it this way or that way." But I can and do create a spirit and
attitude that permeate the entire class, that place an extraordinary amount
of importance on character, that help the students develop their character,
and that place them in value-forming experiences. That is what education
is all about.

Have a good one.

Saturday, 8 May 1993

WHAT A STUDENT NEEDS

*W*ell, it's real early in the morning. It's starting to get humid and warm
down here in south Georgia, even at 5 in the morning. As I was
walking the quiet streets, I was thinking again. This time it was about a
discussion — a vigorous discussion — I had yesterday afternoon with a
colleague from the School of Business at a TGIF (Thank God It's Friday)
faculty get-together. She had come up to me and started talking to me
about my character-based approach in my classes. I was in an excited
mood. I felt that I had had a good week in my classes. There was that one
class that had learned a dramatic lesson in applied ethics through the
cheating incident. Another class had kicked me out of class so that they
could have what one student called some "honest truth talk."

"I'm no Sister Teresa," my colleague proclaimed. "We are here to send the students out into the workplace with a degree that will give them a better job. And that's all my job is!"

"Is that what an education is all about," I replied, "just to get a job?"

"Yes, and the student should have to take only those courses that they need," she asserted.

"Why, then, are we in June becoming a university, at least in name?" I asked.

"It will give our students more prestige. They'll be more marketable if they graduate from a university rather than a college," she replied with assurance.

"Sounds like packaging to me, marketing if you will," I retorted to my colleague, who was from the marketing department. "Pretty glitter that's more show than substance."

While the conversation ended without any minds being changed, it was my colleague's word, "need," that continued to haunt me this morning. What does a student, any person, need? A student needs to be independent; a student needs to be able to think for himself or herself; a student has to believe in himself or herself if he or she is to struggle to reach his or her potential; a student needs to be able to control the forces swirling around him or her rather than let them control him or her. To put it in other words, give me a person who believes in himself or herself and can think for himself or herself, and he or she can learn to be anything at any time.

I think those attributes are especially "needed" in these turbulent times. We see all around us that we are living in a world of rapidly changing job skill requirements. We are seeing what happens to people when the particular job skill they are learning or have practiced is no longer needed. It seems to me that my colleague's myopic definition of an education would not offer people the personal life-skills they "need" in order to be independent of, flexible in, and adaptable to such dramatically changing situations.

Moreover, it seems that such a narrow definition of an education is limited to the workplace and preparing students for a single career. But what about the rest of their daily lives? There is life before a job, aside from a job, and after a job. What will prepare them for life outside the workplace? The truth is that students will become more than just breadwinners. They will become friends, spouses, parents, and citizens. No, an education is about far more than just getting a job. It is about learning how to live as well as how to make a living. The primary goals of an education should be to encourage our students to strive for their fullest potential as whole individuals and contributing members of society. And we, as their teachers, "need" to commit ourselves to developing not just the brains and hands of our students, but their minds and hearts as well.

Have a good one.

Tuesday, 11 May 1993
S H E L L E Y

*W*ell, here I am again. I've just come in from my power walking. I've been thinking about what happened in another one of my classes last Tuesday. It was about 11:30 a.m. A student had just left my office. For almost an hour and a half, I had listened intently, saying almost nothing, as she told me about what had happened in our 9 a.m. intro class. I got up from my chair, walked slowly across my rather expansive and cluttered office, closed the door, slowly walked back to my chair, and sat down. It was all almost in slow motion. And suddenly, in an outburst of energy, I banged on the desk with both fists and screamed out a private and orgasmic (that's the only way to describe it) — "YES!!!!" I've been on a controlled high ever since. Let me tell you why.

What I call a "happening" had occurred in my 9 o'clock class. Last Tuesday, many of the students in that class, at least for that moment, had "found themselves." I had walked into class ready to discuss the day's assigned reading and discussion issue. Before I could utter a word, Shelley — a quiet student who had been afraid to talk in class — got up from her chair. Without waiting for me to recognize her, she firmly said, "Dr. Schmier, when we had our open class evaluation yesterday, there was a lot of bullshit going around. I think we all have to have a 'truth talk' with each other, but we can't if you're around. Could you please leave?"

"What's going on? What are they going to do to me?" I silently asked myself — very nervously.

Shelley had come into my office the day before and said that not many students were honest in their appraisal of the class, and she asked what she should do. I replied that she should do what she thinks needs to be done. And now this!

My feet became jelly; my heart started pounding; I admit I was afraid. The other students turned to me to see what I would do. Words like "courage" and "risk" and "honesty" suddenly came home to roost.

I had told them the day before that I had a tough skin and needed their input in order to improve in the class whatever needs improvement. Talk about being on the spot! Well, I figured I had to put my money where my mouth was. I nervously walked out of the room. For the next hour, I fidgeted on the computer, struggling to write something sensible, but my mind was on the goings-on in that classroom.

From what Shelley told me and later recorded for me, this is the gist of what happened:

> "Yesterday we had a class discussion where Dr. Schmier asked us how we thought the class could be bettered. But none of you spoke up and said anything. You were afraid he'd hold it against you and you were more worried about your grade than helping yourselves or to improve the class for all of us."

> "She's right. We've got to get down to business."

> "I hate these triads. I don't want to depend on someone else for my grade. I don't need anyone else."

> "You play football. No wonder we have a lousy team. Where's all this teamwork stuff, or is all that crap only to sound good?"

> "I'm going to med school. I need good grades. I want to drop this course. My adviser told me to wait for an easy class. He's such a bastard for not letting me."

> "I heard you try to corner and embarrass him at the beginning of class. But he didn't back down. I think he did you a favor. Maybe instead of whining you ought to meet the challenge and stop acting like a spoiled brat. Are you going to take only easy courses in med school? Stay away from me when you get out!"

> "Let's get down to business. How many of you honestly do the assignments every day and come in prepared, or even use the SQ3R methods Dr. Schmier suggested at the beginning of the class?"

> "Some of you don't even read the syllabus calendar and then complain you don't know what's expected or assigned."

"Here's what I think. The reason some of you are complaining is that you're not doing your work and you want a free grade."

"Well, I don't understand the discussions sometimes."

"Ask questions. I've never seen anybody embarrassed in this class when they do. He loves questions."

"Then he makes us answer our own questions."

"Maybe he's trying to show you that you're able to answer the question, but are too lazy or scared to try."

"Maybe he could summarize at the end of class."

"Tell him. He won't bite. I'll tell him."

"Some of the triads aren't working."

"Well, ours has become a study group."

"We're friends and have become like family. We come to each other with our real personal problems."

"It's been hard for us, but we're getting to know each other and starting to work together."

"I think we are becoming family. I know more people in this class than in all my classes since I've been here combined. I see some of you talking outside class. Some of you don't know a great thing when you see it. Like Dr. Schmier says,'You gets out whats you puts in.' "

"I like taking the quizzes and discussing tidbits like we were one. It's not that we can do less work by sharing the load. Hell, I learn more arguing over the answer to a question than when I study by myself."

"Yeah, but some of us aren't together. We haven't been pulling our weight. But we're not giving up. If you can do it, so can we. We have to help each other."

"Why doesn't everyone look at each other and point to the ones who aren't doing their share. Say that we need your help. You're important to your triad. You're part of us and without you we're not operating at 100 percent. Go ahead. Point."

"Look, Dr. Schmier comes in here, come hell or high water, prepared, alert, and ready for bear. We owe him to do the same thing."

"That's his job. He gets paid for teaching us."

"And we pay to learn by ourselves. We owe it to ourselves. If we don't want it, why should he give it to us? Why the hell are you here?"

"To get a grade. This is all so stupid. He doesn't lecture. He doesn't give out any handouts. He doesn't tell us what's going to be and what's not going to be on the quizzes. When we ask him what he wants on the exams, he says, 'What do you think you should do?' "

"Get a life. You ain't going to make the grade."

"I don't like how he asks me questions. He's always asking, 'Why?' He embarrasses me."

"Maybe you embarrass yourself because you come in here unprepared and try to wing it. He's not going to let you get away with it. He's too good and cares too much to let you do less than what he thinks you're capable of doing."

"Hey, I've been in his office and talked with him. Remember, he dragged me in kicking and screaming. He really cares about us. He wants us to care about ourselves. If you don't want to give him a chance, give yourselves a chance. Hell, how many of the profs around here would do what he just did? I really respect him for that. Maybe some of you ought to start respecting yourselves."

"How many of you have a smart person in the triad and say, 'Well, they'll carry my load. I don't have to do anything.' Well, get off your asses. Our triad meets twice a week in the library. We're there about 2-4 hours. Come on over and join us. It's working for us. It can work for you. We'll help anyone who wants to help themselves."

"That's a good idea. We meet in the library too. We'll help anyone who needs it. But you have to come prepared."

"Three of us just have been talking. I know we're not in the same triads, but that doesn't matter. We've decided that we're going to designate ourselves class tutors. Let's start a history lab. We make a commitment to the class to be in the library twice a ..."

"My best time is Sunday."

"OK. We'll also be in the library on Sundays from 2 to 4. We'll reserve a study room and we can discuss. Your obligation is that you have to read the material before you come in to discuss. We're not going to do your work. Come in and join the rest of us for a talk. If you haven't done the reading, come in and read, and then ask questions."

"I hate the tidbits. I tell him what each article is about and he says that he wants to know why it's important and what does it mean. I've never had to do that. It's too hard."

"He wants you to think and understand. Use the guide words he gave us. What we do is read together and talk about the meaning of the article. We consider the points and see how they apply in our lives and society today."

"Sometimes, when we finish talking, we close our eyes and do a quantum leap, like he does with us in class, and imagine what's going on, and feel the article."

"We'll work on the tidbits in the library."

"I'm not sure this is all going to work."

"It won't if you don't want it to."

"I don't know if I can do it. It's hard and I'm not used to it."

"Maybe she and the others are right. Let's see if we can help each other in our triads and between the triads. We might learn something."

"We're used to memorizing things for a test. He doesn't do that. He says he wants us to think. I've never done that. Why doesn't he just tell us what to learn?"

> "Maybe he wants us to take control of ourselves and make our own decisions. That's scary. If some of you are willing to help, I'm game."

> "I know you all said you were going to come, but if you don't, it won't hurt us or him. You'll be hurting yourself. I'm going, and if you don't show up, it's your own fault. I heard bellyaching today. Sometimes I'm one of you, but you're not putting forth the effort. You're not trying."

> "He promised us pizza and drinks on him if we all pass this course. I got a taste for pepperoni and mushrooms. Let's think on it today and meet in the library and talk some more if you want."

Shelley wrote me a personal letter at the end of her written summary of the class events. I want to share it with you. I do so not to brag about myself, but to applaud and praise her. We just had Honors Day here at the college. She did not receive any recognition. She did not receive any awards. She didn't have the grades. In fact, she is among that group of students who my colleagues say don't belong in college. Well, in my book she is an honor to have in my class. She and all the others are the reason I go to sleep each night anticipating the next day's classes. They make all the frustration and aggravation and worrying and hard work worthwhile. They are my encouragement and strength in the face of discouragement. I offer you her letter to show what unique potential lays hidden within these "poor students," and what they can discover with some support, effort, and caring. I cried as I read the letter:

> A few members of the class said today that they just didn't think that things would work out for some reason or another. But it didn't disappoint me all that much, because if they don't learn anything from what I and all the others said, I learned a lot. I learned that I can do things that I never thought I could do. I learned that I could be a leader, and I guess it is something I wanted to do all my life, but was afraid to do and felt I couldn't do. In high school I wanted to be, let's say, an officer in a club, but I wasn't popular. I was shy. I didn't believe I was a leader. And I thought that the people who were popular were better than me. I was sort of a loner in high school.

> I don't know what happened in your class. I don't know. This feeling just came over me. I know I was surprised that when

I came to you and said that something had to be done in the
class because people weren't honest about their feelings in
the open evaluation, you only said that I should do what
I thought should be done. I felt you felt that I was good
enough to be trusted enough that I could decide, not you,
what the right thing was to do. I am so happy with myself
because I'm so much more than I thought I was. I've never
been able to speak in front of people. The one time I had
to stand in front of a class was in a history class in high
school. But I was too shy. I literally passed out on the spot
because I was too nervous. When I got up and asked you to
leave the class so we could talk, I was so nervous that I could
hardly get the words out. I was shaking and sweating. And
when I was up there in front of the class, Dr. Schmier, I knew
I would end up crying, and when that happened I would fall
over and pass out like last time. But I didn't! I didn't do it!
I think the reason I didn't do that was because you trusted
me by leaving without a protest, and more importantly
because my triad had encouraged me to say something.
They were out there supporting me when I said something.
Others were supporting me too, when others were saying
negative things. But I have such a feeling of accomplishment.
I can do anything! I am growing as a person. I think
I stopped being a kid. I learned that I can face people.
I learned that I can face myself. ...

I'm proud of myself! I feel that I have earned this sense of
accomplishment. For the first time in my life, I took a deep
breath and I took a big risk, not knowing whether it was
going to be for the best or not. But I left your office feeling
that you bet on me and I figured it was time I had to try
to trust myself. I've helped myself and found a me that
I thought didn't exist. I hope that I can help anyone who
needs encouragement to help themselves. I'll never stop
trying. But Dr. Schmier, I just want to thank you for helping
me because you helped me a lot by showing that you believed
in me and helping me believe in myself even though you
never said anything. It was just that I knew from how you
acted and talked in class that you really cared about me as a
person. I truly believe now that if I want something, I can
get it. And I am not going to let anyone tell me I can't.
And I'm going to remember forever what it felt like when
someone told me or acted like they were better than me.
I'm not going to do that to anyone if I can help it. I've grown

a lot since I've been in your class. I've learned a lot about myself, about others, and about history too. I'm starting to see now that only I can, as you say, hold my head up.

I can't let anyone else tell me how to think about me. What they think about me is their concern. I think I understand when you say the problem is inside of us and so is the solution. I think I'm beginning, just beginning, so don't expect too much, to understand what you mean when you once handed out: 'To strive to reach the potential that is inside you, you need the will to achieve and the courage to fail.' I taped that on my mirror last night. I'll never, never, never forget that, this class, or you. Thank you, Dr. Schmier, for being you and being there.

On that note, I'll just say a very quiet,

Have a good one.

Sunday, 23 May 1993
MISS TROMBLY

*W*ell, I've been walking the darkened streets again, thinking about OBE, job training vs. education, liberal arts vs. professional programs, etc. I guess it's that time of the year when such things are on everyone's minds as graduates leave the stage with a diploma in one hand and want ads in the other.

I hadn't rounded the first corner today when into my head popped, "It's all in the wrist, people, it's all in the wrist," and my thoughts began to center on diminutive, plump, buxom Miss Helen Trombly. She had been my typing/shorthand teacher in high school way back in 1956. I'd like to tell you about her because I think she is worth knowing about.

She was quite a lady, though no one appreciated her at the time. I certainly didn't. She didn't cut a striking figure. She didn't light up a room when she entered. She was quiet and unassuming, maybe a touch shy. I can't say she carried herself with dignity. If anything, she was bland. She wore her graying hair up in a bun. Her clothing was drab. When her reading glasses weren't hanging around her neck and resting on her chest, held there by a frayed black string, they sat halfway down her nose. I can still

see her eyes peering over those black frames and saying firmly but warmly
— over and over and over again as we struggled with banging on the
typewriter and writing those surrealistic shorthand lines with our pencils
— "It's all in the wrist. It's all in the wrist."

She was a lonely figure. We kids made cruel jokes about her. We didn't take
either her or the course seriously. Why should we? This was secretarial
administration. It was a subject that we college-bound kids were told by
other teachers was "crib," "below" us, and only for the "girl rocks" who
were going into the workforce after graduating high school. The only reason
we were there was because it was, along with shop and home economics
(I took a class in cooking and made biscuits that the Navy still uses as
anchors), one of those "snap," lowly, fill-in electives. Yet, upon reflection
over the years, that course turned out to be one of the most interesting and
influential courses I ever took.

Miss Trombly was not content with teaching us to merely learn how to
type and take shorthand. As I look back, I think she was more interested in
preparing us for life than for a life of typing and taking shorthand. There
were no mindless Gregg typing or shorthand manuals to be found in the
class. No charts of either the keyboard or the shorthand symbols hung on
the walls. Instead, the walls were so draped with hand-printed quotations
that they looked like pages from Bartlett's. She changed them every week.
There were no dull repetition drills. She expected us to learn on our own,
outside of class, how to set our fingers on the typewriter and learn the
keyboard and learn the shorthand symbols — "squiggle stuff," as she
called them.

In class, to sharpen our typing and shorthand skills (so she said),
we copied bits and pieces she had selected from Hemingway, Greene,
Faulkner, Rand, and a few others! With about 15 minutes left in the
one-hour class, she would stop us and ask us how we felt about the
passages we had typed. "Be a thinking person," she'd quietly admonish us
if we hesitated, "not a living typewriter." To practice our margin and tab
skills on the typewriter, we copied passages from Shakespeare, Pope, Keats,
Death of a Salesman, *The Glass Menagerie*, *The Cherry Orchard*, *Requiem for
a Heavyweight*, and a few other plays. And then, she'd ask us how we felt
about the passages. "There's more to life than being a secretary," she'd warn
us. To develop our shorthand speed and typing dictation speed, half the
class formally debated issues while the other half struggled to record it.
And we had to come in prepared to debate! As I remember, we discussed
civil rights and racism, sex, communism, religion, and democracy. This
was a secretarial administration class, but she would not allow us to merely
"get by." I can still hear her firm, caring, melodious voice reaching out and
saying, "Louis, is that really the best you can do?" or "Where's your pride

in what you're doing, Schmier?" "Be honest, Louis." "Stop being scared, Mr. Schmier. Think for yourself."

Miss Trombly had been shunned and even ridiculed by the other teachers, even the ones in home economics and shop. No one ever or would ever have thought to nominate her for the school's "teacher of the year" award. I certainly would not have. Hell, that course was supposed to be a breeze, not a debating-English-philosophy-history-and-God-knows-what-else course, the grade for which we had to work! And I haven't said a thing about her tests — mind-challenging "evaluations" and "opportunity experiences," as she labeled them. No, no nominations then. After class was over, I don't think I ever said a word to her. I am truly sorry about that and wish I could apologize. It was my loss. I don't know about the others, but I learned a hell of a lot more than typing and shorthand, though it took me decades to realize and appreciate that I did. Accolades to her today.

It wasn't until a few years ago that I unexpectedly thought about that … (I won't tell you what we called her at the time). Oh, I had written the books and articles, and made my professional reputation, and I had a reputation of being a crack teacher. But something was missing. I felt off balance, for the scholarship — that damn publish-or-perish garbage — had come at the expense of the classroom. I was a good teacher, really good, but deep down I felt that I could be so much better and do so much more for students. Then Miss Trombly started haunting me again and showing me the way: "It's all in the wrist, people. It's all in the wrist."

I think a lot about Miss Trombly. I wish I could thank her. She helped show me that the true teacher must be far more student-oriented than subject-oriented, that the true assessment of a class or curriculum or major is far more the character of the people who leave it than the content presented in it, and that my dedication to helping the students broadly prepare for life is a far, far better thing I do — for them and for me — than merely training them for a job. "It's all in the wrist, people. It's all in the wrist."

Have a good one.

Thursday, 27 May 1993
LIBERAL ARTS

*A*s I traveled the darkened streets this morning in solitude, I was pondering passages from *Hamlet* and *Julius Caesar*. In Act I, Scene 3, of Hamlet, Polonius says to his son, Laertes: "For the apparel oft proclaims the man." Does, then, the mere taking of a core of liberal arts courses, or even a liberal arts major, proclaim the enriched spirit and mental agility of a person? I wish it did, but there isn't an automatic and exclusive impact by such core courses or programs on a person.

Liberal arts is not a course or a major or a program. It is not a class, but what takes place inside the classroom and what is generated within the student. It is an attitude, a spirit that permeates every fiber of a person's being, that creates a place of questions and initiates the first steps toward wisdom. A liberal arts curriculum should be judged by that ethereal and more difficult measurement of what the student has become, the centrally defining attributes of character that energize and give direction to native talent. But that requires that professors lead the way. They must first have a vision and then give it life in the imagination of the students.

Yet, students are led down isolated, barrel-visioned, pre-determined paths overloaded with "courses appropriate to the major." Liberal arts core courses are often paid little more than lip service. Students are led to believe that every course must have a utilitarian vocational value. They and professors are too often infected with what I call the "I don't need it for the major" syndrome. Departments and schools vie with each other for body counts. Classes are so stylized that few stand free and are alive. Professors package and filter information to students who are under considerable pressure to please them. Professors fearfully seek to please students. Professors divert their energies from the classroom to research and publication. And so it's not all that clear that most present-day institutions of higher learning are the best places to acquire a liberal education, or that studying the liberal arts has a guaranteed meaningful connection with the enrichment of a student. And "the fault, dear Brutus, lies not in our stars, but in ourselves."

Have a good one.

Friday, 4 June 1993

P E E R   P R E S S U R E

*W*ell, I've just come in from an arduous power walk. And though the south Georgia sun has yet to come up, I still feel like one of Noel Coward's mad dogs and Englishmen. At this early, hot, and humid hour of the darkened day, I was thinking about peer pressure. It was not the common variety of peer pressure that we usually think about — the kind that exists among our kids or students. The peer pressure — the deadening, negative peer pressure — that I was thinking about is the one that exists among faculty; the overt kind that frequently demeans the value and professionalism of classroom teaching; the adversarial kind that has the chilling effect of intimidating teaching innovation and extinguishing the flames of experimentation; the subtle kind that forces professors to scale back their efforts, dampens their enthusiasm, and erodes their self-satisfaction; the isolating and ignoring kind that creates a frustrating loner syndrome; the kind that is the enemy of educational excellence and a breeder of stylized classrooms that produce a rising tide of mediocrity; the kind that is spread by the apocalyptic horsemen of arrogance, insecurity, cynicism, self-righteousness, laziness, resentment, jealousy, guilt, lack of personal and/or professional esteem, skepticism, hostility, negativity, disbelief, and disinterest.

It is disappointing to see colleagues not striving to do their best in the classroom or thinking that they have little upon which to improve. It is, however, abhorrent for colleagues to actively seek to diminish the performance of others, and it is that kind of behavior that rightly invites criticism aimed at all levels of education. We don't want to talk about it; we prefer to ignore it, maybe deny it. But it's there!

What got me started on this usually ignored subject was a conversation I had with a colleague, a friend and associate of long standing, a self-proclaimed student-oriented teacher, and a supporter of liberal arts education.

I had just come into my office to "come down" from a particularly exhilarating class. I had begun my intro class with a question about the McCarthy witch hunts. Some of my students took control of the class. I stepped back as they moved spontaneously into a discussion of individual rights and majority rule that ended up in a heated argument about political correctness.

So, there I was with my feet propped up on my desk, a cup of coffee in hand, about to read the latest issue of the student newspaper when in walked my colleague. Without so much as a "How are you doing?" he rather rudely blurted out, in an obviously agitated tone, "Louis, you've done it again. Some of us were talking and we don't appreciate you using students to promote yourself to fill your classes, much less manipulating them to advance your agenda and have it imposed upon us."

"I suppose you're a spokesman," I replied with a calmness that surprised me. I guess I've been around my son's school in Maine too long. "So, Mr. Spokesman, tell me just what are you talking about. What is it that I am supposed to have done?"

"You know," he asserted. "It's in the 'Letter to the Editor' section of the paper. Some think that you actually wrote it!"

I opened the paper and read a letter written by six of my students:

> Hi, we are students in Dr. Schmier's His 200 class. In addition to the assigned triads, we have joined with a few of our fellow students to develop an informal study group. We call ourselves the 'SCHMIERITES.' Our motto is why ask why? BECAUSE WE ARE SCHMIERITES!
>
> If you've heard about Dr. Schmier's class, you are probably wondering about our reaction to his innovative, provocative and radical teaching methods. Well, you could call it a love/hate relationship. Some days we hate him for making us work so damn hard. But most days we love him. Never in all of our education experience have we had to toil this hard. He motivates us to push ourselves to the max and beyond. We have to delve deeper within ourselves to find the answers to the who, what and why questions of American history. He expects us to accomplish his goals for us, and more importantly, to accomplish the goals we've set for ourselves. Never give up, he says, on ourselves or on others. We are learning to not take anything for granted. Question everything. Be critical and skeptical. WHY? WHY? WHY? When the other professors here at VSC get sick of us asking so many questions in class, they can blame Dr. Schmier.
>
> Want to improve your outlook and increase your expectations? Does your self-esteem need a boost? Need better study habits? Want the experience of being a team member or even a team leader? Searching for courage? Want to test your honesty and integrity? Want to read until your eyes bug out? Do you want to learn how to debate an issue? Do you like adventure and seek your unique potential? Are you willing to put forth your best, and then your better than best, and boldly face new challenges? Do you yearn for a permanent, personalized seat in the Library? Would you like to really learn about people in American history and not just memorize facts? Like to argue about today's issues? If you answered yes to any or all of these questions — take the plunge and sign up for Dr. Schmier's History 200 class.
>
> WE GIVE OUR THANKS TO DR. SCHMIER!! He has enriched and enhanced our lives. We have begun to think

> differently, our study habits are better, and our general
> outlook is better. We have opened our eyes and our minds.

"How about that!" I quietly exclaimed.

"Is that all you have to say?" my colleague impatiently asked. "We hear that they sent copies to every administrator on campus. What do you have to say for yourself?"

"It seems that they said it all," I whispered as I focused on those words.

"Look," he proclaimed, "most of us, certainly me, don't care what you do in your classes with your students. But you can't do these things. They're spilling over into our classes and threatening us. And what about the other day when you let your students kick you out of class to talk about you behind your back? The next thing they'll come into my class and challenge my authority. I'm a damn good teacher. I work with the students. You know that. But you're making me look bad. What are my student evaluations now going to say?"

"Am I really threatening you," I asked as I looked up from the paper, "or are you feeling threatened?"

The conversation rambled on for a while, but little was accomplished. You know, sometimes as I roam my campus, I think of a prison. I see the separate cells of offices, classrooms, departments, and schools that unnaturally dissect the living body of knowledge and strip education of its natural sociality. It's almost like everyone is teaching and learning in solitary confinement. Someone once told me, "What a world of love teaching is." Like love, teaching is not an individualistic activity in which professor is isolated behind the lectern or podium from students or is isolated from colleagues. It is a social activity between professor and students, as well as among professors, the lack of which reduces opportunities to acquire new knowledge and attitudes and skills. Teaching is a love whose excitements, fears, triumphs, and disappointments should be joyously shared, not jealously guarded or defensively feared and protected against. A college campus should crackle not only with the excitement of research and scholarship; it should revel with enthusiasm of examining substantive issues, exchanging ideas, and encouraging reflection about one's own teaching; it should reduce, not increase, strain and tension; it should be dedicated to the affirmation of dynamic instruction by acting as a catalyst for sharing, educating, and promoting growth; it should recognize that teaching is not the bastard child to be tolerated, but the love child to be embraced.

I really get tired of the negative, debilitating peer pressure, of trying to be convinced that I am the mutant or that I must climb unending hills or fight endless windmills. Let the dynamic professors come out from the closet and use peer pressure for positive ends. Let the dynamic professors stop feeling self-conscious and band together with confidence to persuade their colleagues to use creative teaching methods that actively involve students in the learning process. I have a dream that when professors will emerge from their cell-like offices and their isolated classrooms to talk enthusiastically over coffee about their exciting teaching ideas, when they will visit each other's classrooms to observe, exchange information, and help each other develop new teaching skills, then they will help students find themselves.

Imagine the teaching experiences, the fresh ideas, the increased enthusiasm by professor and student, and the pursuit of educational excellence that would be generated. I have a dream of when teaching on the college or university campus will acquire a status equal to scholarship, of when it will become a shared and joyful enterprise in which professors will participate with mutual respect for one another. But for that to happen, we all must acknowledge the uncomfortable and sometimes painful truth of Cassius' words: "Men at some time are masters of their fates." The fault, to paraphrase Shakespeare, dear colleagues, is not in some inanimate abstraction called "society" or "administration" or "education," but in each of us.

Have a good one.

Tuesday, 20 July 1993

D I V E R S I T Y

*L*ordy, it was hot and humid out there this morning. It was also like Grand Central Station on the streets. Maybe that's because I went out late to power walk. Anyway, the diversity of people out there was amazing. There I was, in my early 50s — my very early 50s — chugging away on my four-mile route at 8 1/2 minute/mile splits. I know. I'm bragging. With a polite "Good morning," I rushed past a young lady, maybe in her 30s, who was doing a modest regular walk. A young man, in his 20s, later whizzed past me from the opposite direction running at a marathon clip. On the opposite side of the street, a fast-jogging, middle-aged woman passed me. A young college woman was doing a slow jog on a cross-street. On another cross-street, two elderly women were leisurely walking as they talked to each other. Then, there was the pair of bicyclers who passed me in a blur, and a delightful octogenarian couple lazily pedaling on a tricycle-for-two. As I walked, I was struck by that diversity. I began thinking how inappropriate and difficult it would be to compare those of us on the street this morning. It would be silly to talk about the fastest, slowest, longest, shortest, worst, best. After all, we did not have the same starting place; we were not on the same route; we were not traveling the same distances; we did not have the same destination; we did not have the same capacities; we did not have the same purposes; we weren't engaged in the same form of exercise. I suppose someone could compare jogging, running, and walking, the distances we each traveled, and each of our time splits, and relate them to ages and genders. I suppose that might serve some purpose. But it wouldn't say much about each of our distinctive features and personal idiosyncrasies. We were like those proverbial apples and oranges and tangerines and bananas.

Doesn't the same situation exist in our classrooms? We are wrong to assume that students are like one another in their potential and in their capacity for growth, and that each student should aspire to a single image of success and achievement. Students are not tin cans to be produced on some monotonous production line. They are not all square pegs to be jammed into round holes created by some depersonalizing and  averaging psychological models. Our educational system supposedly values the dignity and worth of each student. Yet we ignore the diversity of individuality and act as if the diversity in our classrooms is something brand new. Merely because some students do not have any distinctive age, physical feature, or measurable testing or performance distinction associated with the non-traditional student or the physically challenged student or the learning-challenged student, we have wrongly assumed that they are all alike.

Yet if we are supposed to modify our classes to accommodate these newly discovered students, why can't we use the same approach with all other students? One of the characteristics of a good teacher is that he or she pays equal attention to the "slow walkers," "marathon runners," "power walkers," "bicyclers," and "joggers" in the class. After all, isn't the purpose of education to help the individual become whatever he or she has the potential to be? Students are different, and education should lead to individualization, not collectivization. The diversity of potentials in a class means that there needs to be a diversity of ideas about what constitutes success and achievement for any one individual. If our goal is to educate students, then every student — every student — is worth educating.

Have a good one.

Wednesday, 21 July 1993

T H E " G O O D " S T U D E N T

*A*s I pounded the asphalt streets this morning, I was thinking about grapefruits and students. My wife had gotten up early this morning. Darling as she may normally be, she is not a happy camper in the morning — especially if she thinks that my rummaging through my dresser drawers like a "clunky elephant" (her words), groping in the dark for a pair of jogging shorts, is what awakes her from blissful slumber. To bribe her, I made coffee, cut a grapefruit, and offered her a half. As I sat across the table eating my half, trying to use my innocent smiles to parry her stares and sneers, I dared not disagree when she asked if my grapefruit was as bad as hers. Secretly, I liked the taste of my half.

Having escaped with my life, I ran out the door for my walk. I had not gotten far in my travels when the question of what is a "good" grapefruit suddenly popped into my mind. And I started thinking as my body struggled to cut through the wall of water we call humidity down here. When I got back to the house, I said to myself, "What if I took all the grapefruits out from the two small bags and put them on the kitchen counter to compare and contrast them?" I could arrange them according to size. I could take out the food scale and weigh each. I could array them according to the color of the rind. I could even separate them according to the color of the meat.

Having done this, I thought, what would I have accomplished? I would not have discovered the "good grapefruit." I would not have learned very much about the quality of any one of the grapefruits. No, if I wanted to know whether I had a "good" grapefruit, I first would have to know all about the particular grapefruit I have. Then, I would have to eliminate my subjective judgments, for while my wife likes her grapefruit on the sweet side, I like mine on the sour side. And finally, I would have to discover just what constitutes an absolute "good" grapefruit. At that moment, I recalled John Locke saying something about man's view of nature, which may apply here. He might have said that such things as "good" grapefruits may not have real existence. They may be the creations of man's mind and the quest for order rather than the work of nature itself.

Evaluating students is not much different from my problem with the grapefruit, except that the evaluation problem is even more complex when it comes to human beings. We can try to know who the student we have in our classroom is — that is, if we really care. But, like grapefruits, we only can compare and contrast them by looking at their personal experiences, their past academic performances, and maybe a battery of evaluating tests.

But, I thought, after all was said and done, would we be any closer to knowing what constitutes that Platonic, absolute "good" student by which all real living and breathing students are judged? Or, as Locke said, are we creating an artificial order for the sake of convenience and other less noble reasons?

It seems to me that such constructs are far more in the interest of us teachers than in the interest of the student. Moreover, are the criteria we use in our quest for the Holy Grail of the "good" student legitimate? After all, didn't we once — and regrettably still do in some perverse circles — heavily weigh physical appearance, race, cultural background, and gender in our evaluation? Didn't these criteria color our judgments, distort our decisions, and limit our actions? It seems to me that we have to take great care with such imageries, for they may inadvertently be no less a danger to our essential concern for the sanctity and development of the individual student than any other bias, stereotype, or prejudice. If we have to have such images for the sake of convenient conversation, we can't make them absolute truths. Remember, they are always contestable and fallible.

Anyway, like the grapefruit, we can try to know what a student was and is. I am, however, less certain intellectually, emotionally, or experientially of what the student will be or should be — just as I can never know what an absolutely "good" grapefruit is like.

Have a good one.

Monday, 26 July 1993

A METAPHOR EXERCISE

Hi from hot and steamy south Georgia. It was strange this morning. I hardly noticed anything as I roamed the darkened streets. In fact, my walk seemed to last only a minute or two. I guess I was deeply — very deeply — engrossed in my thoughts. Lucky for me that not even the milkman is out at that wee hour of the pre-dawn morning. I can't remember slowing up for a stop sign or red light to see what was coming. I was thinking about the results of an exercise I had given my students at the beginning of the quarter in an effort to get a sense of their feelings and attitudes about me as a professor, about themselves as students, about the purpose of a college education, and about college itself. I think that this is important, since it is the too often ignored emotional side of the student that energizes or stifles his or her efforts and affects his or her performance.

Going over the results once again, I was again astounded, saddened, angered — and challenged.

The exercise was fairly simple. I asked each student to complete the following sentences, using metaphors, similes, or analogies:

> Education is/is like …
>
> Professors are/are like …
>
> College is/is like …
>
> Learning is/is like …
>
> Students are/are like …

One hundred nineteen students took the exercise. They were mostly freshmen and sophomores. Some were juniors. None were entering freshmen, and about 25 percent were non-traditional. They each, therefore, had some educational experience beyond high school. Let me tell you the results related to their attitudes toward professors:

Nineteen students unemotionally described professors in what I call "either/or" terms: "good-bad," "allies and enemies," "unalike," "an influence," "role models."

Twenty-six students described professors in positive, though inanimate, bland, and unexcited terms: "challenges," "stepping stones to learning," "knowledgeable," "intelligent," "well-running engines," "facilitator," "guides." I found it curious that none of the students completed the sentences using terms dealing specifically with human relations.

Seventy-four students tragically described professors negatively, in such terms as: "unloving parents," "ants at a picnic," "annoying gnats," "necessary evils," "a boat without oars," "a steering wheel without a car," "locked treasure chests," "tops that spin over our heads," "a dark tunnel," "yukkie cockroaches," "holier than thou preachers," "gods that can't be pleased," "ultraviolet rays," "wormy apples," "exploiting bosses," "professional non-listeners," "drill sergeants," "bumps on a road," "nursing mothers with dried up breasts," "dentists pulling your teeth without Novocain," "the opposite of learning," "uninterested guides," "mind-bank embezzlers," "balloons filled with hot air," "devouring wolves," "tyrants," "dictators," "monsters," "St. Peter at the gate," and "a sledgehammer."

About themselves, only 27 students used positive imagery, and then, a few did so with obvious anger and defiance: "reason profs have a job," "real people growing," "THE FUTURE, DAMMIT," "first draft of a mansion," "doctors without a degree," "deserving respect!!!" "budding flowers," "young, exciting, wild, and curious," "just as good as the profs," "creators," "adventurers," and "survivors."

The rest of the students resorted to negative imagery that could be described as passive at best and denigrating at worst: "slaves," "sponges waiting for water to be spilled on them," "victims," "drones in a hive," "an empty canvas to be painted on," "dogs called to heel by their masters," "lab rats," "lumps of clay waiting to be molded," "oxen whipped by the rider," "cows herded together," "pieces on a game board," "blank pages to be written on," "robots," "mimics," "production workers waiting for orders," "parrots," and "babies to be nursed."

Yet when it came to completing the next sentence, "Education is/is like ...", the results were totally reversed. Only six students used negative imagery: "Saturday Night Live," "pure memorization," "useless in the real world," "pure boredom," "a Three Stooges movie," and "a game." The rest of the students had only positive images in terms of vocational advancement and/or personal development: "giving life to a child," "a ladder to the heavens," "an exploration of the spirit," "options for a car," "the doorway to a career," "planting of seeds," "an endless book," "a credit card without limits," "a bank account," "a foot in the door," "keys to the kingdom," "discovering your soul," "a better paying job," "a lover that sneaks up on you," "dieting — hard at first, have to get in the habit, but worth it in the end," "getting in top shape," "a beginning without end," "food," "a rainbow," "paving a street with gold," "an expanding universe," "a never-ending story," "seeking the golden fleece," and "adventurous."

And what did they think of college? Well, 22 students wrote answers like: "a beginning of something," "a place to meet people," "good years," "I'm not sure — yet," "a place to party," "enjoyment before the work in the real world begins," "an opportunity," "being free to be me."

Twenty-four students offered positive answers with a bit more color than their comments about the professors: "a step in the right direction," "a chance to improve," "a place to find yourself," "a challenge to test who I am," "a place to learn," "a nourishing water fountain," "a playground of the mind," "an opening world," "a piece of candy," "a dreamland of opportunity," "a building block," "the future," and "an intellectual vo-tech school."

Seventy-six students, however, regrettably were just as visceral, though perhaps more imaginative, in their disparagement of college as they were of the professor: "a well with no ladder to climb out," "a rat race," "unsupervised high school," "a tug-of-war," "a banquet with lousy food," "growth that's stunted," "a poorly mixed drink," "a prison with a four-year sentence," "a mental ward where you get lobotomies," "Excedrin written all over it," "a church where you're told you're a sinner," "a hotel with uncooperative doormen," "a ball game with pitchers trying to strike you out," "trial by combat," "a tour where the guides won't let you roam," "a confusing maze," "seldom worth the effort," "a boring production line," "a job with insensitive supervisors," "expensively over-valued," and "an opportunity only a few help you to seize."

I thought it was very interesting that the most colorful, creative, and imaginative imagery was negative. It was as if the neutral and positive attitudes were at best lackluster and the negative ones visceral. Now I'm no psychologist, but it doesn't take much to figure out where students get these ideas that professors are authoritarian, unapproachable, uncaring, insensitive, self-centered, and disconnected. My common sense and experience tell me that these students did not come out from their mothers' wombs with these attitudes, any more than I can believe they were written into their DNA code. No, these attitudes were made, not born. They reflect the experiences of the students. They largely explain the source of the "sorriness" and "apathy" about which we often complain. The students are too busy being scared or demeaned to answer that question, ask that question, question that answer, write that sentence, do that exam. It drives me up a wall that almost invariably, whether it is any kind of an assignment or an exam, they want to know from me, "What do you want?" They're coming into class intimidated, terrorized, and denigrated. They're very reluctant to open either their mouths or their minds because, as they tell me, they're afraid of "being wrong," of "being made fun of," of "looking dumb." That's their reality, and it's a reality that we must confront and change.

It seems that at least these students value an education. But from their personal experiences, they do not think that college or professors are up to the task to provide one, or that college or professors care to support and encourage their efforts or treat them with respect. It is a sad, sad situation. It's an indictment!

Now, we can deny it. We can rationalize it away. We can even argue that we had no part in shaping these restricting attitudes. "It's the fault of the public school system," my colleagues exclaim. That is, indeed, part of the answer. But all of that won't alter the fact that these perceptions exist among the students, that they influence both the attitude and effort of the students, and that the reason for such perceptions rests on personal experience. Yet, we professors generally do little to correct the situation. On the contrary, the sad truth is that at the collegiate level, too many of us perpetuate and exacerbate those attitudes. Far too many professors display their own sense of aloofness, aloneness, distance, and defensiveness. They often put themselves in the foreground, forgetting that they are a channel for education, not its source. To them, the classroom is about power, and the students are the weak.

Let us, the powerful, use our power in the students' interest. We set the tone of the classroom; we are the role models. We should take the first step to connect with them, understand their hesitancy to reciprocate, and keep trying until the connection is made. That can be accomplished only if we, at the least, stop, look and see, and listen and hear. We must have the courage to reflect, examine, and admit more. We have to fear, defend, deflect, and accuse less. After all, it's the interest of the student, not the professor's interest, that I'm talking about, and isn't that what we are all about? Then, and only then, can both student and teacher start attacking those stifling stereotypes the students expressed in this exercise. But we cannot connect with the students unless we come to know them, and to do that, we must become learners of the students. To strive for that goal, we must have an eagle eye for each student's body language, facial expressions, and voice tones. I think the real power of the teacher is knowing the student for the individual human being he or she really is.

Some of you will argue that it would be a struggle. I answer by saying that the purpose of a teacher is greater than the teacher and should be more powerful than the teacher's ego. Teaching is a struggle — especially when you expect a lot from it.

Have a good one.

Tuesday, 27 July 1993

MORE ON THE METAPHOR EXERCISE

*W*hy are so many of us educators so blasted defensive, so over-sensitive to criticism, and so inclined to deflect criticism, however constructive and revealing it may be? Are we so fearful in our person and insecure in our job? Do we not have sufficient pride in our craft to know we can do a better job, that our "best" can *always* be better? Such soul-searching, in my book, is a sign of strength and courage, not an indication of weakness and incompetency.

I ask these quick questions because one teacher contacted me and wrote the following about the metaphor results:

The problem may stem from our society's general attitude that education, in and of itself, is not valuable. I don't think this idea has been particularly stressed or furthered by K-12 teachers or Univ. profs, but by parents and by societal members.

Whether an education is valuable or not is not the issue. Besides, I think that is bunk. No one denies the value of an education; it is a question of the extent to which education that is presently being provided is valuable and valued. I strongly feel it is valuable, but that it can be greatly — very greatly — improved. The perceptions of the students deal with the critical matters of the attitude and behavior of the teachers toward the students, the nature of the classroom spirit, and the role models the teachers present, all of which seem to be destructive and denigrating. After all, why has the innate curiosity of the toddler become virtually extinct 15 years later? To say that it is those awful parents and those ethereal, elusive "societal members" makes as much sense as saying it is in the water.

Ah, everything would be so wonderful for us educational professionals, us "experts," if it wasn't for "them." It's so very seldom "us" who are at fault and bear some responsibility for the situation; it's always "them" who are the culprits. Give me a break. We're in denial. Do we really think that parents and "societal members" have nothing else to do but sit down and propagandize their children against us teachers? Do we really think that strangers — those "societal members" again — are lurking behind every corner, whispering into the students' ears, or that small cells of "them" are secretly gathering in homes to conspire against the teachers? Besides, you would think that with all the time spent with the students, we teachers, by our actions and words, could offer the children some effective, alternative, constructive, and encouraging imagery.

And isn't it true that, in this day and age of the educated baby boomers, these "societal members" and parents of whom you disparagingly talk are the people whom we have educated? And if they do indeed possess such perceptions and pass them on to the kids, it still comes back to haunt us, the source of these attitudes.

There's no conspiracy "out there." I think some hard honesty is in order — an honesty that will direct us to ourselves as the true source of these perceptions. We are the painters, sculptors, and architects of those mind constructs. That might be scary, but it is closer to the truth. We educational "experts" must have the courage to engage in self-reflection, assume the responsibility for the situation, and change both our attitudes and our ways. Until we do, little will change.

This teacher used the following quote to end her message: "We often find stones in our way; we can stumble over them, we can climb over them, or we can build with them." I would add, "or we can let them bar our way."

Have a good one.

Wednesday, 28 July 1993

INTELLECT OR CHARACTER

*W*hy is it that we seldom think in terms other than "either/or": we are either student-oriented or subject-oriented; we are involved either in process or in content; we concentrate either on a student's intellect or on the student's character; we value an education either for its vocational goals or its loftier ends of self-development; and so on? Surely with all of our teaching experience, our concern, and our learning, we could be sufficiently creative and imaginative to do it all at once. Let me tell you what I mean.

One assignment I have in my freshman history class is for the students to read Andrew Carnegie's *Gospel of Wealth*, discuss it among the triads, and then come to class prepared to discuss the issue of whether Carnegie, the robber baron, was a moral person. In one one-hour class, the students — with little help from me — bounced all over the place. They were discussing, raising questions, debating, arguing, disagreeing, and almost fighting each other over such matters as: a definition of morality, the subjectivity or objectivity of morality, business practices and ethics, charity, individuality, social responsibility of government, capitalism, science and society, unionism, welfare, Republicans and Democrats, government regulation vs. laissez faire, evolution, and something called "traditional American values."

True, the thoughts were partial, but that was OK; the ideas were incomplete, but that was OK; and the supporting evidence was lacking, but that was OK. There was thinking out loud, but that was OK. There were no clear, finished, supported thoughts, but that, too, was OK. It was only their first step toward uttering a completed thought in a convincing manner. I think they were surprised with themselves when they left class. There was no *either/or* in this class — only *many/and*. There was knowing, thinking, doing, feeling, and asking; there was self-confidence, diminished fear, honesty, and self-esteem. In other words, there was content, process, character, and value that had vocational and aesthetic applications.

I don't know what the lasting influence of this class might be. But I do want to believe that classes such as these can serve the students in all their professional, vocational, personal, and societal walks of life. If I'm right, all it takes is effort, concern, creativity, and imagination. That's enough.

Have a good one.

Friday, 30 July 1993

L L O Y D

I was thinking about my metaphor survey this morning. Yes, the results are troubling. I wonder if these students are a sample of what's out there. Unfortunately, I think they are. I think part of the problem is that if professors were to accept even partial validity of the results, they would have to redefine themselves. First, they would have to redefine what they do, that is, what is the function of a professor. That's somewhat difficult, but you know, I think too many of us define ourselves by what we do rather than by what we are. The exercise of redefining ourselves deals primarily with attitudes, or the "what we are's," and that requires courage, and I don't use that word lightly. We can't transform the system unless we transform ourselves because we *are* part of the system, and we wouldn't be on any moral ground if we asked students to do as we said rather than as we did.

I approach each student as having a unique potential worthy of receiving my attention. Instead of using the term "good student" or "bad student," I prefer "different student." I see each of them as a "fellow traveler" or an "equal partner," and act accordingly, both in and outside class. I guess those are my metaphors, similes, and analogies.

I do know that if we do not respect the student, and if we do not see teaching as an art or a craft or a calling, and if we keep being taken with ourselves, we can hardly expect ourselves to do whatever it is we can do when we are at our best. I work hard to demolish mutual stereotypes so that we can understand each other for the faulty human beings that we are. In class, I engage students in honest, open, and, at times, uncomfortable and painful conversation. I find it to be releasing, exhilarating, and insightful.

As part of the metaphor, the students exchange their sentences with each other for comment. (By the way, I do one myself and throw it into the pool.) Then, we openly discuss our impressions. We also talk about how and why they feel the way they do about themselves, about each other, about me, and about college and getting an education. We also discuss why I feel the way I do. The gist of the conversation is, "Let's see what we can do together about all of this."

Sometimes the effect is dramatic. Let me give you an example. One student, Lloyd was his name, wrote that students are like lumps of clay waiting to be molded. In the course of the discussion — now this is on the first day of class, mind you — another student asked what role did the clay have in shaping itself. Another commented that the clay is totally dependent upon the artistry of the professor. Still another talked about how worthless dirt is. Lloyd, whose facial expressions betrayed his insecurity, sheepishly commented that his experience in high school in Atlanta, and generally here at VSU, was that his views were unimportant and that he didn't have anything of value to contribute to his own education. He and I made a commitment  to each other that we would be "potter-partners" who, drawing upon the artistry within *both* of us, would mold that clay into a fine coffee mug *together*. He hesitantly agreed.

As the quarter has progressed, he has seen that I have been serious. I have seized every opportunity to remind him of our pact: "We're potter-partners, Lloyd. We can't do it without each other." He has started trusting me. I've found out that he talked with the other members in his triad about taking a chance because he thought I really cared about him. Slowly but surely, as we have learned to trust and respect each other, he has become a major and significant contributor in the class. It has astonished another student, who had known him the entire year as a "scared mouse in class." Lloyd's sheepish expressions have changed to a more confident expression; he holds himself better; he has displayed some leadership; he has challenged me in discussions. Some would say his performance, study habits, and insights would only earn him a "C." But he has put some effort into himself, and he has studied, and he has struggled, and he has come a long way, and that is worth an "A+" in my grade book!

Have a good one.

Friday, 30 July 1993

GRADING EFFORT AND ATTITUDE

*S*o many of us believe that the grade is an absolute indicator of achievement, and that a college degree is an absolute indicator of competency. Our idea of success is so hung up on performance. Let me try to make myself and my approach clear. First, I operate on the assumption that every one of my students is capable; they just have to dig to deeper levels within themselves to tap what's down there and use it. Second, my motto, my approach, my philosophy is: "Effort more than performance." The students know that I value effort and incorporate it into my grading because I tell them that in the course syllabus, and because I openly value it every day, in and out of class.

I don't measure success by how many words they speak in a discussion or how many minutes they talk, but by their attitudes or change in attitudes. I keep an eagle eye out for their effort. My eyes are forever and sensitively roaming. I am roaming all over the class rather than being glued to the podium at the front of the class. I watch their facial expressions, their body movements, and their interactions with other members of their triads and the class, and I hear their vocal tones. I encourage, support, and value the struggle to take a risk to overcome fear of failure. I always tell them that the will to achieve is non-existent without the courage to fail. I explain to them that learning to appreciate their mistakes — what we call "being wrong" — is important to learning. I urge them to ask questions and develop a curiosity for everything, instead of being a puppet dancing to the professor's manipulating and controlling strings. In short, character development is the foundation of my class.

Now, I know what you're going to ask. Let me guess: "How can I evaluate effort? How can I put a grade on it?" My answer is simple: "Intuitively!" I ask each student if he or she is doing all he or she can reasonably do to give it what he or she truly has. Is the student approaching his or her potential? I ask the students to evaluate themselves each week during the quarter and at the end of the quarter. I find that those self-evaluations, with few exceptions, are amazingly similar to mine. The evaluation is subjective because there is no absolute scale by which to measure effort, improvement, the pursuit of excellence. Moreover, my evaluation is comparative — comparative to where the student was at the beginning of the class and where he or she is at the end of the class. That's why I believe that I must know my students and establish a bond of trust with them — connect with them, if you will. Hard work? You bet. Time-consuming? Heck yes. Worth it? Well, let me briefly tell you of a happening during this discussion about Andrew Carnegie.

There is this one young woman — a very, very shy, "can't talk in front of others" type — who was scared to death to answer questions or enter any discussion in class, and with whom I've had several conversations. In this particular discussion, everyone was saying that Andrew Carnegie was moral because of his charitable deeds. Suddenly, I heard this voice interrupt and I turned my head.

There she was. I could see her shaking, getting heat flashes, terror flashing in her eyes. I am not exaggerating. "I don't think he was such a good person since he hurt a lot of people getting his money." That was all she said during the class. That was enough. I knew what she had gone through to say those few words, and what she felt to have challenged herself. That she altered the tone of the class discussion was merely icing on the cake. She exerted a Herculean effort to do something she had never done before and saw for an instant what potential lay within her. I gave her a rousing, "Excellent, Elizabeth! Who can add to that?" And her eyes lit up like lighthouse beacons. I turned back to her, winked my eye, and slightly nodded my head as I gave her a subtle thumbs up.

I spoke to her after class to offer all the encouragement and support I could. "Don't lose the feeling of that moment," I told her. "Grasp it as tight as you can and build on it." She gets a higher evaluation in my book than a senior in my class who is doing only what he has to do to get a passing grade. His effort grade sucks!! So does his attitude. He'll be surprised at the end of the quarter because he doesn't believe the syllabus or me.

Have a good one.

Monday, 9 August 1993
PERFORMANCE AND ATTITUDE

I don't grade on effort and attitude instead of performance. As I once said, it is not a matter of either/or. It is a matter of both. I value both, but I use the subject as a tool to assist the student in developing his or her potential as a person. It stands to reason that if a student does not have the proper attitude to guide and energize his or her effort, the prospects of performance in that subject are commensurately and adversely affected.

Why are students' attitudes important to develop? A friend of mine offered this analogy as an explanation. Make a fist. The fist represents a student's potential. Then cover your fist with the other hand. This hand represents some of the attitudes the student has developed, which restrict the movement of the fisted fingers. As long as the clenched fingers are enclosed by the second hand, the fingers cannot freely perform the delicate maneuvers of which they are capable. No one will ever know if those are the fingers of an artist, a violinist, a sculptor, a carpenter, or a surgeon until that person has the courage to struggle to cast off the covering hand and reach for his or her potential. That is an effort to be appreciated. What, then, is so wrong about appreciating a student's struggle to cast off the envelope surrounding his or her attitude, to learn how to learn, and considering the effort as a worthy component in calculating a grade — a grade which, in itself, has no absolute value and is not an absolute indicator of anything except that someone gave that person that particular evaluation?

I feel strongly that we too often tend to think of success in terms of the end point of a particular experience — reading that book, answering that question, handing in that written assignment, getting that grade — rather than the value of the experience itself. We often ignore the fact that, as Jesse Jackson wrote to his son, "struggle builds character." And so the true development of the student occurs in the journey rather than in the destination. The reflection of a student's development is not in the arrival at a destination, but in the nature of the path that he or she walked to get there. To explain, let me give you a personal example of an incident that took place outside the classroom.

I went on a wilderness retreat, part of which was to free climb a 100-foot sheer cliff. I have more than a touch of fear of heights, but I am in very good shape. To climb that cliff, I had to confront my fears, not only about the height but about whether my ego could stand "defeat" if I froze while climbing; for I was not sure how I would react. I was not comfortable with the situation. I sweated. I shook some. I had a lousy feeling in my stomach. I hesitated. But with support and assurance from my belayer, a beautiful man named Curry, and shouts of encouragement from the others, I slowly climbed my first cliff.

There was another person in the group — my wife. She was out of shape and had a severe self-confidence issue. I have never seen a person with such fright in her eyes. She sat off by herself. There were tears in her eyes. She kept angrily saying, "I am not going to do it. The hell with them." Her legs were shaking as her turn to climb was upon her. But she started climbing, clumsily, fearfully. I could see her lips moving as a tirade of silent curses poured from her mouth, aimed at those who "made" her put her life in such jeopardy. About one-third up the climb she froze. She had become so scared and so afraid to move that our group leader went up to climb next to her. She clung to that little ledge for dear life for about 15 minutes. Then, as if in slow motion, she started once again for the top. She froze again; she cried; we encouraged; the guide assured her; she moved a bit. This cycle repeated itself a few times. With one-third of the climb to go, the guide came down and she made it to the top by herself. Below, we were shouting encouragement until our throats hurt. Some of us, myself included, had tears in our eyes at her display of courage. Yes, courage. Damn, I was proud for her. And even though we all reached the top, guess who got all the attention on the way back to the lodge, all the congratulations, and all the admiration. And if we must compare — compare each of those climbers with themselves, where they started on that day and where they arrived — guess who had come the farthest way, made the most progress, had the most significant experience, and deserved the most credit. Don't you think that that is an important consideration at day's end? I do.

But to make that judgment, you must have gotten to know each climber. The challenge is not to reward only those who reach the top by whatever means. The real challenge is not to punish or ignore or embarrass those who can't as yet climb or have difficulty climbing. The trick is to find ways to get them all to believe in themselves, to believe that they each are capable of climbing, to tell them that the effort itself is a worthwhile consideration, and to get them to start climbing. I don't see how these climbers are much different from the students in the classroom.

Have a good one.

Tuesday, 10 August 1993
THE CLIMB

*W*hew! I just came in from my power walk. The dog days are upon us down here in south Georgia, barking loudly as ever. The humidity was so thick I could have sworn I was wading through the Okeefenokee swamp. But at 4:45 a.m. it is so quiet on the darkened streets that, as they say, you can hear yourself thinking.

I was still thinking about climbing that cliff and what it took to climb it, just to make the attempt to climb it. I will say without embarrassment that it was for me a spiritual experience, a moment I came in contact with myself and saw my potential as I never saw it before. I have a piece of my safety rope hanging on the wall in my study. A day does not go by that I don't look at that rope and think about that experience, think about the self-confidence it instilled in me to have the courage to face the personal, professional, and communal challenges that were to follow. It made me realize once again that the will to achieve is impossible without the courage to fail, that there is value in the effort if it is seen in a positive and learning light. That was the lesson of what my wife and I call "The Climb." The issue was not successfully facing up to the cliff; it was facing myself. It was not the mastery of the cliff; it was overcoming myself. But I didn't do it alone. I could not have done it alone.

So this morning I was thinking of Curry, our guide. And suddenly I found a solution to a problem I have had for several weeks. A colleague had said, "Professors are not teachers; they are guides to learning." I remained silent as I struggled unsuccessfully to find a way to answer that statement meaningfully. Now I think I've found the way. So, I'd like to tell you briefly about Curry.

I met Curry at the lodge the night before our climb. As our group discussed the next day's event, my legs became jelly. "What climb?" I asked myself silently in a panic. "I thought we were going hiking or canoeing or communing with nature." The rest of my body parts weren't feeling too good either at that bit of good news. After all, I was the "professor" in the group. I had an image to maintain, as if my Ph.D. made me into something apart from the others. All night I wrestled with disturbing questions that I preferred not to address: Did I want to find out — really find out — about myself? Did Ph.D. really mean "piled higher and deeper"? Could I tolerate possible public failure? Did I want to discover what others thought about me — really thought about me? I felt like a student in a classroom, suddenly asked a question by the lord high master behind the lectern.

Curry came over and talked with some of us, as he must have done many times with others. The others drifted off, but he and I talked quietly about things into the wee, wee hours of the morning. He talked assuringly about himself, a lot about himself, his love of the outdoors, occasionally, in passing, mentioning his climbing experience, his enthrallment with Indian folklore, and his outlook on "things." I talked about myself, a lot about myself, my love of teaching, my fear for my youngest son's future, and my outlook on "things." We never talked specifically about the climb. But in that short time, as I now look back, I felt a kinship forming, a bond of trust, a mutual commitment that I would be there to give it my all and he would be there to give it his all and together *we* would make that climb.

It was dawn. He quietly invited me to join him in an Indian cleansing ritual for wiping out all the "evil spirits" of fear and doubt before going off on a hunt. The air was still and crisp. It was about 35 degrees outside that early morning. And there we were, stripped down butt-naked, sitting on the banks of the mountain creek that flowed about 50 feet down the mountainside from the lodge. We talked a bit. Then Curry and I stood up, arms out reaching to the sky, chanting an Indian incantation. Curiously, I did not feel cold. We then slowly immersed ourselves in the freezing waters and washed our bodies with oak leaves. I could have sworn I felt the cold waters entering my veins and purifying my blood.

After a few minutes, we emerged, sat on the banks, dripping wet, and talked. He talked about the inner him and Indian warriors going out on a

dangerous hunt; I talked about the inner me. We never mentioned the
climb. I have never felt as clean and pure as I did then.
Every nerve fiber was tingling with sensation. My thoughts
were crystal clear. Putting on my clothes seemed to stain
my soul, hurt my skin. My wife later told me that she and a
few others had been watching our return to the lodge. She
said that she had never seen me look as I did in the 25 years of our loving
relationship, that I came into the lodge with an emotional glow that had
overwhelmed my intellectual posturing.

As we all walked up the mountain, my fears started returning. We practiced
the technique of climbing on a huge, slanted rock slab. I kept sliding off.
I screamed, "I'm going to die today!" We reached the face of the cliff by
way of what seemed a very narrow path cut out from the steep mountainside. When we reached the ledge at the base of the cliff, I immediately
started pacing back and forth, back and forth in quiet anxiety. When it
came my turn to climb, I looked up from the bottom of the cliff and saw
Curry on the upper ledge, belaying the safety rope on the most difficult
and sheerest of the three routes up the cliff. I remembered, realized, knew,
and climbed.

The climb for me was an indescribable experience. As I climbed, I felt
myself entering the rock. I felt myself becoming one with the cliff as I had
become one with the creek. When I reached the top, I felt myself literally
emerging from the rock. Overcome by an exhilaration which to this day,
almost three years later, remains as vivid, and upon which I constantly
draw, I turned to Curry and blurted, "WE did it!" And then, a bit subdued,
I said in acknowledging gratitude, "You're not a guide, you're a teacher."
Never turning to look at me as he prepared to help the next climber,
he quietly replied, "What's the difference?" a faint smile of accomplishment
belying his matter-of-fact manner. There is none.

And that is my response to my colleague's implication that a "professor"
is something far above and something better than *only* a "teacher."
His kind of guide is little more than an aloof tour group leader mouthing
some memorized script, moving along a prescribed path from tourist
attraction to tourist attraction just to keep on schedule, oblivious to
whether the people in the group behind him are listening or understanding, demeaning them if they don't follow at his pace. No, a professor
or teacher or guide or whatever term you want to use should be far more
interested in the persons the students will be after they attempt to climb
their mountains than in the climb itself. The professor, however, can't
help the students climb their mountain, can't show them how to climb,
unless he or she climbs it along with the students. That kind of effort is
far more personally rewarding than being a distant and uninvolved tour

guide — for, as you help that student climb, you will get closer to the top yourself.

Have a good one.

Thursday, 19 August 1993

A T R I A D

*W*ell, here I am again, dripping wet and, much to the disdain of my wife, bringing some of the south Georgia humidity into *her* house. A lot has been happening in my freshman history classes this past week as we wind down the summer quarter. I've wanted to share much of that with you.

This dark morning, as I roamed the streets, I couldn't stop humming Billy Joel's "Piano Man," and I couldn't stop thinking about Lloyd, Elizabeth, and Juwarna. They are a personal, very human response to any discussion about education.

These three wonderful people formed a triad in my class. I called it my "fearful threesome." They sat clumped together in the left far back corner of the classroom, where two cold, cinder-block, windowless walls meet, symbolically darkened by the overhang of a large a/c duct. You may remember Lloyd. He's the student from the metaphors who thought of himself as a lump of clay and with whom I committed to be a "potter-partner." You might also remember Elizabeth. She was the shy young woman who finally talked during the class discussion on Andrew Carnegie.

As the class progressed through the second half of the quarter, I could see the self-esteem and self-confidence appear on their faces. They increasingly contributed to the daily class discussions, encouraged by each other, by others in the class, and by me. But I want to talk about Juwarna.

She came into class almost as a recluse. For about two weeks, she ambled into class, no fire in her eyes, no firmness in her step. She never said a word to Lloyd or Elizabeth, and never voluntarily or involuntarily spoke out in class. And while she was silent, her face and voice and the way she held herself shouted fear and self-doubt. I talked to her in the hall one day before class. To put it in a nutshell, she was carrying a lot of personal baggage. She was distrustful of others, of me as the professor, of the overwhelming majority of white students, and especially of Lloyd and Elizabeth. She had little self-esteem, at least in the classroom and, I suspect, outside it as well. Teachers, because of their racial prejudice and classroom "herd" style of teaching, had constantly told her, by word and attitude, that she had little of value to say, if she had much worth in the first place. She was fearful of saying something that would be wrong and would make her, at least in her eyes, look stupid in front of others. Her attitude was paralyzing her, and she could not achieve.

I told her that I could see in her more potential than she thought she possessed. I made a deal with her. If she made the effort to tap what I believed was in her, if she displayed the courage to trust herself and others, I would grade her on her effort, not on whether she was "right or wrong" or "good or bad." Secretly, I knew that if she made the effort, she could achieve. She agreed with great hesitation. I think it was just to get me off her back.

During the next three weeks, she refused to make an utterance in class. She wouldn't volunteer a question or statement. She wouldn't attempt to answer my questions. BUT, she began to discover that she had a good deal in common with Lloyd and Elizabeth; they had shared anxieties. I could see that they had begun to talk with each other, at first about academic stuff and then about personal stuff. They began to trust each other, rely upon each other, care for each other, support and encourage each other. From the weekly self-evaluations, I saw that Juwarna was increasingly contributing actively to the triad, and at times taking on responsibility. During the weekly quizzes, I could see how she got more and more involved with Lloyd and Elizabeth to answer the questions. But she still wouldn't talk in class. I talked to her in the hall again. I encouraged her to do in the class what I understood she was doing in the triad. I asked if she would answer my questions if all I requested was a "yes" or "no." Again, she reluctantly agreed, and again she did not come through.

Then, with two weeks to go in the quarter, Lloyd and Elizabeth came to me. They wanted to do something different for the final exam. Instead of writing an essay, they wanted to write new lyrics for "Piano Man" about racial prejudice in the U.S., tape their performance, let the class listen, and initiate a discussion. "Go for it," I quickly responded.

A week later, Elizabeth nervously came to me and said that Juwarna had volunteered to write half of the six stanzas, and that she wanted to perform the song live, "up there in front of everybody in the class." Elizabeth nervously told me that when she protested, Juwarna said that the triad "had to do it that way" because it "was the right way to do it."

Well, they did it, and they had the class sing the chorus after each of the six stanzas. It was substantive, and it was "good." For me, the most important stanza was the last, the one that spoke of contemporary racial issues in the American experience — one that Juwarna wrote. It went like this:

> Now Lloyd, Beth and Juwarna were strangers;
>> strangers who had never met before;
> But when it's time for the books;
>> who gives a damn about looks;
> 'Cause now there's no company they enjoy more."

All of us sat in silent awe. I felt very humble at the display of their courage, quietly overjoyed with their discovery of themselves. Juwarna later wrote in her class evaluation, with a spunk, an anger, she had never previously displayed: "I never believed I had a best in me, but you did, and fuck them who always said I didn't and two (sic) those who said I was worth shit. I hope I can keep at it." She, Lloyd, and Elizabeth had begun to climb their own cliffs.

At the end of their presentation, I gave each of them an unspoken thumbs up. I am going to give Juwarna an "A" in my class. Lloyd and Elizabeth also, for that matter. I have found that developing their potential is a far more powerful agenda than the bland dispensation of academic information, that gauging a student's success in terms of character growth is more meaningful than in terms of academic achievement. By "character" I mean the courage to accept challenges, the integrity to be yourself, a concern for others, the curiosity to explore life and yourself, the leadership to make things work, and letting go of images that keep you from being genuine. In short, it is to be the best *person* possible, to voluntarily find the best in ourselves.

And to those who think in terms of either/or, I answer, as I have so often, that character growth is the foundation of and the means to achieve excellence; it is the pursuit of excellence that is an integral reinforcing agent of character development. You cannot have one at the expense of the other; you cannot concentrate on one and ignore the other. That is true not just for my students; it is true for me; it is true for all of us out there.

Have a good one.

Friday, 27 August 1993

CLASS CONTROL

It was eerie out there on the streets this morning. It had just rained, and even at 5 a.m., the asphalt streets were still warm enough to cause wisps of steam to rise. There was a hypnotic, surrealistic beauty to it all. I felt as if I were walking from cloud to cloud. The street lights shimmered as if a faint St. Elmo's fire danced around them. As the storm cloud passed, the returning pre-dawn moonlight covered the grass, bushes, and trees in glowing gossamer, while draping Spanish moss sparkled as it moved gently in the remaining breeze. I was sure Puck would jump out from behind a glistening bush and mischievously walk with me.

It was an intense scene that served to intensify my thoughts about the summer classes that had just concluded. I've been going over in my mind the student evaluations and events that occurred in class, and what I learned in my classes about the students and about myself that I can apply in my upcoming classes.

As I reflected between my huffs and puffs, I saw that the students taught me a great deal this summer — maybe, in a way, more than I taught them. They taught me the need for constant humility to accept criticism and suggestions; they taught me that there is always room for me to improve and grow; they reinforced my belief that I truly cannot teach those whom I do not know; they taught me to listen more intently; they helped me to realize that I cannot ignore *their* overall needs and solely rely upon my authority of being the "prof" to do my job; they continued to remind me that the professor is not the center of *their* class, much less of the universe.

What brought all this home was the almost universal comment in the evaluations that the atmosphere of the class had changed dramatically for the better about two-thirds into the quarter, as if everything had come together. An overwhelming majority of the students echoed one evaluation:

> After lots of struggle and adjustment to the triads, during that discussion we became a trusting and loving family in the triads and the class. I started believing that what I have to say counts because they listened to me. No one done (sic) that before. After that a lot of us talked outside of class and agreed that we could participate and express our ideas without fear of being made fun of and looking stupid. I guess I felt that I owed it to me and the others to learn and keep the class going. I knew that the others in my triad and the class would help me if I needed it. Some came to me for help. No one ever done (sic) that before either. I learned that I had something that I could help them with.

I wish I could take sole credit for what one student called "a turning point," but I can't. It was the result of a strong suggestion to try another approach, made one day by students from two triads. In my class, we discuss the meaning of the daily reading assignment scheduled in the syllabus. The triads are required to bring to class a half-page written summary of the chapter, a sentence statement of how that material ties in with previous material and/or discussions, and a sentence statement of how the material relates to one or more of the final exam essay questions. At the beginning of class, the triads would swap their summaries and sentences, talk about them for about 10 minutes, make written comments, and hand them back to the original triad. Then, we would launch into a discussion of the material, usually centered around the issue questions I gave them in the syllabus.

One day, about five weeks into the course — the day after we had an open class evaluation — this group of students came to me after class and asked if the triads could "scrap" the summaries. Instead, they wanted to come into class with questions that they would throw out to the class for discussion.

I answered curiously, "What's wrong with the questions in the syllabus?"

"Nothing, but we've been talking and think we can get better discussions and more out of them. You know, those are your questions, not ours. We only ask questions when we don't know something. We want to ask questions of each other that will help others to understand the material, and you could sort of guide us along."

I guess that I hesitated and they sensed what I was thinking. "You know, you said it was our class and that you wanted us to take as much control as possible. What do you think?"

Talk about throwing down the glove. Boy, they had me on that one. What's that about putting your money where your mouth is? I have to admit that I felt a grip of fear generated by old prejudices and distrusts. I believed that they had potential, but I was worried about the quality of their questions. No, I had to trust them as I had asked them to trust me. And I always told students that you don't know if you're right or wrong until you try. A flash of climbing that cliff literally whizzed through my mind. I said, "Let's do it. You want that responsibility, you've got it. If it doesn't work, we'll go back to the way we've been doing it."

It was rocky at first. The questions were the simple "Who was" or "What was." I was nervous that it wasn't working, but each day I told myself to have patience. They've never done this before, and education is more journey than destination. Then, one day, that day, one of the students volunteered a question. She was not one of the "vocal" students. She asked a "why" question: "Why did Gertrude Stein call the 1920s the 'lost generation?'" Silence. God, I hate silence. I think I'm afraid of silence more than anything else in my classes. It's as if it's more of a sign of my failure than the students' indifference. Like nature, I hate a vacuum, a vacuum of sound. But I bit my lip, struggling to convince myself, "They're thinking, they're thinking." Then, it started to happen.

One student quietly said, "Values."

Silence.

A moment later another student quietly uttered, "Morals."

More silence.

A third student hesitantly said, "I think it had to do with Einstein and Freud, and what the book called the new science that said people had to rethink about themselves and others."

"No," said a fourth, "it was those flappers and sex and wild dancing."

"Do you think it was that new invention of the movies," a fifth asked, "showing all that Rudolph Valentino stuff?"

"I think it was the challenge to religion. That's why Darwin came under attack in the Monkey Trial when Carnegie talked about him and capitalism," voiced still another.

"It seems to me it was just like in the '60s that I had been reading about in one of my tidbits. New ways fighting with old ways and no one knew for sure what to think."

"You know my grandmother was a flapper, but she doesn't like women's lib and women today, and tells me how it isn't like her day. I don't understand. I think she doesn't want me to know what she did at my age."

This went on for the whole class time, involving about two-thirds of the students. I barely uttered a word. Just before the class ended, one student asked, "Where did the KKK get all its influence up north at this time?" Time had run out, and I said, "The next chapter for ..."

"Dr. Schmier, we're not finished with this chapter," shouted one student. "Let's talk some more tomorrow." So much for the calendar schedule.

The next day, the class jumped into the issue of the KKK, nativism, and prejudice during the 1920s. Then, from one side of the class came a loud "dammit to hell!" We all turned. "I just don't understand how my grandfather could be a bigwig in the local Klan and be so hateful. You know,

I've worked hard not to be prejudiced like the others in my family. But every now and then, and I gotta say this, sometimes in this class, in my triad, I find it creepin' into my thoughts and attitude. It's like this history book is living inside me and influencing me. I'm real sorry, Dee (an African American student in his triad). I just hate it, and I have to fight it. Dr. Schmier, I guess having been a civil rights activist so long ago (I wasn't wild about the 'so long ago' crack), you don't have to worry about dealing with those feelings."

Truth time. I told them that I had been something of a civil rights activist, though I didn't have the courage to go into the deep South and put my life on the line, that I had fought for integration here at the university, that I was almost at the Washington march (our "car" had broken down), and that I briefly had dated an African American girl as a teenager. But I, too, have to fight those subtle feelings, those culturally ingrained attitudes, and have to "kick myself in my head" for having them.

"I know what you mean," blurted out a non-traditional African American woman. She told us about her grandfather, who was white, not being able to take his dark-skinned children into the stores with him, how she and her sister had very dark skin while her three brothers were white. "We didn't know racism in our family." Tears came to her eyes when she told of her daughter who came home from school after being told by another child that "nigger skin is dirty" and threw her dark-skinned doll into the trash can. "I cried. I surely cried, and people like those KKK called themselves 'defenders of American values.' "

Stunned, a woman in another triad solemnly said, "I just read about *Brown v. the Board of Education* in *American Heritage*. Now, I know what Thurgood Marshall meant."

"So do I," Lloyd called out. "My mother was Filipino and my father's family treated her like dirt. They liked me because they said I had my father's white blood in me, but her they ignored. It hurt; it hurt a lot. It made me quiet around whites. I only chose Spanish Americans and black Americans for friends." I noticed Juwarna looking intently surprised at him.

"I guess them KKK folks would have reacted the same to the people with AIDS," Amy suddenly commented.

"AIDS is God's scourge against an abomination. I wouldn't be caught seen or associating with a homosexual or lesbian," said Maryann (not her real name).

In a huge act of courage, a girl in Maryann's triad arose and said to Maryann, "I'm gay and we've worked together all quarter and enjoyed being together. Is that going to change?"

Silence. Dead silence. With only five minutes left in the class, I quietly said, "Let's go home."

The next day, at the beginning of class, Maryann arose, said she had done a lot of thinking that night, and apologized to the class and to her triad partner. They continued to work closely together with the third member.

Now, not every day was as magnificent, not every question was as provoking, and not every comment was as personal. But the class there-after had a different tone. It was as if — as the students themselves said — the class began to hit its stride. For me, it was another realization of how our prejudices can be unproductive. We call the students "adults" and treat them as young and immature adolescents; we say that they are "responsible" while we act as if they do not realize the value or extent of learning; we say they don't know what's best for themselves and that they are the best judges of what is good for themselves, but we don't know who "they" are. But I learned more graphically that students are quiet or passive in class not because they are indifferent, hostile, or childish; they are afraid, they feel devalued, and they are "not connected."

I, the professor, created the class for them; they didn't organize it around themselves. They responded to things better, channeled their intellectual and emotional energies, and altered their attitudes when they helped to create their own environment, when they asked their own questions, when they could better relate to things, and when they could see the benefit of their participation. And by becoming partners, most of the students started on the road to becoming independent thinkers. At their urging, I am going to incorporate this change into my classes next quarter.

I started this class thinking it would only be a "summer class" rather than a class taught during the summer. Shame on me.

Have a good one.

Tuesday, 14 September 1993
OFFICE HOURS

What humidity! Walking this morning, even at 5:45, was almost like slogging through a deep swamp. While I was sweating as much water as I was inhaling, I was thinking about my office hours. It sounds like a silly or insignificant thing to which to devote my thinking time, but it's not really.

Have you ever noticed professors' office hours? It almost seems that the professors establish office hours at the most inconvenient times in order to ensure that students won't "bother" them — something like "between the hours of 2:30 and 3:45 a.m. every other Saturday." But I strongly believe that making yourself readily available to students is another very important aspect of how professors and students ought to connect in order to form that bond of trust so essential to learning.

Officially, I have office hours, but I don't really have office hours. I post office hours outside my office door, list them with the department secretary, and include them in my syllabus only because some administrator says I must. Once having posted them, I proceed to generally ignore their limitations. I also never see students in my office. I have discovered that having students, especially freshmen, come into my office is more often than not intimidating to them. Aside from the fact that they can kill themselves if they do not step lightly in what has often been described as an annex to the local landfill, once they do find me, there I am, behind my cluttered, busy desk covered with ignored administrative memos dating back a year or two, sitting in a high-back, black swivel chair, looking like Louis XIV graciously granting an audience to one of his lowly subjects.

Picture this. They enter a very large, long office. It's an old seminar room. They have to walk about 15 feet before they get to a chair. With each step they are bombarded by constant and frightening reminders of my authority and their weakness, of my "superiority" and their "lowliness." There is a huge file cabinet with one overflowing drawer that is invariably open, rows and rows of cluttered, book-filled shelves, a table overflowing with stacks of papers and photographs and open books, and another table on which rests a computer that never sleeps.

As they approach my desk, I loom larger. Almost always, I find them asking me, in self-denigrating wonderment, "Did you read all these books? I could never do that," or saying "Boy, this is a busy office." It reminds them of their difficulties with discipline and concentration, or with study habits, or with poor performance, or with whatever. And then there are the interrupting telephone calls, during which, even when I say, "Call back" or "Take a message," they nervously fidget and feel even more unimportant.

At first, I dealt with the situation by coming out from behind my desk and sitting next to them in a comparable chair. But it was to little avail. The effects of the surroundings on the students were still there. Their eyes still roamed. They still felt out of place. They couldn't feel that they were being treated as equals. I was still THE MIGHTY PROFESSOR and they were still the puny students. They were on *my* turf.

Now I meet them on *their* turf, more often than not at their convenience rather than mine, where and when they are most comfortable and at ease, where we will not be interrupted, and where they know they have my fullest attention and that I am listening intently. We meet and sit and talk on the floor in the carpeted hall, looking like a re-enactment of a '60s sit-in. There's a worn spot in the carpet outside my office. The students call that spot "Schmier's real office." We'll have coffee in the Student Union; we'll walk around campus; we'll sit on a bench; we'll even meet at my home, which is only 300 yards from campus, and lounge on the backyard decks. In this way, we are more partners than lord of the manor and serf — maybe friends, having an open and honest conversation. I find that they will talk more openly and more honestly in this environment than in the intimidating environs of my office.

One more point about not keeping strict office hours anymore. We always denounce the medical doctors for keeping "banker's hours" and for rarely being available when they are needed during the times their offices are closed or on what seems those innumerable days off and weekends not on call. How many times have we grumbled that, like the police, "You can't get a hold of a doctor when you need one," especially on the weekends, which the kids reserve for their sicknesses and accidents. We complain that we are shuffled off to an office partner, a stranger, or sent to an impersonal emergency room or to a foreboding after-hours clinic. Yet we academic doctors turn around and do the same thing. We protest that students encroach on our "valuable" time when they ask to see us at times other than those very, very few hours that are convenient to us — that they want to intrude on our scholarly research time, invade our reflective private time, trespass on our personal family time.

I admit that the non-regiment I have is time-consuming and demanding and inconvenient. I admit that students can knock on my door or call on the telephone at the most "inconvenient" times. Over the years, I've been called to dorms to settle arguments or deal with the break-up of relationships, to wild parties to get a female student out of a difficult situation, to bars and clubs to drive an incapacitated student home, to accidents, and even to the police station or sheriff's office. There was a time or two I had to get help for a student threatening suicide. But sometimes, a bond of trust is formed in the classroom and they feel I'm the only "someone" they can talk with or get help from when an academic or personal emergency arises, and I can't leave them out there slowly dangling in the wind.

In my syllabus, this is what I tell them:

You are cordially invited to drop in on me for just a friendly chat or to discuss academic difficulties and any other stuff that may or may not be affecting your performance in the class. My office is located on the third floor of West Hall Annex, Rm 301. Look for a door that is loaded with a bunch of junky cartoons about timely subjects. My office hours officially are Monday through Friday, 8-9:00 a.m. & 11:00 a.m.-1:00 p.m. If these times are inconvenient, we can arrange an appointment at a mutually convenient time. Actually, I never remember appointments and I hate talking in my office. It's so stuffy and messy. I much, much prefer that you tackle me as I walk through the halls or across campus. Don't hesitate to stop me. What I was going to do was probably boring, and besides, I really would like to talk with you. Anyway, if you do come to the office, I'll drag you out and we will sit on the floor in the hall or on the building steps, or on a bench. If you prefer, we can chat at the Student Union over a cup of coffee (your treat), in the Library, or on the lawn (if you have an unlimited laundry allowance). It's more relaxing and informal. If you're really daring, you can meet me while I race walk at 5:00 a.m. and we can talk. If you first want to reach me by that marvelous invention of the telephone, my office number is 333-5947. If I do not answer, please leave a message with the History Department secretary. If you do not like telephones, you can stop in at the History Department, which is located at West-229, and leave a message in my mail box. In extreme emergencies, you can reach me at my home. I live a stone's throw (don't take that literally) from the campus. Come by and knock on my door, but I warn you my wife's toy poodle loves to lick people to death. My telephone number is 242-3049. No obscene calls, please; I have Call-Trace. No real late, late calls, please, except in cases when your life is on the line. Otherwise, you will put my life on the line. The telephone is on my wife's side of the bed and she is not a happy camper when suddenly awakened at strange, late hours. If you're really up on modern technology, you can contact me on campus e-mail anytime and say anything you want. My e-mail address is:

lschmier@grits.valdosta.peachnet.edu

So my advice is: Get out of your office!

Have a good one.

Friday, 23 September 1993

T O M M Y

*I*t was muggy, muggy, muggy this morning. Walking the streets today was like slogging through congealing Jell-O. Anyway, I was thinking about two conversations I had yesterday. One was in the empty student union for morning coffee with four colleagues still roaming around the empty campus. The second was a telephone conversation with a "B+" student, a rising senior majoring in personnel management, who had received a very poor grade in my class. They were separate, but they were strikingly connected.

The initial conversation centered at first around small talk about our summer classes. It didn't take long before we were bragging about our kids. When it came time for me, I told them how my 24-year-old son, Michael, had just received a huge salary increase and promotion as the head of a newly formed department of cardiology in his Washington DC-based medical consulting company, with which he has been for the past 18 months.

"That's an unusual double major, bio-science and business," my biology colleague stated.

"What area in business did he major in at Chapel Hill?" the professor from the management department asked.

"He didn't," I answered, knowing full well what was to follow. "He was a Russian Studies major."

"Well, he must have taken some management courses," returned my friend in a half-question.

"No," I answered nonchalantly. "The closest he came to business courses was when he took a couple of courses dealing with the economics of the Soviet Union."

"What kind of company would make him the head of a department without any training in management?" he asked with a tone of annoyance.

"A very successful one," I answered with a nod of exaggerated nonchalance.

"But," the biology professor jumped in, "he had to have a strong science background."

"No," I quietly answered. "Besides the astronomy course he took in his freshman year, only what he took in high school."

"No science or business? What, then, were his credentials for being hired and promoted?" she asked.

"He was," I answered with an air of finality.

Later that afternoon, I received a call at my house from a student I'll call Tommy, who couldn't understand why he had received a "D" in the course. The gist of the hour-long conversation went something like this:

"I did all my reading," he argued.

"But did you study the material? Did you understand it?" I asked.

"I read it all," he kept replying.

"You didn't contribute to your triad. You were little more than a bump on a log, and you certainly didn't participate in the class discussions," I said.

"I'm a listener. I don't feel comfortable talking up," he retorted.

"I can understand that when it comes to the entire class. For some students, it takes time," I replied. "But from your own evaluations and what the others in your triad wrote, you made no effort to participate in the triad. Remember, I stopped you on the lawn and we talked, twice."

"I came prepared," he said.

"For what?" I calmly asked. "You never said a word in class; you never looked interested. During the quizzes and when people were jumping up and down, roaming around and discussing the questions, I noticed that you just stayed in your seat. You just sat back and never contributed. You're going to be a senior. The others were mostly freshmen. You have experience. Why didn't you take some leadership?"

"I'm not used to your type of course. I'm not good with talking," he lamely replied. "I'm kinda shy around people. I just like to sit back and take notes. I don't like being called on, even in my other courses. But I'm a good student. I get A's and B's on the tests."

"Did you read the syllabus?"

"Some, but not most of it. Just the calendar."

"But didn't we discuss in the class the emphasis on class participation, attitude, and effort, and the value I place on it? I even talked with you outside class and we made a commitment to each other (the same as I had made with Juwarna)."

"I don't think I believed you. I figured that was a bunch of rah-rah hot air. I was afraid of being wrong or askin' a stupid question and lookin' dumb."

"Maybe you were afraid to believe it?"

"I guess."

"What's your major?" I asked.

"Personnel Management," he answered, to my surprise.

"How are you going to deal with people? How are they going to respect you and listen to you if you're uneasy around people?" I asked quietly, with as much caring and understanding in my voice as I could muster. "Have you spoken to your advisor or anyone else about it?"

"No, you're the first one who asked. I know I gotta do something about it," he quietly replied. "I will."

"When?" I asked. "How are you going to handle an interview when you go out for your first job? What do you think you should do?"

"Well, once," he hesitantly replied, in a way that stirred my juices of both sadness and anger, "I told my advisor I thought I needed one of those speech courses to help me. But he told me that I didn't. He said my grades showed that I was a good student and I didn't need to waste my time with that useless stuff and told me to use my electives in business courses. So I did."

"Tommy, do you have any electives left?"

"Yes, but I'm taking some accounting course."

"Do you want to?"

"Not really."

"Do me a favor," I said. "I want you to sign up for a speech course with Dr. —— or a drama course with Dr. ——. I'll talk to either one of them and they'll work with you. Promise?"

"Yes. Are you going to change my grade and give me a C?"

"No. Do you really think you deserve one? Be honest with me; no bullshit."

"Not really, but I tried. Don't that count for something?"

"Trying is lying, Tommy. Don't settle only for 'try.' Do!"

"But I learned a lot."

"What do you mean by 'learning'?"

"Well, I memorized all that stuff, just like I always done."

"Did you give it your best shot? Did you try to improve or just get by? Be honest."

"Not really."

"I don't think you did either. I wouldn't help you by giving you something you yourself know you don't deserve. You going to take that course?"

"I guess. I'll think on it."

I thought about Tommy all last night, wondering if he will take that drama course and challenge his inhibiting issues. I have my doubts. I wondered what I could have done better. Tommy will probably graduate with a 3.something or other. He will walk across the stage thinking he is educated and receive his diploma that says "with honors" thinking he is competent. What he won't know, and what most of us do not care about, is that he will have graduated only with what a colleague calls "book experience" and received only a "Bachelor of Grades."

My son, a University of North Carolina Johnston Scholar and an honors student, graduated cum laude with a very high 3.something or other, with a Phi Beta Kappa key and a few other UNC honor society memberships, and with all that other stuff we take too seriously. But more importantly, he graduated with a "Bachelor of Experiences." When I once asked him what he thought were his most formative moments at UNC (besides watching basketball), he replied, running for president of his dorm and being defeated, later being president of his dorm and president of his resident area, being on the student council, helping develop the cultural exchange program between UNC and the University of Rostov in the Ukraine, challenging the vice chancellor on a financial matter, and having been exposed to those few professors who cared to help him develop as a person. He was not impressed with his awards, grades, scholarships, or honor memberships.

I once talked with one of his executives and asked why my son was hired without any business or science background.

"Michael was hired because of who he was, not because of what he did. His *gifts* told us more about what he would do in the future. His school *experience* only told us what he had done in the past. We talk with our prospective employees. That's more important than some grade sheet or letter of recommendation. We want to know," he went on to say, "if he enjoys life. Does he have a sense of humor? Does he have a vision? Can he relate to people outside the company? Does he have other interests? Does he take pride in his work? Can he work with others respectfully? Does he have the courage to make a decision? Does he have imagination and creativity? Does he have judgment and the confidence to use it? Does he have critical thinking skills. We don't want 'yes men and women.' That's been too big a problem in the past."

What the executive said came back to me as I thought about those two conversations. It seems to me that the problem with book experience, and even expertise, is that it is static. It fits a person with a specific vocabulary; it gives a person specific answers to a specific set of problems that may or may not be pertinent to the future. My son's CEO didn't feel that grades, diplomas, and/or awards accurately indicated in and of themselves the presence of what he called *gifts*, much less expertise and competency. What he wanted was not so much specific knowledge, but intellectual agility and strength of character to know how to ask the questions, move from idea to idea, stay ahead of issues, be creative and imaginative, see what is yet to be, and be self-confident and courageous to act on those visions.

I don't think that book experience is bad. If we measure such experience in terms of developing character, maturity, or judgment, it's desirable. You need the information, as well as the ability to utilize it. But for the likes of Tommy, the problem is too much faith in specific information and total faith that grades and diplomas accurately indicate possession of such a bank of information. Life isn't a series of short-answer questions or memorized answers. In this respect, grades are not a substitute for even the slightest deficiency in acuity of judgment or for any shortcomings in *gifts*.

I wonder how many Tommys are on this country's campuses, and how many of us perpetuate the Tommys by ignoring them as persons. It's a tragedy not to have helped Tommy help himself to develop the life skills he needs. The real tragedy, perhaps cruelty, is that the Tommys are almost

DOA in life — dead on arrival. This wonderful and likable young man, and too many others like him, are operating unaware of the constraining glass ceiling — the very low glass ceiling — that has been placed over him, partly by us.

I hope Tommy takes the drama course. I believe in him, and I believe he has potential that is yet untapped to crack that invisible ceiling and ultimately shatter it. Rest assured that I'm going to contact him at the beginning of next quarter and see if he did.

Have a good one.

Friday, 1 October 1993
MORE ON TOMMY

I called Tommy last week. I wanted to see if he had signed up for that drama or communications course. He hadn't. I wasn't surprised. He told me that his advisor wouldn't agree. He had to take another accounting course. When I asked why hadn't he ignored his advisor and telephone registered by himself, he said he had talked with his parents and they had agreed with the advisor. So, as he said, "I just went along."

"You knew what you had to do. You have to start taking control of your own future," I told him with a sadness in my voice.

A day or two later, I received a letter from Tommy arguing his case for a better grade. Portions of it went like this:

> Evan (sic) though I did learn a lot about
> history and learned to be more responsible, I think I missed
> one of the main points of the class, and that was to stand up
> and be more aggressive and to not be afraid to say what you
> feel. When I first got my grade I was really ticked off. I knew
> that history, but when I talked to you on the phone I realized
> that you have to go after what you want and you just can't sit
> around and expect a grade. I have to stop being afraid of being
> wrong if I'm ever going to do anything that's right. I guess
> I just didn't trust anyone in my triad or you. I guess I thought
> your class would be like the rest of the classes that I had before.
> But you were the first teacher who has seen me in class, even
> though I tried to hide by being quiet. You moved around in
> class and looked at me. That scared me even though I never

told you. You thought more of me than I did of myself, more than my advisor or parents. Like I said, I thought this was just another class, only with chairs moved around and a weird teacher, but I found I was wrong and it was a different kind of learning experience in more ways than just history. I've given this a lot of thought and I've learned a lot about myself even though it was after the quarter was over. ... You might not realize it, but you've helped me a lot in my future classes and you will never see me sitting around in class even if it causes a fight. The teacher will know I'm there! Thanks for caring.

I called Tommy soon after I read the letter. "You see, I really learned something," he said, "about my attitude. I'm going to take that drama course next quarter. I'm going to take a chance in my classes and start believing. Now can I get a better grade?"

"No," I said. "Talking is easy; it's walking that's tough. But this is what I will do. You take your classes for the next two quarters. I'll talk with the professors. If what you say isn't bullshit, I'll call it 'effort and performance after the fact.' And then, I'll change your grade."

"That's fair enough. You watch!"

"Good luck, and I'm here if you need an ear or a shoulder. Have a good one."

"You, too. And thanks again."

Tuesday, 14 September 1993
B L U E B E R R I E S !

*B*lueberries! That's what I was thinking about this morning as I knifed through the water-laden, warm, darkened, south Georgia air. Now, you may ask why I was pondering those luscious, succulent, squishy, blue pearls. Well, it's because of blueberries that I can teach a class of about 60, still be aware of and sensitive to the needs of that single student, and get the results that I have discussed in earlier Random Thoughts. Blueberries help me to *focus* and to *care*.

It all began when I climbed that cliff almost two years ago. I vividly remember the scene as if it were yesterday. There I was, pacing back and forth at the foot of that rock face, waiting for my ever-approaching turn.

I was unaware that I had begun to focus intently on that rock as I never had been able to concentrate on anything before. As I started to climb, I stopped thinking and began feeling. All sound blacked out. I was aware of nothing else but that cliff. Looming above me, I found gaping hand-holds and protruding ledges to place my feet upon that I had not seen from below. I felt myself becoming one with the rock. While belaying down, I was stunned to discover that those protruding ledges were no more than one-eighth to one-quarter of an inch wide! The cavernous hand-holds were mere indentations in the rock. As I got back into my head, I called my experience an "adrenalin surge." Curry — you remember him — said, "Louis, you stopped looking and began to feel."

He was right. The next morning, a Sunday, long after my hormonal levels had returned to normal, I still felt a tingle along the surface of my entire body. It was as if, no, I *was* aware of each and every follicle. As I gazed out from the porch behind the lodge, I was struck by all the distinct sounds I heard: the singing of different birds, the sounds of the animals, the movement of the trees in the breeze. Each and every needle on the trees, each and every leaf on the bushes, each and every petal on the few flowers, each and every blade of grass was clearly distinct, as if I were looking through a microscope. I told my wife I swore that I could hear them all talking to each other. As we in the group talked about our experiences, I was amazed to find that my mind was not drifting; all the  normal distracting chatter to which I usually succumbed was filtered out. I was listening intently to each of their words as I never had listened before; I was seeing each of them as I had never seen anyone before. I felt connected, and it was exciting and fulfilling!

The next day, Monday, I walked into class and my skin was still tingling. And this is the God's honest truth — it was as if someone had taken a grip on each end of the room, pulled and expanded it, as you would do to soft taffy. The desks seemed spread farther apart. The mass effect of the class was diminished. The separateness and individuality of each student was accentuated.

I have always prided myself on being student-oriented, but on that day, I saw far more intensely than I had ever seen before. The student in the seat was not a student. That student was a person. That person was a somebody. That somebody mattered and was a somebody who is unique. I heard each of those somebodies with a clarity I had not heard before. The normal distracting chatter was blocked out. My thoughts were totally concentrated on the student at whom I looked or the student whom I heard, and the students responded as if they had received a shot of adrenalin. I experienced an exhilaration that was as indescribable as climbing that cliff, a sense of connectedness and a sense of meaning and purpose more intense and true than I had experienced at any time in my life.

After class, however, when I returned to my office, I suffered a revealing and educating "letdown." I studiously sat at my desk, slowly, very slowly, sipped on my coffee, and thought deep thoughts. I did not like what I was thinking. It was uncomfortable. Hell, it was painful, because while it was a long walk from the classroom to my office, it was just a short step to realizing that, while I *am* a student-oriented professor, I was not the teacher I thought I was. I was not actually in close touch with the students in my classes as individual persons as much as I had prided myself on. I was far more detached than I wanted to believe. I was not "showing up" for my classes and paying attention to the students anywhere near what I should be doing and was capable of doing. I was looking far more at the mass of the entire class than seeing each individual student. I was hearing sounds far more than I was listening to their words.

I decided that I was not sufficiently focused — that I had been unwittingly tuning out all sorts of things because I was too preoccupied with other concerns: myself, combat with the administration, committee meetings, research, grants, writing, publication, personal and family problems. I knew for a long time that this was the case, but I would not admit it. This experience made me confront the reality that I was far more the professor than the teacher, and that was not *me*, not *the true me*.

As the week passed, I found the tingling diminishing. It was harder to maintain my focus. I was losing it, and I was both scared and angry. That following Saturday, I came in from a wee-hour walk and was once again struggling to think how to keep my focus. Going to the north Georgia mountains and climbing that cliff every day as a booster shot was out of the question. I had just about surrendered to the inevitable as I sat down to a bowl of Wheaties and blueberries. Because the blueberries were out of season and expensive, I decided to savor slowly each and every one of them, knowing they'd be the last until the following summer. Just then, my wife staggered out from the bedroom, groped for a cup of coffee, plumped down in the chair next to me, and said, "Honey, why are you eating so slowly? Not feeling good this morning?"

And then it struck me. While I loved blueberries, I always ate them so fast that I rarely tasted a one. My lovely wife always has chastised me that I gobble and gulp my food. "How can you appreciate what you're eating? I don't understand how you even know what you're eating," she'd always ask and admonish me as I was invariably the first at the table to finish my meal. So this time I picked out a blueberry, slowly rolled it in my fingers and felt it, brought it up to my eyes and saw it, put my nose to it, slowly inhaled and smelled it, slowly drew it to my mouth and felt the expectant saliva gushing forth, took it into my mouth and let it sit on my tongue, and began to taste what I had unthinkingly always eaten and swallowed automatically. My wife thought I was "going blueberries." But later, I told her that I realized that slowing down, sensitizing myself to that single blueberry, and tasting it made me appreciate it and focused me on the immediate moment.

I realized that none of us can appreciate the most valuable things in our lives if we let them whiz by unnoticed and unappreciated. It's almost like reading a newspaper or watching television or engaging in a conversation and eating without fully experiencing the wonders of taste. I was so busy physically or mentally rushing from one place to someplace else that I was inadvertently missing things. Sometimes, we eat so fast or are so distracted that we're out of touch with the whole process of tasting.

Since then, I have been focusing on that single blueberry — or strawberry or slice of banana (a bit messy) or raisin or almond or whatever — every day. It's a daily exercise that complements my power walk thinking time. It all has to do with concentrating on the experience of tasting that blueberry in that particular moment. It's not magical meditation. It's training that anyone can do in the same way someone trains himself or herself to do anything. It's about awareness and sensitivity. When you're tasting, just taste. When you teach, just teach. Be completely engrossed with the tasting — and the eating. Be completely engrossed with the teaching — and the student.

As I've learned to concentrate on that single blueberry, I've trained myself to focus on each and every student as a meaningful, unique person. It tells each student that "you matter to me." That's important, because the opposite of love is not hate; it's indifference. We need teachers who teach with their hearts wide open. I think education is evoking the will to learn. It's evoked by letting the student know that he or she matters. It's not evoked by being indifferent.

I don't think it is too much to ask those at the head of the class to have mastery of a subject *and* to possess social and personal skills as well. It isn't enough to be just competent and efficient. Being competent and up-to-date in your field is essential. But a teacher is a caregiver and must pay attention to the underlying relationship with his or her students. We cannot teach those whom we do not know — just as we cannot teach that which we do not know.

Have a good one.

Wednesday, 15 September 1993

THE HUMANITY OF TEACHING

*H*ad an interesting but brief conversation this morning with a friend of mine in the hall of one the buildings on campus. He asked me how the triads were working out. I told him that they were a reasonable success, but that it was a never-ending experiment, since the students in each class each quarter are different. He next lamented how he wished he could try "some similar ideas that I am toying around with."

"Why don't you?" I asked.

"I'm not sure how the others in the department would take it if I broke with using traditional lectures," he replied, as I remember, in almost a whisper, as if he were afraid someone might overhear him. "I'd probably get a lot of complaints."

"From the students?"

"Oh, I think they'd like it even if it means more work. It sure would be better for them and I'd be a better teacher."

"Then what's the problem? Don't you think they're what it's all about?"

"I'm not like you. What if it doesn't work?"

"If it doesn't work, go back to what you were doing or try something else. Hey, don't think that I'm not nervous at the beginning of every quarter and almost every day. I always think about if the class is going to work and what will they say if it doesn't come off."

"You're tenured."

"So are you!"

"I can get fried on the student evaluations if it doesn't work or if the students don't like it."

"I guess that is something that you have to decide."

"I'm no rebel. I'm not the kind to challenge the system. I know some of them. They'd see what I'm doing as a threat and an attack on their competency, just like some around here look at what you're doing. Besides, what if it all fell apart? I've never told anyone this, but I'm afraid of failing.

I'm not sure that the results are going to be worth all the effort and aggravation. I sure wish I was like you."

"I am me," I sympathetically replied. "I can't tell you what to do or how to do it. My teaching boils down to what I do with *me* and how I use *me*. But I'm not the me I once was. I've changed me and I'm still changing me. It took me years, struggling years, to get wherever the hell I am and do whatever it is I do, and I'll be working on it 'till the day they bury me. You can do the same thing if you want."

"I don't know. Maybe. Whatever."

You know, my friend reminded me that it's not really the method that we use that's important. There's more than one way to skin a cat. It's what motivates us to do what we do, our inner selves, that's important.

There is a myth going around that somehow something particular, some-thing external to us — a technique, a method, an approach, a technology, a piece of equipment — is going to bring us the automatic solutions. "Ah, if only we knew how to ... ," they sigh. "Wow, with this new technology we can ... ," they exclaim. So many want a quick fix. They want instant answers. They want immediate and total success. They search for the "easy" way. However, I have learned the hard way that I can experiment with techniques from now until the cows come home and I can get involved in the new technologies, as I have over the years. But until I addressed myself — until I sincerely asked, was forced to ask, "Who am I?" little truly came of my efforts.

My friend told me that his anxieties sometimes get in the way of his teaching and the students suffer. He's admitted that at times he's so busy worrying about giving the best lecture that he's distracted from the students. No, what you do is far less important than who you are. What you do will be affected, maybe determined, by what you are and what you strive to be. I believe that teaching rests far less on technique than most suppose; it rests far more on the personality, identity, and character — on the humanity — of the teacher. The measure of a teacher is not determined by the number of degrees, the number of publications, the number of committee assignments held, the number of awards received. None of that earns an automatic reservation for a seat on the summit of Sinai. I know colleagues with national reputations and professional vitae a mile long who are bores inside and outside the classroom, who are lonely and need to be the star of the classroom, who lack self-confidence and cower before a challenge, who are controlling, egotistical, power-hungry, dishonest, arrogant, and self-righteous. I know some who are all talk and no walk. I know some who misuse and abuse their authority. I know some whose fire is extinguished. But I also know some who are independent, humble, confident, enthused, curious, sensitive, compassionate, and loving. We do not leave ourselves at home when we come on campus, and we do not leave ourselves outside the classroom.

My friend is a crackerjack in his field. He knows much about his academic subject. But how much does he know or want to know or understand about himself? And he's not alone. Most of us may have the technical skills, but do we know or want to know or understand the drives and desires that energize us or limit us? How can we help our students develop, transform, or change as persons if we can't or won't develop, transform, or change ourselves? We cannot give what we don't possess, and we cannot keep what we don't give. Maybe that is why so many of us clutch the lecture to our bosom, keep a distance, put on protective airs, wear masks, fondle the image, exercise control, and use the impressive jargon rather than engage. Is that why some of us cynically pander to the students or dismiss them? When we engage someone, someone might engage us back and we might have to listen. Maybe that's why too many of us exercise power in our classrooms rather than create a sense of community. Maybe that's why so many of us deal more with facts and information than with knowledge and wisdom, more with the subject than with people. If we get too close to our students, they may get dangerously close to us. Maybe that's why our schools are far more academic than educational institutions.

To the degree, however, that we recognize and acknowledge that our own behaviors and attitudes are a significant contributing factor to the classroom situation in particular and education in general, we can do something about it. We can take an honest inventory of our inner selves, our strengths and weaknesses; we can learn about ourselves. We can identify and deal with the baggage we carry around through life, onto the campus, along the halls of ivy, and into the classroom. That is what I call real empowerment.

I know that if you want to change attitudes, it requires a more fundamental change than most of us think we have to make or are willing to make. I know that it's stressful, to say the least, to alter lifestyles and professional styles, not to mention the bedrock of attitudes upon which they rest. I've taken a few of the many uncomfortable, painful, humbling, and soul-searching steps that I need to walk. They may not be fun, but, oh my, they are releasing, and they have changed my life for the better.

I think a true education may not be so much about getting "better" as about letting go of everything, of expectations and beliefs, forsaking images and masks, and becoming a "truer" person. We were born with a brain, hands, and feet, but we were not born with beliefs and attitudes. Those were taught and learned. Some help; some hinder; some I'm not sure about. I've discovered that they have to be sorted out because only those ones that are true and help and promote are the ones to keep. I believe that there are things each of us need to do, should do, and can do if we are to have the chance of being a truer person as well as a truer teacher.

Have a good one.

Wednesday, 29 September 1993
WHOSE SCHOOL IS IT?

"Whose school is it anyway?" That question has been swirling like a hurricane through my mind all this past first week or so of classes. And it was on my mind as I walked this morning in the brisk morning air that is our one day of south Georgia autumn.

I was thinking about an incident that had occurred early last week in front of the mail window in the Student Union. It was a madhouse, as opening days of class are prone to be, especially in the Union. Tired, frustrated, and angry students were lined up, snaking into the college bookstore. Cutting across them was a line of tired, frustrated, and angry students standing up in front of the mail window, waiting to receive their mailbox assignments and combinations. There were masses of tired, frustrated, and angry students struggling to practice their mailbox combinations as herds of other tired, frustrated, and angry students leaving the bookstore bumped into them. And through them weaved people going in and out of the snack room. It was crowded; it was noisy; it was hot; it was smelly; it was crazy; it was inhuman.

I was standing in the mail line behind four students, waiting to get two stamps for some personal mail, when a young man, neatly bedecked in a tie and jacket, rushed up to the window and broke into line, interrupting a student who was trying to get her mailbox assignment.

"Hey, get in the back of the line," a harried student angrily yelled from behind me. A supporting chorus of "candid comments" quickly arose from the other students.

He snapped his head around toward the student. "I'm a professor and I'm in a hurry to get to my class," he loudly pronounced, with obvious authority and annoyance.

"Oh, I'm sorry," the student sheepishly apologized, as if she had done something wrong. Everyone backed off and submissively went quiet. But they were not happy campers.

"You can still get in the back of the line and wait like the rest of us," I calmly said.

He whipped his head around so fast I thought it was going to be wrenched off from his neck. Lordy, you'd think I had challenged both his manhood and authority. Probably did. The annoyed look in his eyes was immediately replaced by an anger. He looked at me as he proclaimed with deliberate emphasis, in an obvious attempt to cower me, "I ... am ... Dr. ——— ... in ... the ... ——— department. Who are you?"

I didn't know him, and he surely didn't know me. I think, since I was dressed in jeans and was sporting my UNC NCAA national basketball championship shirt — teaching attire for that day — that he thought I was merely a graying (only *slightly* graying), non-traditional student.

"I'm Louis," I innocently and quietly replied, "Louis Schmier." Then, with increasing firmness and a deliberate, and admittedly mocking, authoritative emphasis to match his, I added, slowly emphasizing each word: Dr. ... Louis ... Schmier! Professor ... of ... History! Who are you?"

He didn't answer. I continued, "Now would you please get in line and wait like the rest of us?"

The angry expression remained fixed on me. The smiles appearing on the faces of those students didn't help his disposition, nor did their snickering. He turned abruptly and I watched him go into the snack bar. So much for integrity and for being in a hurry to get to class.

"Doc," said a student behind me who lightly slapped my shoulder, "that was worth standing in line for."

After getting my stamps and mailing the letters, I went into the snack bar. Out of the corner of my eye I saw Dr. ——— sitting with a few other professors, none of whom I knew. He apparently said something and they all gazed in my direction. Ignoring them, I got a cup of coffee and sat down with some students. Here comes Dr. ———. He didn't know when to give it up.

Ignoring the fact that the students and I were talking, he interrupted, "You know, you embarrassed me out there in front of all those students, and I don't appreciate it."

"I thought you did a good job of that on your own. I don't think there was much I could do to improve upon it," I replied in a tone of obvious irritation as I looked up at him from my chair.

"Well, I think we, as professors, should be entitled to some respect. Students don't give us that anymore."

"I can't imagine why," I matter-of-factly said with feigned ignorance.

"Well, the likes of you don't help the situation," and he abruptly walked back to his table.

Now, I admit that Dr. —— may be an extreme case, but he is symptomatic. If we are bold enough to be honest, there is a general attitude out there permeating the educational establishment that students exist to serve the administration, faculty, and staff — that it is *we* who deign to grace the students with our presence, that *we* take time from our valuable scholarly pursuits to engage in the lesser task of teaching, and that the students should be humbly grateful that *we* would grant them an audience in our presence. But whose school is it?

Dr. —— said that students don't give professors respect anymore. Personally, I think what he and others really mean is that the professors aren't worshipped. If it were up to the likes of him, there'd be separate faculty and student water fountains or separate faculty and student bathrooms. I may have climbed mountains, or at least mountain cliffs, but I've never reached the summits of either Olympus or Sinai. I'm glad the students have given up the image that professors are almost priestly, mystical people. Gods are distant and unapproachable. Fear, not respect, is what Dr. —— is talking about. He is talking about a power relationship. He wants to wield power over the students who would feel the brunt of its exercise.

Dr. —— talks of respect. Respect, however, isn't automatically bestowed by a degree or publications or an administrative position. He has to earn it through his attitude and behavior toward the students and his colleagues. Respect is a mutual engagement of and sharing among individuals to the benefit of all. Let the likes of him be focused on student concerns, not his authority; with tending to students' needs, not controlling them; with empowering them, not overpowering them.

Yet schools have been organized for the administration and professors, for everyone but the student. The prevailing attitude that runs rampant on our campuses is a condescending, "What do students know?" In the classroom, far too many teachers demand blind obedience; outside the classroom, administrators require equal homage. Students are so intimidated, they don't feel like they're part of a team. They're so terrified and passive, they let professors and staff and administrators do things to them few others would tolerate. They feel depersonalized because their individuality is so often ignored.

A colleague of mine — an enlightened colleague — developed an interesting exercise. She had the students stand up in class, put their hands on their heads, and march around the room. She then asked them how they felt. "Stupid" was the general consensus. "So why did you do it?" she asked. "You're the professor," was their innocent, sincere, and very revealing reply.

Sometimes, I feel that colleges and universities are far more business and academic research institutions than educational ones. We manipulate and school rather than educate; we ask students to be seen rather than heard. We may be good at lecturing, writing on blackboards, assigning rooms, scheduling classes, doing committee work, crunching numbers, developing budgets, holding concerts, attending conferences, constructing edifices, naming buildings, winning athletic championships, beautifying campuses, writing flowing goal statements, and researching. Administrators and faculty and staff play the numbers game, placing dollars above students and herding students into large, depersonalizing classes, maneuvering them into courses. Students are caught in turf wars and power struggles between and among professors, departments, schools and colleges, professors and administrators, professors and staff, and staff and administrators, ad nauseam.

Professors may grumble privately, but their own self-interests, not those of the students, prevent most from speaking out in public. It's little wonder that students may like a particular professor or staff member or even an administrator, but they don't like the educational system that tends to demean them. Providing a building, a course, a program, a championship team, or an academic or bureaucratic talking head is not the end of the social contract with the student. We need far fewer administrators and staff personnel on our campuses; we need far fewer "scholars" and "experts" in our classrooms; we need far fewer information transmitters among our faculty. We need far fewer people dealing with "things" or coldly treating students as things.

We need a heck of a lot more "teachers" who know how to deal with, and want to deal with, students — *people* who will talk to students, listen to them, respect them, and make them a part of their own process of development.

Have a good one.

Saturday, 9 October 1993

ON BECOMING A UNIVERSITY

*A*s I was gliding over the asphalt this morning, I happened to look up and catch sight of a colorful and artful banner, eerily spotlighted in a field of black by the lamp post it was bedecking. Surrounding a decorative logo were the words: "Celebrate Valdosta State University." It is one of hundreds that are still hanging from every light and telephone pole on the streets surrounding the campus. They were part of the celebrations marking the college's attainment of university status. It was quite a show. On July 1, after months of meticulous preparation, utilizing time and energy comparable to that which goes into a presidential inauguration, with all the glitz of a Wal-Mart opening, with the sights and sounds of a gala debutante ball, a bar mitzvah, a confirmation, and a Sweet 16 party all wrapped up into one, Valdosta State College became Valdosta State University!

It was a media event that resembled one of the 1930s film extravaganzas. There were laser beam shows, rock bands, food tables, balloons, orating politicians, puffed-up administrators, receptions, hot-air balloon races, road races, faculty rushing to alter their vitae, souvenirs, a huge celebration cake, fund-raising, roaming crowds, secreted fraternity alcohol, fraternity bashes, a final countdown, and the inevitable fireworks. So few questions about purpose, lots of assumptions.

I've seen those banners and posters and God knows what else everywhere I've gone for the last four months, but I guess a conversation with some students the other day in the Blazer Room about the idea of what a university meant to them made me particularly aware of that banner this morning. Part of our discussion went like this:

"I wouldn't have come to VSU if I had to graduate last year," one freshman admitted.

"Why?" I asked.

"Well, it wasn't a university."

"Does that make a difference?" I asked.

"Sure."

"Why?" I asked.

"Coming from a university looks better than having gone to just a college."

"Why?" I asked.

"My diploma would look more impressive."

"Why?" I asked.

"It means more to people."

"So?" I asked.

"It'll be easier to get a better job."

"So?" I asked.

"I can make more money."

"Why?" I asked.

"I can be happier!"

With each set of questions and answers, the students were giving me looks and twisting their faces as if I were becoming an increasing menace.

"Damn, Dr. Schmier, can't you say anything more than 'why' and 'so'?"

Finally, I said, using an approach I learned at my son's school, "What if I could give you all the money that would make you happy, on the condition you could not get a job? Would you still come to the university?"

They were confused. There were strange looks at me and each other; there was silence; there was hesitation; then, there were the stammering "uh ... well ... uhs."

These students will go into the world on the treadmills of success that we have helped to construct, operate, and perpetuate, believing that happiness is connected with material gain. The tragedy is that we too often are reinforcing their visions and values. They and I hear the same words coming out from our Admissions Office, Counseling Office, and Student Affairs Office; from our president, vice presidents, deans, department heads, and too many faculty. I hear these same words from local legislators, businessmen, parents, and community leaders. I hear teachers, principals, members of boards of education, and superintendents talk eloquently of "university track" and disparagingly of "vo-tech track." I hear it from other institutions rushing to acquire loftier titles, develop bigger programs, enhance reputations, inflate egos, grab the respect and clout lacking in being a mere community college or junior college or vocational school or college. They are all charmed by the flowing pronunciation of the "U" word; they are seduced by their assumption of the meaning of the word; they are enticed by the marketability of the word to attract students and sell job-seekers; they are satisfied by the uncritical image of the word. Make a wish upon a star, click your ruby glass shoes together three times, wave a magic wand, just change the name from "college" to "university," and the institution automatically becomes a better place to get better credentials to get a better job to better keep up with the Joneses. So few questions about meanings and purposes, so many assumptions.

While some people are satisfied with the image of the "U" word, others are satisfied with the "objects" associated with it. "Come see our university," say our recruiters and foundation personnel. They take prospective students and their parents, prospective donors, and alumni on tours of "objects." A professor or even a student can walk by their entourage. Is he or she stopped and introduced to offer a human dimension to the institution? No. Our tour guides are too busy pointing at objects. "Our student body is this big." "We have this many fraternities and sororities." "Have you seen the national standings of our so-and-so team?" "We have so many attractive buildings." "See that fountain." "Look at our lovely grounds." "All that grass, all those trees and flowers." "Here are the labs." "See all those computers." "We have so-and-so many Ph.D.s on our faculty." "Our professors go to so many conferences and give so many papers." Still, so few questions and lots of assumptions.

Some people speak with pride about what I call the "toys" of the "U" word. They brag about the growing number of programs, degrees, and courses. Everything has to be on a professional track: the pre-thises, the pre-thats, and the pre-everything elses. The "toys" are all designed to provide the most efficient and effective way of making the students marketable, to package them, to give to the students the tools to make it "big" out there. Still, so few questions and lots of assumptions.

I don't think the "image," "object," or "toys" of the "U" word constitute the essence of the "U" word. So few of us are concerned with the substance of a university: to liberate us from images; to break our chains of preoccupation with objects; to enlighten us about the purpose and meaning of the toys, rather than just how to use them; to endow us with broadened understanding, rather than limit us with barreled sight; to instill in us a love of learning rather than just a technical skill; to launch us on a never-ending adventure of self-development, rather than end the quest with a diploma; to expand the range of our experience, not to narrow it; to urge us to take the risk of challenging and examining uncritically held assumptions, not just play the game or go with the flow.

Above all, a university is a place to find a calling, a life's work, to combine the technology with the substance. A university is not just a place to get a job, but a place concerned with the kind of job that is done and with the character of the person doing the job, with the deeper visions of pride in craftsmanship and the skills needed to produce or provide, the deeper dimension of dedication to excellence of what is produced and provided, and the deeper values of concern for and ethical dealings with all others. It's bad enough that students think a course is valuable only if it satisfies a major requirement. But if they walk across the graduation stage thinking, "Wow, I'm finished with this rat race. I'm educated; I'm a professional. Now I'm going to be a so-and-so and make as much money as I can by hook or by crook, no matter what I have to do to get it or no matter whom I have to run over," they have not received a true university education.

If we professors tell them that a course is valuable only if it fulfills a department requirement, and we watch them walk across the stage thinking, "They've completed their so-and-so major with a so-and-so GPA and are now getting the degree that's going to open doors for a good job," then we have not given these students a true university education. The students have been brainwashed; we have brainwashed. Maybe we have been brainwashed as well. Still, so few questions, a lot of assumptions.

None of us have asked ourselves or others about the meanings, the "what is the good of it all?" I'd like to have a conversation with students that would go something like this:

"What is the good of coming to VSU?" I would ask.

"To be the best I can be."

"Why?" I would ask.

"To help others."

"Why?" I would ask.

"To leave the world a better place."

Have a good one.

Sunday, 24 October 1993

TEACHING AND RESEARCH

*T*his has been a heck of a week or so. As I have been roaming the darkened streets during these last 10 days, I have been reflecting on the exciting happenings that have occurred in my classes. To be honest, I just haven't been in the mood to sit down and write. Maybe a low-level reaction to a flu shot had something to do with it. Maybe it was being emotionally drained from working closely with a particularly large number of students on their personal issues: listening to them; sharing my personal experiences with them; and though I *never* offer advice, getting some of them to see the need to talk with a professional. Then again, maybe it was a subtle fear of not being able to "keep it up" — of losing my spontaneity and feeling the demon of contrivance breathing over my shoulder as I sit at the computer.

Then, this morning, I received a "sign." I had been thinking about an e-mail message from a professor about research vs. teaching. He said something to the effect that his mind was sinking because the students were bringing him down to their low level of active knowledge, and he could not find much excitement in teaching them. Ostensibly, the professor was talking about research vs. teaching. In reality, his message reflected his demeaning attitude toward students, the second-class status he gave to real teaching, and how he felt the demands of being attentive to the needs of students encroached on what he considered more prestigious research and publication activities. I have to admit that my immediate reaction was to write a blistering response. But I heard a voice inside saying, "Louis, take it easy. Stop and think. Don't be so arrogant, so self-righteous. Don't be so dishonest."

It would have been a dishonest response because I had been there once, saying that I had to do research to "keep my mind alive." In fact, it wasn't my mind with which I had been concerned so much as it was my ego and desire for recognition. The responses to my efforts to introduce innovative programs, to experiment with costumed presentations in my classes, and to develop interdisciplinary courses had been ignored as "non-professional."

There is so little reputation in teaching, so little impact on promotion and tenure, so little influence on salary. And to be really honest, as I approach retirement here at the university and my scholarly reputation has waned because I have given up research and publication in order to concentrate on my classes, I ask, who would want to hire a teacher rather than a reputed ever-publishing scholar? It's scary.

Anyway, I remember saying in those days — to myself and my "better students" — as this professor wrote, "Research is making me a better teacher." Heck, it may have made me a better lecturer, a better transmitter of subject information, but not necessarily a better teacher. It wasn't helping me adequately and properly address the needs of the students. Perhaps worse, during all those years when I concentrated on research at the expense of my classes, it may even have made me more distant from those students who needed me the most, more arrogant and disdaining toward them.

So I was thinking about all of this today when, after I finished my walk and went to get my newspaper, I found a short letter stuck in my mailbox. I'd like to share it with you. That letter was the sign:

Damn you, Dr. Schmier! I came into your class thinking I was going to get what I get in all my other classes, the usual lecture, facts, memorize for the test, quickly forget the stuff kind of class ruled by what my friends said was a hard, unreasonable son-of-a-bitch who didn't care anything about the students. I was ready to be bored, and I was ready to be angry and I was ready to play the game and I was ready to waste my money. I wasn't ready for you. I wasn't ready for the way the class ran. And I sure as hell wasn't ready for me. I came into the class to memorize historical facts, and you give us lessons on life! You and your damn triads. I've learned more in this class than in all my other classes combined. But you've forced us to learn how to cooperate with each other, to be more compassionate with others, to hear other's opinion, to debate our position, to learn to think. But, worse and better, to evaluate ourselves and look at ourselves. That I hated, but that's what I needed because I had to admit that I was strangulating me. I said at the beginning damn you, it was a nice damn you. I really mean thank you for being concerned enough to care about me. It was crazy but when we were talking in class about the submissive slave mentality and then —— said she knew exactly what that meant being a woman and treated in the same way and we talked some about that and then —— said something like as students we were taught that the teachers were our masters, inside I felt myself saying, "Hey that's all me, too. And add my family to that." Then, you pulled me over after class for a talk, it blew my mind as if you could read my thoughts. At first, I said to myself, "Here comes the rah-rah lecture." But, all you did was to ask, "What's going on? Why aren't you giving it what you're capable of doing? Why don't you believe in yourself?" And then waited for an answer. None

of the usual routine lecture, none of the noble advice, all you
did was just to wait to listen. It really surprised me that I
opened up to you, a stranger, and all you did was to listen. I
was stunned that all you did was to share with me your own
experiences. I found out that I wasn't alone. I mean you
respected me enough to have the guts to spill yours. I guess I
figured if you could do that with me, I could take the chance
and do it with you. I was really touched when you warmly
said you weren't a know it all and couldn't help but suggested
I go to the councilor and when I reluctantly agreed you
walked with me to make an appointment. You forced me to
start opening doors I would have preferred to stay closed but I
really knew had to be opened. And I found someone
caring enough just to listen and to give me the courage to put
my hand on the knob and slowly start to turn it and see what
I am really made of. You always say in class that you can't
succeed until you're ready to risk failure. Well, I think I'm
about to start getting ready. I'm scared. So, I ask only please
stay on top of me and don't go easy. I can't do it alone — yet.
I trust you not to give up on me or anyone else in class.
You are a son-of-a-bitch, but a special one.

To the professor who thinks, as I once rationalized to myself, that teaching
lowers his ability, I ask him or her to think about this letter. I can tell you
that no research grant, no conference paper, no award, no reputation, no
book or article, no promotion or salary increase is as rewarding, satisfying,
fulfilling, exciting, encouraging, and stimulating.

I have come to realize, from reflecting on my own personal experiences
inside and outside class, that it hurts to have someone look at you who
sees so little worthwhile, whose eyes and demeanor say, "You're a drag.
If it weren't for you, I'd be off doing something meaningful, some
important research and acknowledged writing." When students leave the
class, when those uncaring eyes are no longer looking, the imprint still
remains deep in the soul. And if they are looked at long enough that way,
they begin to look at themselves as those eyes did; they find it difficult to
go to the mirror and see someone worthwhile. They become small in their
own eyes because of those eyes. The loss of self grows.

But why should they have to go through that dehumanizing experience,
and am I not supposed to combat it? Nothing so beautiful as a student
should be made to feel less than something that deserves respect. I work
hard to help students get back that feeling that there is something worthy,
beautiful about each of them. Wouldn't it be so simple for teachers and
professors to care? It's easy to stand off and say that it's the students'

responsibility to learn. It is that kind of thinking that allows us to shirk responsibility. It is that kind of thinking that blames the victim for being victimized. It's the same kind of thinking that is directed toward the rape victim, toward the homeless, toward the poor, toward the ignorant, and toward the student.

We don't always address the students' problems by dealing with what causes them. Most campus counselors will say off the record that so many professors don't want to be bothered with such things, that they feel that it's not their concern. But if you start with the assumption that intellectual ability and academic performance are the professor's sole concern, you won't ask certain questions. You won't realize that you are using one-dimensional terms to discuss a three-dimensional reality. But if you believe, as I do, that attitude is an integrated and inseparable part of performance, then there is a whole new set of questions to be asked.

We can't perform emotional surgery. Intellectual performance is married to what students say, think, feel, and do. Attitude affects performance and performance affects attitude. But I don't think they are separate; it's not one and/or the other; it's how they are related. I'm getting nervous because I'm neither a philosopher nor a psychologist, and I feel myself approaching another realm and discipline. I am getting nervous because I am not the honest man carrying a lamp in the night. But from what I have observed in my classes, from my conversations with students, and from students' evaluations and criticism, it's just so obvious that it needs to be said because all students are important. They all are building blocks of society. We must not be satisfied with describing student and professorial behavior. We must be concerned with why so many students lack self-confidence, self-motivation, with why so many students are silent in class. Perhaps it has something to do with their past educational experiences. Maybe it has something to do with family issues. We can begin to ask questions about how they got into this situation and what we, as teachers, can do to address the issue on a fundamental level.

It's ridiculous to theorize, philosophize, rationalize, and intellectualize about education and teaching without dealing with the humanity, the strengths and weaknesses of those to be educated as well as the educators — without addressing those things that can make both students and us wholesome.

Have a good one.

Saturday, 30 October 1993

CLASS HAPPENINGS

*I*t was deliciously brisk this morning. The late Saturday morning air was fresh and clean, having been washed by a torrential evening downpour. The chill was just enough to excite my bare skin, enough to make everything feel alive, enough to sharpen my mind. After the months of debilitating heat and humidity, this encounter with autumn, however brief, is exhilarating. And though I had to walk between occasional rain drops, nothing could dampen my soaring spirits. I walked like I had wings on my heels, not just because of the uplifting climate, but because I can't get my students out of my mind.

I can't stop thinking of Marguretta, normally quiet in class, who, as we were discussing the antebellum (pre-Civil War) South, raised the issue of the demeaning slave mentality and how it related to and compared with the black experience since the Civil War and with racial issues on campus; of Heather, who made the connection with women's issues as she said, "It's no different from what we face as women around here and in our families," — and raised the issue of women's rights; of ———, who then told the class of how struggles with an unsupportive, demanding husband affect her sense of self-worth and her performance and hinder her efforts "to make something of myself, other than just to serve others as a wife and mother and cook, that I can be proud of"; of Holly, who carried the idea on to include students and said, "And as students, we were told to be quiet because we didn't have much worth saying. And most of us still believe that stuff we were handed from the teachers. And darned if it still isn't that way in almost all the classes on this campus"; of Matika, who took the discussion in another direction and talked about children being treated like, as she said, "nothin' but garbage" and got us to think about the effects of child abuse; and of ———, who talked haltingly about her abusive childhood horrors.

"Let me tell you about being mixed," said Pryn as he jumped in. When he was finished, Ivelysse and Sylvia added their perspectives of being Latin American. Then Ben told of being Catholic in a small south Georgia town and how it created a reverse prejudice in him. "It looks like there are still a lot of know-nothings around," he concluded.

I can't stop thinking of Sharon, who burst out in tears, demanding, pleading, shouting that we should all start to see each other for who we are and not for how we look. "How many of you are prejudiced?" she sobbingly asked. Everyone raised his or her hand, myself included. "Well, why?

And what are you doing about it?" Wow, that triggered a vigorous discussion that lasted two days about the origins of racial prejudice, regional prejudice, religious prejudice, and prejudice in general in this country. And these are supposedly freshmen who "aren't university material."

There was Barbara, who said to me as I was passing out the weekly quiz last Friday, "I have to say something to the class. Dr. Schmier, the quiz can wait. This is much more important." Then she got up and said:

> I just want to tell you guys that last night in the library our triad talked honestly about what was going on in class for the last few days. It got real emotional and we were crying with each other. We decided that we have to respect each other and understand why we think and do things the way each of us does, and that we each have a heritage of our own and a heritage that we share, and that we ought to be proud of both of them equally, and we should celebrate them every day as a reminder of what we have accomplished. We're good with each other now. Natasha, me, and Trey feel like we're one and a family, and will be there for each other. And I want you to know what we did and I think each of the triads ought to do the same thing.

And these are freshmen, who so many say "only know how to copy."

There was Laquanda, who came to me at the start of Wednesday's class and told me she had something to say to the class. And she did. With a great deal of courage and humility, she walked up to the front of the room and she said that she had been "firmly spoken to" by some of her African American friends in class, whom she respected, after her outbreak of anger the previous day during the discussion about slaves and racism and women, and that she had telephoned home and spoken to her father that evening seeking comfort and support. Instead, he "gave me a yellin' at." She told the class that she had stayed up all night "doing some heavy thinking about why I have a 'log-size' chip on my shoulder" and, with tears in her eyes, said, "This is hard because I never done this before. ... I have to admit I am wrong with my attitude and I apologize to anyone I might have hurt with my cruel words."

And she is a freshman who "just wants a grade."

And there was Arden, who answered a classmate protesting that we weren't talking about the "facts in the book that you're going to quiz us on":

That's our responsibility to get that stuff out from the book as a triad. In class, we're learning more history than I ever did in any class. We're using the facts and understanding Dr. Schmier's 'whys' and our 'whys,' not just memorizing them to pass a quiz or test. I'm starting to see how we're linked so close to the decisions others made in the past. It's like a movie, and I'm part of it. We're using the book as a springboard to discuss all kinds of issues and how those facts influence me and you. We're learning a lot of history, but we're also learning about life and about ourselves. I know a lot of us really look forward to coming to this class.

And he's a freshman who "doesn't care about learning."

I can't stop thinking of Regal, who missed class and, in tears, tackled me as I crossed the campus. "Dr. Schmier, I know everyone in the triad sinks or swims together, but don't punish the others in my triad because I screwed up and didn't hand in my part of the assignment. Give me the F. I deserve it. I failed them. But it's not their fault. I swear I won't do it again."

I can't stop thinking of Chrissy, Elana, Elaine, Calvert, Greg, Mike, Ivelysse, Natasha, Yolanda, Melanie, Melinda, Shannon, Jeff, Peter, and a bunch of others who participated in these wondrous reflections and discussions. Some contributed a phrase, a word, a sentence. Some bared their souls. Some gave discourses. Some offered insight. If I were to tell how each participated and contributed, I'd have to write a transcription of a week's worth of discussion for two classes. I talked very little these past days. I just stood on the side and watched with respectful awe. These "poorly prepared" freshmen initiated and carried on all the discussions; these "unskilled" freshmen did all the connecting; and these freshmen "who can't think for themselves" asked all the questions of each other; they did all the analyzing. I am so proud of them.

I always start each quarter with great anxiety, wondering if things in class will successfully work out with this particular group of students, if the perseverance will pay off, if having to defend myself will be worthwhile. Things are starting to work out and pay off in this class, and these great people are worth the effort. Even most of *them* feel it.

Yeah, this has been one heck of a week or so, maybe a watershed week, for almost everyone, including me. I am not sure I really have the ability to describe the spirit that embraced all my classes. All I can say is that sometimes, when and if it clicks, it sure does click. It has been a difficult week, a good week, a tiring week, an exciting week, a rewarding week, a satisfying week, a fulfilling week, and a magnificent week. It has been a week of great intellectual curiosity and exploration, of high academic accomplishment, of deep emotional self-examination and discovery, and of extensive social struggle and growth. It has been a week of courage, honesty, trust, openness, sharing, and humility. It has been a week of debate, argument, admonishment, discomfort, pain, anger, and tears. It has been a week of laughter, joy, and camaraderie. It has been a week of communication, the beginning of mutual understanding, and, hopefully, of some healing. I now am beginning to see in so many eyes, unfortunately by no means all, a gleam where there was once emptiness, a brightness on once bland faces, smiles on once stoic lips. And I see others now struggling to have that gleam, brightness, and smile. Some remain bumps on a log. "But," said Lisa, "we'll work on them. We owe them that much, to try."

Have a good one.

Sunday, 31 October 1993
C O M M U N I T Y

*L*ordy, it was COLD out there this morning. I had to rush back into the house, an icicle forming on my nose, to get my jogging suit, gloves, and stocking hat. The cold air was stimulating enough to fend off depressing thoughts of my impending 53rd birthday tomorrow. I always say that it is appropriate that I was born on All Saints' Day. My wife says I was born a few hours too late because there's too much of that little devil in me.

Anyway, as I fought fears of frostbite, I was thinking about what had been going on within the triads and in the class this past week or so and during past quarters. I've been poring over written student self-evaluations, end-of-quarter evaluations, and some student journals, bumping into veterans from my other classes and talking with them, and just reflecting on my own experiences as I walk or struggle with the scales on my flute.

It seems that whatever the students wrote or said, they always felt that they learned more history in the triad-oriented class than in any other class. But, having said that, I noticed that they always zeroed in on the personal associations that developed in the class and within the triad. The words that obviously had most meaning to them were those of emotions and intentions, words that dreams and hopes are made of, words that touched their spirit, words such as "care," "concern," "knowing," "sharing," "respon-sibility," "personal," and "friendship." But above all, so many talked of beginning the class, as they do every class, feeling that they were "alone" and, unlike in other classes, ending it feeling as a member of what they frequently and warmly and tenderly called a "family" and "community."

"Family" and "community," I think, explain the mysterious and exciting happenings that often evolve in many of the triads and in the entire class. These words say to me that many of the students may be changing or facing a challenge to change on a much more profound level than simply engaging in a cooperative effort to learn a subject, pass a test, write up an assignment, or earn a passing grade. They seem to be undergoing a change of consciousness that allows them to develop a different relationship with themselves and with others. This is what the students are telling each other and me.

One student, Karen, who took the class this summer, told me Friday, "I got to meet new people, really got to know them. The triad got us into some really deep thinking beyond just learning the material. It made us all analyze our personalities, our future thoughts, our goals. It helped me grow as a person. It was hard to adjust to, but I got to love it." Meat (that's his nickname) got up in class Friday after the quiz and wanted to read a journal entry aloud: "I really like this class. I felt alone at first like in the other classes. But here it's fun to learn, and you learn a lot, and you get to know about a person more than he or she just being in the same room. You get to know their personal life and about your own. Our triad had a discussion last night about some personal stuff and found that we weren't alone in our feelings and could help each other." Now keep in mind, I'm not a trained sociologist, psychologist, or any other -ologist, and I haven't collected statistical data in an objective and scientific study. Having said that, I do have some ideas, subjective as they may be. So I'm going to go out on a limb.

So many students come to our campuses afflicted with a varying severity of "LD"; Learning Dependency. It's a pernicious disability that drains the intellectual and emotional excitement, drive, energy, purpose, and meaning from the student. Since attitudes have an effect on performance, this LD stunts or arrests intellectual development, academic achievement, and emotional growth. Blank faces, hollow gazes, silent voices, and unexcited movements are the easily spotted physical symptoms of this malady. The intellectual disabilities are legion: shortage of creativity and imagination, deficient sense of curiosity, lack of initiative, weakened technical skills, addiction to dull and meaningless plodding, satisfaction with copying and memorization and drill, preoccupation with test scores and grades, contentment with being controlled, inability to exercise empowerment. The emotional impediments fundamentally are a difficulty in believing in themselves, acceptance of mediocrity, a lack of pride, eroded self-confidence, weakened sense of self-worth, and an overriding fear of being wrong or "looking stupid."

The causes of this LD are what I call a "woundedness": physical woundedness inflicted by the chance throw of genes, accident, and disease; intellectual woundedness resulting from a less than supportive educational system that plays with students in dumb-smart games; emotional, mental, and spiritual woundedness resulting from a host of personal, social, and family situations, pressures, abuses, and prejudices.

In that woundedness, the students often think they are the only ones in the world with pain. They feel separated from everyone else; they feel different. A sense of isolation envelops them in an opaque emotional curtain that doesn't allow them to see others and makes them think others cannot see them. They believe that other people don't want them, don't want to listen, don't care about them, aren't concerned with them. They feel mediocre at best, worthless at worst. So they hide in silence; they hide in aloneness. So many have been betrayed and hurt and demeaned; so many have learned to build defenses of varying thicknesses and heights. The walls that protect, however, also isolate and restrict.

I think students who feel isolated, or isolate themselves, perform at lower levels. I find that anything that promotes isolation and perpetuates loneliness is debilitating. Anything that promotes a sense of intimacy, connectedness, or community can be releasing, exhilarating, and, in some cases, healing.

Participation in a triad and sharing, however uncomfortable and challenging, is good for everyone. As I form the triads at the beginning of each quarter, I see so many frightened, lonely, self-denigrating people. They are uneasy about participating in a group. Their isolating woundedness does not make it easy for them to rely on someone else. They are at first very reluctant to begin to make connections with others, to begin to rely upon others, much less address and begin to talk of their personal issues. But, at least in my classes, they cannot hide from me or each other. They must deal with my "blueberries"; they must look at each other and talk with each other; they must see that there is a face on the other side of that head sitting in front of them in a traditionally arranged classroom; they must get to know at least each other's names; and they must work together.

Yet eventually, for many, it seems that their woundedness affords them an opportunity. Many want to reach out, but never knew how or were too scared to try. They want to share with each other and trust each other and to find support and encouragement in each other. It's as if the triad contains a comforting salve. Many find that they can trust another person because they can sense that the others, too, have woundedness, have pain, have fear. Out of that trust, many begin to pay attention to their own wounds and each other's, to teach and be taught, to make the effort,

and to start to discover the wondrous potential that lies within them.
As associations and friendships form, they start thinking about their feelings, share themselves, let the walls down, and start testing their abilities.
They invite the others into their loneliness. They get to know each other
and gain insight into themselves and others that they may never have
gotten. I see emerging relationships between strangers, put together by me
but brought together by their attitudes and finding each other through
their struggles and sufferings.

I'm trying to create a situation in which the students feel better about coming out from behind their walls, share who they really are instead of being
socially isolated, and risk discovering the extent of their learning potential.
We are separate, distinct individuals, but at the same time we are social
beings. If our craft is to be noble, its purpose must be noble. I cannot think
of anything more noble than to assist the process of making the individual
whole, to help bring together not only intellectual, emotional, and physical
parts of the individual, but to bring individuals together and instill a sense
of community.

I am struck by the students' constant use of the word "family." It seems that
many of the students are breaching the isolating, inhibiting, and demeaning
"walls of loneliness" with a powerful, supportive, encouraging sense of
community. It is hard to believe that such a simple idea as "community,"
of sharing, seems to have such a powerful impact and dramatic effect for
so many.

Have a good one.

Tuesday, 2 November 1993

M A T I K A

J ask my students to journal voluntarily, reflecting about themselves,
others, me, the operation of the class, and life in general. I journal
along with them. I don't collect the journals; I don't read them; I don't
grade them. As a sidebar, at the suggestion of the students, next quarter
I will start making the journals mandatory, and I will collect and read them
each week. At the beginning of each class, I ask if anyone has a journal
entry he or she wants to share with the class. It's a way for us to share with
others our feelings and attitudes, to come out from behind our walls, to act
as role models for the more reluctant members of the class. I read entries
from my journal to the class as well. No one volunteered to read an entry
today. So I read one of mine. Then, as we were about to end class, one

student, a female African American, called out that she wanted to read two entries from her journal. She said that she felt "you all ought to hear what I'm thinking." We sat down and listened. It proved to be worth being late for the next class.

At first, we all thought she was talking about a new boyfriend. I soon found out how wrong I was. She caught me way off guard. When she was finished, I was stunned, speechless, my eyes a bit glassy. We all left the class without a murmur. I was hesitant about writing about her entries, even though she gave me permission to do so. A little voice whispered in my ear, "Louis, if you do, you'll get your butt pinned for tooting your horn." I listened at first to that voice and sent personal messages to a select few. But another voice was making me uncomfortable. "Coward," it screamed. "You believe in what you are doing. Don't you trust your colleagues out there? There's a lot of academic learning and personal growth going on here with what you are letting the students do. Her entries reflect that. Let everyone else see that. What the hell is wrong with the celebration of teaching?" After receiving the advice from those few to whom I sent the message, I've decided to risk the heat and send it out. It's a testament to the brilliant light that can flood a classroom, a campus, and the world if only we care enough to help the students turn on the inner glow that lies within all of them. Here are her entries. I think she was courageous in sharing them. I'm thankful she did. They are pearls that encourage me, uplift me, and tell me the effort is worthwhile:

> When I first walked in class I saw many different people.
> When I saw dark faces a sigh of relief came over me.
> I felt comfortable with people that looked similar to me.
> In high school it started out that way but then I began to change. It is so easy to talk to people of the same race but it takes a little more to talk to people that's different. Although I learned a lot about people in my high school the same cycle occurred when I got in college. The more I sat in the class the more I began to talk and interact with people different from me. Now I sit in class with all of these people not looking at them as being black or white but as being people. We are all unique and have similar goals and objectives. I know that if we disagree we can talk about whatever and we can agree to disagree. In this class I have learned a lot about myself. If I seem to be extra happy in this class it is because of the people in the class. I am happy because I know many years ago I wasn't allowed in a class full of people not of my race. I think that I am privileged to be in this class with all of those unique people because I know I can learn something from each one of them and they can learn something from me.

She then added an original poem:

> There's a new man in my life now.
> I see him every day.
> He makes me feel so good inside with the words he say.
> I talk to him about my thoughts.
> He never tells me I'm wrong.
> He's always encouraging me, making me feel so strong.
> If there is a day when I'm feeling confused,
> He guides me in the right direction acting as my muse.
> I'm not sure if he knows the way I feel.
> But, he makes me feel special; he makes me feel real.
> He not only teaches me the things I need to know,
> He teaches me how to understand, how to learn, and,
> most important, how to grow.
> Please don't get me wrong.
> This new man is not my lover.
> He's one of the best teachers I know, not like any other.
> This unique man's objective is very clear to me.
> It is to help and encourage me to be the best that I can be.
> Because he is so caring in my heart he'll always be near.
> This man has done a lot for me, this man named
> Dr. Schmier.

Have a good one.

Friday, 5 November 1993

R I S K S

Watch your ego! That warning was bouncing around my brain as I struggled to walk on an aching wrenched knee in the black south Georgia morning. But that counsel had nothing to do with my physical agony. It had been issued in gentler words by a Canadian professor of English with whom I have become friends and with whom I talk on an e-mail list. He was uneasy that I might be stepping over the line and inadvertently creating a cult of personality in my classes. He was trying to alert me to the possibility that if the students became dependent on me, they would not learn or want to learn how to learn about things without my urging, without wanting to please me, without needing the support of assignments and textbooks and exams and marks. He worried that the student who works hard because I inspire him or her would not continue to do so after he or she leaves my class. He worried that

I will have given the students, in his words, "a good, big fish — but I won't have taught (him or) her to fish."

It was a timely caution as I thought about some discussions I had with two students and about another's journal reading in class. It truly is all so easy to let one's ego get in the way and step over the line. It is something to which I am very sensitive. I think about and have to deal with it almost every day. Are there risks? Of course there are risks, but we shouldn't let the fear of failing stop us from striving to succeed. If we did that, none of us would have struggled successfully as tots to walk.

I think that anyone who is concerned with students must be careful as he or she struggles to become that proverbial "guide on the side" instead of the "sage on the stage." We do little good if the students' eyes follow our movements; if, while being physically off-center, we remain psychologically in the center. To replace one form of "Learning Dependency" with another accomplishes very little, and to perpetuate such LD is not my goal. I firmly believe that more often than not, it's not what we do in class that makes a difference, but often what we allow to happen. For that process to develop, however, a kickstart and encouragement often must occur, just as we once hand-cranked the car to start the motor running.

There is so much pain out there, so many albatrosses hanging around necks, so many impairments. Even a teacher or professor who wishes to assume the identity of a guide, to be meaningful and effective, must have the trust of those he or she guides. Trust has to be earned by the human display of respect, caring, concern, and ability. We just have to struggle to know when to let go and/or to push away. If we are not successful at that, then we will be exercising just another form of control and self-gratification.

It's curious, but things just keep popping up in my classes that are to that point. I had conversations with two students today. The first student is quiet, shy, laden with low self-esteem. He came up to me before class and said in so many words, "Dr. Schmier, I really felt good about myself when I took that risk you urged me to take and spoke up for the first time in class to disagree with Melinda. The others in the triad congratulated me. They've been trying to get me to talk for a long time, but you know I was too scared about being wrong and looking dumb. I felt really good about myself. Thanks for kicking my butt. Keep doing that each day."

I answered in so many words, "You did it. I and the others only believed in you and encouraged you. I'll encourage and support you, but it's you who has to start kicking your own butt. If you depend on me, then you've accomplished nothing. Your drive must come from in there (pointing to his chest) not from me. You have to want to do it; you have to do it, not me or anyone else. I may be icing on the cake and the class may be a place where you can take those first steps, but what are you going to do if you get into a class where the prof doesn't care? Don't use me as a crutch. Don't do it for me; do it for you. Think of how you feel this moment about yourself. Don't let that feeling out of your grasp. Build on that. Take another risk; keep taking steps. But only you can walk."

It wasn't but a few minutes later that a second student came up to talk. "Dr. Schmier," he admitted what I already knew, "I've been fucking up all quarter and bringing my triad down. I've had a bunch of shit on my mind, a lot of pressure from the folks, and I've had it with myself and all this crapping around. If I give it everything I have, can I still pass the course? I want to make my parents proud of me."

My answer was something to the effect: "Make yourself proud of you. What really should matter, the grade or the realization and the effort? Should the grade be more important than your commitment to excellence? The truth is, John (not his real name), that you can't have the first without the second. Read the syllabus. What does it say about climbing mountains and putting in effort? Besides, what does your sense of self-pride say you should do, rise to the occasion or tuck tail and run away? You've got four weeks left. That's a long time. You're talking now, but will you start walking? I believe you will surprise yourself, but only if you believe it as well." And so on and so on.

My conscious craft is more concerned with empowering the students than merely informing them. But I can do only so much. Ultimately, the ball is in their court. And if what I do results in expressions of appreciation or gratitude, what's wrong with that? I still remember and acknowledge those few — very few — teachers and professors who cared enough for me as a person.

Let me end by quoting from a student's journal. I had noticed Monday that she was different when she came to class. Something had happened. She had a glow of confidence about her. She was interacting with the others in the triad differently. She suddenly was participating in class, asking questions, answering questions, challenging positions. It was as if she had decided to come out from a shell. We all discovered why when she surprisingly volunteered to share these two entries with her classmates. I was so struck by her words that I got her permission to share her thoughts with you:

> THURSDAY, OCTOBER 28: Today, revelation and knowledge struck like lightening (sic). Dr. Schmier read one of his journal

entries about blueberries about when he became aware that
he needed to connect with his students and how he had to
struggle to face the truth about himself. When he read that,
my last (I hope) barricade fell. This guy is for real. If he can
do that why can't I face me. Then tonight I had an intense talk
with Dave (brother). Dave started talking about me being
submissive & getting an identity. My jaw dropped. I asked
him why he said that, and he said that it needed to be said.
Dr. Schmier had asked the same exact thing a couple of weeks
ago. ... Well, I thought a lot about what they had said and
wondered how to get my identity. I'm still not sure, but at least
I have something to strive for now. Also, tonight I realized the
significance of our self-evaluations. They are to get us started
in evaluating ourselves in general. We can apply the same
principle to other aspects of our lives. For ex. in our class that
we had the big discussion about prejudice, I began to evaluate
myself. Do I or don't I? Against who? Why? Do I like it? How
do I change? Can I change? I just feel I learned so much today.
I'm excited! Even though it had nothing to do with history,
I learned about me. That's the most important thing I can ever
learn. And I'm ready to get my self-evaluation today!

FRIDAY, OCTOBER 29: Today is quiz day over 15 & 16.
I got the guts to ask my question about the Indians.
Dr. Schmier delayed handing out the quiz to let the class deal
with my confusion. Also, on the quiz there was a question
that I knew the answer to that my triad disagreed with. But,
I had studied hard and this time I wasn't going to back down.
I persuaded them to use my answer and low (sic) and behold
I was RIGHT! Since I stuck to my guns and wouldn't let them
change it, we got it right. But the important thing is not that
we got it right, but that I stood my ground. I'm going to
participate in class next week. I know I'll learn a lot more
that way.

To be a part of that transformation, I will take any risk.

Have a real good one.

Monday, 22 November 1993

THE RIGHT TO SUCCEED

*I*t has been a while, over three weeks I think, since I last glided through the quiet, early-morning streets. A knee wrenched by stumbling over a raised crack in the asphalt saw to that. It is amazing how quickly you lose it if you don't keep up the walking.

This morning I wasn't consciously thinking at first about anything much except the ache in my legs, the searing heaves in my lungs, and what seemed like the very real possibility of a heart seizure. If anything, I was wondering why I couldn't quietly accept the slowing physical momentum of age instead of putting myself through such torture. Then, about halfway through the route, my mind began to play its games, probably from pain-induced delirium. In the midst of the surrounding darkness, I caught sight of the moon and I suddenly started thinking about "the brightest." It may seem odd to think about brightest in the midst of darkness. But the gray of dawn had begun to make its faint appearance on the horizon, and I began to wonder about its relationship to the receding darkness. The dark sky, I thought, was merely a present, but not necessarily permanent, state of affairs. It seems to say little about the coming of the dawn that can herald an unknown future brightness.

I guess I really had something on my mind. It was the matter of the "brightest students" and the supposed "not-so-bright." I have to admit that when it comes to the issue of those people who elevate and brag about "bright students" and the so-often ignored and supposedly embarrassing "not so bright," I cannot be coldly objective. About such matters I do not wish to be abstractly intellectual. I will not be scientifically theoretical, and I do not wish to be idealistically philosophical. I cannot be detached. Education is a human issue. It's about human life, human hopes, human dreams, human futures. At least for me, there is nothing impersonal, detached, abstract, theoretical, or cold about issues dealing with real people. We can fool ourselves into believing that our job is just to teach a subject. But the truth is that no action by a teacher is impersonal, no attitude detached. Like it or not, by gesture or word or glance, by display of concern or disinterest or disdain, by inclusion or exclusion, we touch students' lives. We open or close minds and hearts and souls to what's out there. We foster or shatter dreams. So I admit that I can't be impersonal.

I was reminded of that reality in a self-evaluation a student wrote last week before I left for a conference in Washington, D.C., on teaching college freshmen. It posed an agonizing topic that tugged at me all weekend.

After my walk I went back to re-read it. My heart ached no less than when I first read it. It glassed my eyes with sorrow and anger.

"I know you believe in me," she agonized as she explained why she felt she had not reached her academic and personal goals for the week. "You support me and encourage me. But it is so hard. No teacher but you has ever cared about me. I have been told so many times with so many words and so many gestures by so many teachers and by so many other people that I am mediocre or worse. I want to believe you. I am so afraid to believe you. I am afraid to find out who is lying to me, if I am what they say or any better than what they say."

No, I can't be impersonal.

If that entry weren't enough, that passage stirred memories — excruciating memories — of my ADD (Attention Deficit Disorder) son being thrown about by the winds of an uncaring educational system. Those words also stirred memories of an event that occurred a few years ago as I was climbing my own cliff.

It was the beginning of the school year. A teacher from an elementary school in a nearby county called me. She wanted me to come and talk to several classes of fifth- and sixth-graders about old photographs that I had been collecting for my photo history of Lowndes County and Valdosta. I initially balked at the suggestion. Though I've coached tee-bat baseball with this age group, I had no training in dealing with them in a formal classroom situation. To this day, I vividly remember her reply to my hesitation.

"Oh, it won't be any trouble," she blandly assured me. "They're *only* first- and second-level students. They probably don't even know what a camera is all about. Some can hardly read. All you have to do is show them a few pictures and say a few words about each. They get bored quickly and start getting unruly. You shouldn't have to take more than about 10 or 15 minutes of your valuable time and then you can go."

Her tone of voice was so matter-of-fact, so ho-hum, so resigned, so unexciting, so uncaring, so demeaning. It really annoyed me. The more I thought of that telephone call, the more upset I got. Here were children who needed encouragement and support the most, who needed caring attention the most, who needed to be told by word and deed that they mattered. Yet I got the feeling that they were getting the least, that they were being tagged and sold down the river by teachers who felt there was little prestige in teaching at that level — teachers who felt that the second they first set foot in that classroom, the students were beyond learning and weren't worth the effort.

I decided that I wasn't going to go to that school and go through the motions to give the teachers some relief time. Those kids weren't going to be just another line in the "Community Service" section of my annual self-evaluation. Those kids deserved more than they were getting. I thought and thought and thought. After a while, I got an idea.

The teacher and her two colleagues were somewhat surprised when I walked into the library room toting all sorts of paraphernalia: camera, camera bag, copy stand, lights, and original photographs. The students were all quiet and orderly, their hands folded on the tops of the desks, blank looks on their faces. The teachers were "shhhhhing" and whispering to remind them not to move. As I laid my equipment out on the table, I noticed one young man in the back of the room stretching to see what I was doing. I invited him up to the table.

"Oh, no," one teacher exclaimed. "They'll all want to come up."

"That's OK. That's what I'm here for," I replied, and, as if I were playing *The Price Is Right*, enthusiastically invited the students to "come on down" and look close hand. They rushed up, giving out little screeches of excitement and noisily shoving chairs aside. I could see one teacher annoyed at my disruptive influence on his class discipline — or should it be called "crowd control"?

One curious youngster immediately picked up the camera.

"Don't touch Dr. Schmier's camera," one frowning teacher lunged forward as she sternly warned with a threat. "It's very expensive and if you break it you'll have to pay for it."

She scared the hell out of me! I could see the brief glimmer of interest and curiosity in the student's eyes disappear as she quickly, with fear and disappointment screaming out from her facial expression, placed it back on the table as if it were a proverbial hot potato.

"It's OK," I softly said. I picked the camera up and handed it to her. "You'll be careful." The little girl smiled; her eyes beamed as I put the camera strap around her neck, and she carefully began caressing the camera and looking at it from all angles, showing off to the others who crowded around her.

"Now," I announced, "how many of you would like to copy one of these pictures for my book?"

Their hands excitedly shot up.

"But," I warned with an impish, but encouraging, smile on my face, with a deliberate, confident tone in my voice, "you're going to have to do all the work."

The children poured over the equipment like ants at a picnic. I could see the nervousness on the faces and in the movements of the teachers. With lots of encouragement, a nudge here, a demonstration here, a suggestion there, a question now and then, these students figured out how to copy a photograph. With a minimum of guidance from me, they opened the camera, loaded the film, mounted the camera on the copy stand, turned on the lights and directed them, placed the photograph on the stand, and even focused the lens, and took a picture. It took time, more than 10 or 15 minutes. It took the entire period. Out of the corner of my eyes, I noticed the teachers were periodically checking their watches. I didn't care. I looked at one straight in the eyes and quietly, but noticeably, shook my head in less than subtle admonishment, and moved my lips in silent murmur as I telepathed like a Betazoid (that's Star Trek talk), "How can you be bored? Look at those kids. Notice them. There's electricity in this room. How sad for you." It was exciting to watch the facial contortions of determination, reasoning, decision, concentration, curiosity; to listen to the cacophony of squeaking "What's this for?" "What's that?" "Silly, do this," "Let me show you," and "This is how it goes," "No, it doesn't," "Yes, it does," "See!"

To the surprise of the students themselves, they did it! And when all was said and done, they had such a sense of pride in what they had accomplished. As I hugged some of them and clapped in praise of their achievement, their eyes shone, their lips smiled, their faces beamed. In sad reflection of their attitude, all the teachers could do was to stand quietly. It was almost as if they resented the students' achievement because it was proof of their less than committed devotion to their craft. No, I can't be impersonal.

These students, the students in my class, and my son have been marked absent from classes. The teachers assumed there was something wrong with them because test scores or grades said that they are the "ones you can't do anything with," or the "ones who just aren't smart," or the "ones who won't ever pay attention," or the "ones who ... ." These students are not dumb. They are not without potential. They have gifts and talents to be nurtured. They are just caught in and thrown about by a smart-dumb, socially segregating game. They are not without feelings. They are made even more marginal in these classes that reinforce the notion that their place in society is inferior. They are caught in a conspiracy of low expectations. They are being educated to be invisible, to be life's failures. They are placed among the "outs": sorted out, weeded out, cast out, left out. They have been told in subtle and not so subtle ways that they don't have much of a chance to make anything of themselves, that nobody needs them, nobody wants them, nobody cares about them. Shovels, mops, dust rags, dishes, and fast-food spatulas are the only images in their crystal balls. Yet it has been my experience, both as an educator and as a parent of a bright, but almost discarded ADD son, that learning occurs not just when someone sees how it materially benefits him or her, but when that person realizes he or she can learn and when he or she believes they can learn.

I am not loyal to an educational structure that is dedicated to academic selection, personal exclusion, and intellectual elitism. I have a deep, emotional, unswerving commitment to an educational structure that affirms the right of each student to succeed, to an institution of inclusion dedicated to the principle of individual and personal cultivation and reclamation, to an educational approach that provides standards of opportunity no less than academic standards, that believes there is more to education than academic achievement, and that is convinced that it's not what you *can't* do, but what you *can* do that counts.

By the way, the photograph those students took did appear in my book. No, I can't be impersonal.

Have a good one.

Saturday, 11 December 1993

MELINDA

*M*y walk this morning seemed like it was over before it had begun. After turning the corner that began my uphill stretch, I don't remember seeing anything, I don't remember hearing anything, I don't remember feeling anything. I was deep inside myself, really deep, enveloped by what you might call a profound and serene curtain of purpose.

I'm not embarrassed to say that I have been very emotional since yesterday, when one of my freshman history classes met for the last time. Several triads had just completed their final exam presentations, and we were about to scamper out of class, when Melinda excitedly stood up. With a broad, confident smile sweeping across her face and a brightness shining in her eyes, she said, "Before we leave I want to read my class evaluation. I know Dr. Schmier said he would treat them confidentially if we wanted, but I don't want to." As Hope, an African American young lady who was a member of Melinda's triad, sat to her right with a quiet, supportive smile on her face, Melinda continued. "I want you all to hear how important this class was for me and Hope."

"On day one ..." She hesitated, got teary-eyed, and choked up. As she struggled to regain her composure, an image flashed across my mind. This was Melinda, a member of what I had labeled by the second week of the quarter "my hateful triad" of Melinda, Hope, and Eric. Three separated students with stern and unapproving looks on their faces, sitting stiffly apart, circling their chairs reluctantly only after my daily "urging," staring ahead with blank faces and looking past each other, refusing to converse at the beginning of class, surrounded by a heavy cloud of cold, silent animosity.

As Melinda struggled, Hope quietly leaned over and softly and caringly put her hand on Melinda's arm. And Melinda read:

> On day one, I was excited and terrified at the same time. You seemed funny and humorous and interesting, but rumor had you as 'evil.' Then came your syllabus. It was a book. I had to set my mind for a challenge. I was thinking that 10 weeks of you and I would be drained. But, the opposite happened. I was "filled." I learned more history than I could have imagined, but you took history and made it a part of my world. When I came to this class I had my box and my boundaries. I was prejudiced towards blacks and could care less to carry on any kind of conversation much less have an in-depth relationship with one. How my views have changed. I was skeptical at first to open up to Hope and work with her in class. But mysterious things took place in the triad that I can't describe. Maybe it was the honest class discussions about race, or your conversations with each of us, or simply that you gave us no choice but to work together. But my hatred and Hope's and Eric's began to disappear. The barriers began to break down. Now Hope knows some of my deepest secrets and I know that I can confide in her. And I always had trouble talking to my sister about who she dated (an African American) and especially about the baby on the way. Well, now that little boy is 5 1/2 weeks old. He is to me family, and I love him dearly. His skin may be dark, but I am now proud to openly call him my nephew. Three months ago I barely even acknowledged that he was soon to be. I wouldn't trade him or my sister now for anything. I just wish that I could have opened my eyes and heart a little sooner.

As I looked around the class, I could see through my glassy eyes that there literally wasn't a dry eye in the class. Tears were rolling down Hope's cheeks. Eric's head was bowed. Melinda read on:

> Now a little about the triad. I love it. At first I hated the idea. I prejudged those in my group and pre-decided that I would hate it. But not only did we learn to study together, we learned to laugh together. We've cried; we've hurt; we've become friends.

As she glanced at both Hope and Eric, she continued:

> We call each other family. Thank you for the opportunity. Without this class I would not know these two wonderful individuals and I also would not have realized a lot of stuff about myself. You opened the doors and allowed us to take the steps that we needed to take.
>
> Now they say that often there's that one course, that one professor, who enters your life and changes it. You're that person for me and I know for a lot of others in this class. And are we lucky. I didn't always agree with your values, but that's OK, and you never held it against me or anyone else. As a prof and as a friend — yes, a friend — and as a person you truly are great. I learned a lot of history; I enjoyed doing it most of the time. You make history a work of art; you bring it alive for all of us and bring it into our lives. Yes, a lot of it hurts, but we're better for it. Thank you. Thank you very much.

That, to me, is what teaching is all about. The quarter has come to an end; the class is over. But as Melinda reminds us, we teachers leave a lot of ourselves behind in each student. In that sense, the class is never over. To the extent that too many educators do not reach for the future beyond the classroom, do not reach for the stuff of life beyond the subject, are not aware of the students, are not touched, react rather than respond, do not see and hear others, students see no reason to reach for themselves beyond the grade or major. And so the students too often come away from their college experience with the narrow sense that the purpose of life is merely to be a doctor, a lawyer, an artist, or just a specialist of this or of that rather than to grow in wisdom and to learn to love better and be a truer person.

Have a real good one.

Wednesday, 15 December 1993

FINAL EXAMS

*I*t was kind of nice walking this crisp morning. The air had just enough nibble. It made me feel alive. It sharpened the images that were dancing in my mind like sugar plum fairies. After almost a week, I can still feel the excitement. I am still thinking in wonderment about my students during the last week in the quarter.

That last week started off as if we all had anchors around our minds and feet. There were just five days left. We had just come back from a week-long Thanksgiving break, and I think they were still concentrating on all that food in their tummies rather than the forthcoming food for thought. It was hard to get back in the rhythm for the remaining week. Many triads were about to make "final exam presentations." I was anxious. I didn't know what any of them were going to do. A four-triad group in my morning class had been scheduled to present, but eight of the students weren't in class when the class was supposed to start. I waited a few minutes. No students. My palms were just a tad sweaty. I was thinking, "What if this idea of mine falls flat on its face? What the heck am I going to do then?"

I had told them in the syllabus that they could use any format for their final exam: written essays, music, painted pictures, performed plays, sculptured figures, written diaries or letters, or whatever. The only requirement was that whatever they did had to capture and communicate the essence of their understanding of the historical issue. "Anything goes," I constantly told them in response to their nervous question, "What do you think about … ?" I always threw it back to them. "What do *you* think? If you think it's a good idea, run with it. You don't need my approval. Trust yourselves." Of the 40 triads in both freshman classes, to my surprise 35 scheduled to do presentations at the end of the quarter. This was to be the first presentation. I kept telling myself, "Calm down. They won't let themselves down. You know what they can do." Then, I nervously second-guessed myself, "But do they?" I guess I wasn't as sure of myself or as trusting of them as I should have been. I need not have worried.

Just as I was about to say something apologetic, Holly jumped up and yelled, "It's time to play 'Schmierpardy'!" To the theme song of *Jeopardy*, into the classroom trotted four students carrying a home-fashioned, large 6-foot by 6-foot Jeopardy-like board with the categories "People," "Religion," "Slavery," "Land," and "Government." More students poured in, pushed me aside, divided the class into three groups, and for the next 30 minutes proceeded to involve the class in a full game of "Schmierpardy," double "Schmierpardy" with a new set of categories, and, of course, final

"Schmierpardy." There was an "Alex Trabek," the *Jeopardy* jingle with new lyrics, commercial breaks — for sponsors such as the Erie Canal Company promoting westward expansion on "clean, safe, and speedy water travel," and for such public service announcements as those presented by William Lloyd Garrison, calling on people to "rouse themselves from their moral slumber" in support of the abolitionist Anti-Slavery Society. The place was joyous bedlam as the three groups vied to be the first to answer the questions. Each member of the winning group received a Tootsie Pop and the "right to return to Dr. Schmier's class next quarter." I got a courtesy Pop. After all, I am the professor and I am entitled to a perk or two!

That was just the beginning! Next, a triad went to the front of the room while the place was still abuzz. The class quieted down as Debi began reading an entry from her journal: "As I sit here only one day away from Thanksgiving, I find my mind wandering to History class. I'm thinking about some of the discussions we had in class. The topic was a very sensitive one — prejudice. One thing that I think would help this country is to ask ourselves one question. Could we walk a mile in the person's shoes that we condemn?"

So the members of the triad, in answering the question dealing with the issue of unity and division in American history, wrote an original song entitled "Could You Walk a Mile," with six verses and a chorus. Each verse dealt with a different issue of division and unity: religion, abortion, slavery, women, and sex. The last verse, about Vietnam, was dedicated to Don, one of their non-traditional classmates. It went like this: "He'd known the Ten Commandments from the time that he was five. But in the jungles of Vietnam, there was no wrong or right. He was a decorated hero when he stepped down off the train. But some folks in his hometown only made him feel ashamed." Don, a Vietnam vet, had tears in his eyes. When they finished, you could hear a pin drop. We quietly left class anticipating the next day.

The next day proved to be no less exciting, nor did the rest of the week. As each triad or group of triads presented, these freshmen — whom a colleague just before the holiday break had described in frustration as "airheads" — cooked up a smorgasbord of creative, imaginative, entertaining, innovative, and *substantive* learning dishes. Everyone, myself included, rushed to class each day with great anticipation to see what was the next surprise, the next treat, the next accomplishment. I wish there were time and space to describe all the recipes they concocted, all the delicacies we tasted. I wish I had command of the language to convey the supportive sense of family that bound those students together. There was no sense of cutthroat, backstabbing competition. No losers; no winners; no embarrassment. It was astonishing.

There was respectful laughter when one triad sang an original song off-key, a "negro, black, African American folk spiritual" entitled "Slave Folk Can Survive"; there was clapping and dancing to the rap, "Let's Talk About History"; and there was reflective silence as the class listened to original poems "And They Call Me Racist" and "A Woman's Lot." There was a 50-word down/across crossword puzzle, worthy of any Sunday supplement, dealing with the impact of science and technology on American culture, and we all had fun struggling to solve it; more original songs and lyrics; poems about the American Revolution, the Civil War, industrialization, women's issues, and racial strife. One poem, "The Good Ole Days," was submitted and accepted for publication.

Julie, who was scared to say a word in class all quarter, stood up and told the class, "This poem grew out of this class. The way I see it, if it's good enough to win a contest, it's good enough for a final. Besides, Dr. Schmier said time and time again that it's our class. So I figure, why not turn a poem into my answer to one of the final exam questions? This poem says to me what a five-page essay would say. I hope you all agree. But this is our choice." It took guts for her to say that in front of me, and she had prodded the other members of the triad each to write an original poem of their own.

From other triads came an oil painting of a slave mother holding her child in the middle of a cotton field entitled "No Future"; another oil, a two-color oil, on slavery entitled "A Study in Black and White Anger"; a pen-and-ink drawing of a faceless slave called "Ain't I a Man?"; a talk show called "Makers of American Society," in which Andrew Carnegie, Sojourner Truth, and Dorothea Dix were interviewed and fielded questions from the class; a magnificent eight-page, desktop-published newsletter bannered "American Culture," complete with a multitude of short articles on a variety of sub-jects, a crossword puzzle, political cartoons, a comic strip, a colonial Erma Bombeck column, and a victorian Dear Abby column; a puppet play in three short acts entitled "Let's Outrace Race."

There were collages dealing with religious diversity, racial prejudice, industrialization, and one entitled "United States, a Country of Unending Revolution." One triad put together a 40-minute musical anthology, drawing together religious tunes, revolutionary songs, country folk tunes, Negro spirituals, tunes from *West Side Story* and *Hair*, depression songs, and so on. Another triad created a 30-minute videotape on the role of women in American history. A third did a videotape on the issue of individual rights. And a fourth merely gave me a large envelope as its presentation. It was entitled, "America, the Magnificent Jigsaw Puzzle." Inside was a note. It read: "You made us work our tails off. Now if you want to give us a grade, you have to work yours off." Inside was a collage cut into a 200-piece jigsaw puzzle. It took me two hours to put it together!

It's a good thing I'm a nice guy. And, as if a grand finale was planned, the last group of triads on the last day had the class playing on a life-size game board called the "Magic of History," modeled after the game "Sorry." There we were, rolling oversized dice, moving each other, answering very good question cards, discussing wrong answers. Winners got Tootsie Pops, me included.

After watching the awesome raw intellectual and artistic talent that surfaced, after reading these students' final self-evaluations and some of their journals, which I wish you could read, I have come to believe that self-worth, creativity, and learning are in some way very close to each other. I'm not sure how, but during the last week of classes and on into exam week, I saw evidence of that relationship. I saw students putting aside their self-deprecating "I can't," "I'm scared," "I'm a listener," and "I'm not" parts of them that they so often let get in their way. I saw them take the chance on themselves and, to their surprise, be creative, imaginative, exciting, entertaining, different, risky, and substantive. I saw them find a way of expressing their uniqueness, of listening to the part of themselves that knows what's the truth about them and that speaks in a simple, real, common, and yet powerful way. I saw them move closer inside themselves, to see a part of themselves that they can know is true about them.

You know, I am amazed by students. We teachers should look at them, and they should look at each other, in wonderment. We should give ourselves half a chance to believe in them, to give them half the chance to believe in themselves. Students do not come to school to fail. Getting an F is not high on their priority list. They do not expect to fail. With few exceptions, they continue to try. They struggle to stay awake. Yet as we all know, too many quickly start to fall into a defensive sleep. And though it doesn't make teaching fun for us, we let too many of them remain in the blissful arms of Morpheus. A "Silent Majority" still unfortunately exists in all too many of our classes. Maybe one reason is that most teachers and parents motivate students to perform out of fear. They admonish, scream, advise, warn: "You're going to fail if you don't … " or "You'll be on proba-tion if you don't … " or "You won't be good enough to …" or "You won't get into graduate school if you don't …" or "You won't get that job if you don't …" or "You'll be a 'loser' all your life if you don't … ."

I've heard them all. In past years, I've even used them. But they are terrible images. Fear has an adverse effect on the students' performance. I know that. I don't think education is a reward and punishment system. It's not about getting people to change out of fear of being ignorant or jobless or left out, as if they were lab rats in a psychology experiment being prodded by an electrified grid. It is about showing people how they can improve the quality of their lives — and if they can get a good job, as they probably will, that's great too. It's a matter of educating students, of showing them how they have potential. It's about getting them to believe in themselves. It's about creating new hopes, new dreams, and new opportunities they probably didn't think or know about.

Our students are a heterogeneous mix. Different students bring different perspectives, different preparedness, different talents, different gifts, different this, and different that. Why is it so terrible to play to those differences? *Different* means only assorted, diverse, unique, distinct, separate, or varied. It does not mean better or worse, right or wrong, good or bad, smart or dumb, intellectual or "high schoolish." That's why I always say that education is not a thinning out or sorting game, separating the supposed bright from the supposed average or dumb based on an arbitrary, one-dimensional, measurable scale. The trick is to have each of them develop his or her own voice and acquire the confidence to sing solo. It's about teaching people to learn that there is so much to learn out there and inside them that they didn't know was worth learning. It's about lighting up lives, not dimming them. And these students have been lit up. My, oh, my have they been lit up. So have I.

And as I retain the memories of these classes and I am constantly reminded of them by their creations, which I have on exhibit in my office, I remain lit up. I'm already looking forward to next quarter, anxiously and expectantly asking myself, "What unexpected wonders will come into the classroom?"

Have a good one.

Wednesday, 22 December 1993
FACULTY BOREDOM

"*T*edium ergo sum: I'm bored, therefore I am." How's that for a variation of the Cartesian first principle? For the last several days, I have been poring over my student evaluations and reading student journals. I do that as I prepare to make needed changes in the coming quarter's classes. I noticed that one of the prominent themes that ran through almost all of the students' descriptions of my performance and the nature of the course was what they described as the *uniqueness* of the enthusiasm, the excitement, the stimulation, the inspiration, the animation, and the spiritedness that permeated the class. "It was so wonderfully a different learning experience," wrote one student, "from all my other dull teach-test classes that are so routine and boring where I only have to memorize a lot and forget it later just like in high school."

But I wasn't only thinking about the students' evaluations this morning. During the first part of my walk, I was also thinking of how this morning I felt particularly invigorated and excited, as far as power walks go. Anyway, I felt different. The briskness was not due to the chill in the air or to anything I was thinking about. It was simply the fact that everywhere around me there was relative newness. I was consciously experiencing the thrill of a series of mini-discoveries. I was more turned on, more alert. I had changed the route of my walk. I do this periodically because after a while a particular route begins to lose its challenge. It starts to become old hat, a drag, that same ole thing. It loses its zip and has a wearying effect on my body and mind. I had memorized the walking course and could run it in my sleep. I think sometimes I do. It was now fraught with an uninter-esting, bland sameness: same houses, same trees and bushes, same streets, same signs, same turns, same, same, same, same. I knew every crack in the streets. I knew when I was going to breathe hard and feel it in my legs on the incline, and when I was going to feel a resting relief on the decline. And in self-fulfilling prophecy, I did. I was losing the joy of the walk, and was increasingly finding that I not only had to force myself to go out there, but I couldn't wait until the damn thing was over. I was getting bored. I had grown "accustomed to its face." It was time for a change of scenery and experience.

Putting together the nature of the student comments and the atmosphere of my walk is what caused me to abuse Descartes. I began wondering whether my revised Cartesian theorem might regrettably be a first principle applicable to campus academic life. I started thinking about why the students felt so much of the excitement and the inspiration of learning apparently has been squeezed out of their education. Why, I asked, is it that when, at the beginning of each quarter, I ask the students to describe a meaningful classroom experience or a meaningful association with a teacher that they have had, they seldom can?

It wasn't long before I found myself thinking the unthinkable, something many of us have danced around and have been afraid of touching, afraid of seeing, afraid of mentioning. I wondered about how many colleagues I know who walk through their lives and academic professions, walk onto campus, walk through the halls, walk into our classrooms, and walk through their presentations on their same old stagnating, unchallenging, spiritless route. Probably far more than most of us want to admit publicly. I know, professors are supposedly intellectual Jasons, captivated by the pursuit of the golden fleece of wisdom, in perpetual cerebral motion, drawing sustenance from knowledge, drawn by the unknown, obsessed with curiosity, compelled to grow and explore. Nah, professors are never bored or boring, never lackadaisical, never languid, never accepting of anything less than excellence. Students are; professors are not. Most professors bounce into class with great animation, oozing adrenalin through their sweat glands, putting students on the edge of their seats, setting a mood of great expectation. "Ah, the game's afoot," their demeanor shouts out. "I'm here! Let's go at it! I'm ready! This is good stuff! Let's dance!"

If that's the case, I wonder, then, what all those jokes and comments about "yellowing lecture notes" are about. I wonder why students constantly, though not openly, complain that so many of their college classes are, as one student said, "as exciting as listening to myself breathe." The students feel that they come to campus and too often find that it's really the "yawning of a new age" for them, and the challenge for them is far more of a "yawning experience" than a daunting one.

I'm not naive — when many students describe a class as boring, it's often a transparent diversion from the fact they go to class unprepared or don't do the assignments or don't study. I think, however, that there may be another side. The fact that so many students are turned off by their classes can also reflect that what is really going on inside the classroom *is* too often dull. "Dull classes" translates into dull and disinterested professors.

Wander the corridors of the university or college, as I often do. Wander through your memories of the classes you took as a student. What do you see? I'll bet you will see and recall more often than not the traditional, indifferent, impersonal, cellular, structured, stylized, institutionalized "box and one" class: robot-like students, passive and disconnected observers sitting separated and isolated from each other, moving their heads up and down in monotonous unison as they play the cadence of their note-taking role, a cold, unemotional, zombie-like glaze covering their faces, minds shut down, forcing interest.

Many of us say that if students are apathetic, it is totally their fault. If they doze, if they daydream, if they doodle, if they kibitz, while we at the podium are waxing brilliant in our oration, we condemn the students for being rude, arrogant, and disrespectful as well as unappreciative of the opportunities presented to them. It could be, however, that they're just bored and have every right to be bored. I have heard so many colleagues say, "It's no fun anymore," and leave it at that. They make little attempt to make their classes fun for themselves and fun for the students.

We teachers have to bear a large measure of responsibility for the boredom in the classroom, because all too often, we're bored and are boring. We are the role models; we create the spirit and atmosphere of the classroom; we set the pace. Yet, with too few exceptions, we perpetually continue to administer intellectual and emotional anesthesia, drop by drop, into the students' minds and hearts through the classroom catheter: drip, lecture-memorize-test; drip, lecture-memorize-test; drip, lecture-memorize-test; drip, lecture-memorize-test; drip, drip, drip. Class after class, term after term, year after year, into the students' spirit flow these academic barbiturates.

So many professors are just as robotic as their students, just as unexcited, just as apathetic. With their backs to the students, they talk to the black-board on which they're madly scribbling, thinking that their voice will ricochet off the walls, seemingly oblivious to those behind them. So many professors, with an obvious lack of enthusiasm, recite from their notes or from the textbook, or read words on a screen from overhead projectors. We complain about students' apathy to each other, but do we listen to the students? If we did, this is what we might hear; this is what I hear:

> "Do you know what it's like to sit quietly, do nothing for a full hour, and look and sound interested. Now that's hard. Not worth much, but hard."

> "What am I going to do? Dr. —— in my English 101 class (freshman), his lectures are one 45-minute-long sentence. He's just about convinced all of us that English is a dead language!"

> "She's so dull. She talks her lectures as if her whole entire vocal range is one note! It's like she's reading us a bedtime nursery story to put us to sleep. And it works! The only work we do in class is to work to stay awake."

> "We don't know what he looks like. His face, I think he has a face, is always down in his notes. He talks to them, not us. He knows them better than he does us! I don't think he'd notice if we weren't there. I'm not sure he'd care."

> "He's a walking metronome in class. Now that's exciting!"

> "I've been in the military. It's like a snail's pace marching drill: lecture ... 1 ... 2 ... 3; lecture ... 1 ... 2 ... 3; lecture ... 1 ... 2 ... 3. If he was my drill sergeant, we'd never get far from the barracks."

> "He just reads the textbook. He won't take any questions
> because he says he has to finish the material. Who needs
> him?"

We've all heard them all because we have said them all when we were
students. What perplexes me is that so many of us experience amnesia,
turn around, and do the same thing. We have forgotten those legions of
stories detailing how it usually, except for that one teacher or professor, was
like for us and how we were treated when we sat on the other side of the
podium. It's almost like too many teachers are saying, "If I went through it,
so do you. If I made it through, so can you. It's a test of endurance and
commitment."

Maybe one aspect of being an effective teacher is to remember what it was
like being treated as a student. Instead, the academic "good ole boys and
girls club" keeps such things quiet and perpetuates the proper image. "We're
all good, conscientious, caring teachers in the classroom" is the official line.
Never show feet of clay; never show humanity; never do anything to show
a chink in the academic armor; never admit to the existence of the problem;
never say anything openly, however constructively, about or to a colleague;
never talk about changing and improving. Yet the fact remains that, in
and around the classroom, there are so few needed smiles, there is so little
laughter, so little enjoyment, so little curiosity, so little joy, and so little
excitement of learning. It's as if so many professors think that any display of
gaiety and love in academia is so unprofessional. "You've got to be serious,"
I remember a colleague arguing with me. "Learning is no laughing matter."
If that is so, we've squeezed life's juices out of learning.

"Hey, I'm told that I don't have to like college, just do it," a student
explained in an evaluation. "So why should I care if I am bored in a class?
Most of my professors don't care. They just want me to do it their way. So,
I just want to know what the professors want me to know to pass a test.
It's a tedious lecture-memorize-test routine. But, hey." If that's so, we in
academia have succumbed to the greatest of life's dangers: we take
ourselves too seriously.

I will go out on a limb to say this: nothing is more revealing about a
teacher than how that teacher teaches. Classroom behavior of far too many
professors, however, is far more a reflection of their disinterest in teaching
and in students than it is a sign of a weakness of teaching techniques.
In some cases, professors have gotten into a rut. They have taught the
same course the same way term after term, year after year. Their classes
have become so routine that they can teach them in their sleep, and often
do. Like me on my old walking route, the professors have lost the sense of
adventure, the thrill of the hunt, the anticipation, and they have little to get

their juices flowing. But they have done little to change the situation and, tragically, they continue to inoculate those sleep-inducing attitudes into the students. They go into class with a faked excitement that is transparently so unauthentic. Sometimes they don't ever bother to feign intellectual orgasm. They exude all the excitement of a Gregorian chant. There's no zip in their steps, no energy in their movements, no alertness in their manner-isms. It's, as one colleague in the English department bemoaned of the coming quarter, "the same old hum-drum course with the same poor students; another day and another dollar. Just a few years to retirement, and boy I am counting. Oh, well, I guess I can hang on."

Many professors use the students as their own red herrings. "They have to excite themselves," so many of my colleagues righteously proclaim, as if the love of learning is built into the human genetic code. I admit that students have to assume some responsibility for their learning, but that's only a half-truth. Teachers use these excuses to distract themselves and others from the real issues, to throw themselves and others off the track. Putting all the onus on the students for being disinterested and placing all the responsibility on their shoulders to become excited is a way for pro-fessors to escape from a connectedness with themselves and the students.

It is far less threatening, less uncomfortable, less painful, and certainly less honest than saying "I don't really care" or "I'm tired" or "I don't really understand" or "I won't change my ways" or "I only teach because I have to, not because I want to" or "It's my job to lecture and it's their job to learn." Professors will say the students are indifferent when they really mean they themselves are indifferent; professors will say the students are bored when they themselves are bored; professors will say the students have surrendered to mediocrity when they themselves seldom struggle to improve; professors will say the students don't think the courses are important, when they themselves often feel that teaching freshmen or even undergraduates is unworthy of their talents. "After all," an acquaintance at another university proclaimed, "neurosurgeons didn't kill themselves to get where they are just to take out splinters. Ph.D.s shouldn't have to teach surveys."

Some professors are going through a checklist to achieve promotion, tenure, and professional recognition in which teaching has no significant role to play. They don't have time for devotion to such distracting, time-consuming, unacknowledged, inconsequential nonsense as teaching students. Others, having achieved the safety of tenure, and maybe professional recognition, don't know what's left to do but to continue to go through the motions of teaching as they always have done. They settle down into a smothering routine, a safe and distant routine. Only the other day, as I, with great animation, was trying to convince a colleague to adapt a character-based approach to her teaching and use the triad structure in her classes, she remarked with a tone of disbelief, "Louis, stop killing yourself. Why are you doing all this? I can't believe you're still at it. You've got tenure. You're an old horse with only three years to go to retirement. You ought to be relaxing and counting your days. I know I would!"

Sad. If we want students to think about why they're bored, we have to think about why we're boring. Going back to my walking route, it wasn't so much that the route had become dull. There was always something new to see if I really made the effort. It was that *I* had made it routine. So the disinterest is not totally outside ourselves. It is an attitude, our attitude, over which we have some control. We created it; we can address it; we can change it.

The simple truth is that if we go into a class expecting the students to be bored, we will not be disappointed. But if we go into a class believing the students are interested, we will see them as a gift of excitement, bombarding us with a challenging array of variation and diversity. But that takes a lot of work, a lot of effort, a lot of involvement, a lot of interest, and, above all, a lot of commitment. Moreover, I think we have to remember that teaching the same particular course is not the same as teaching it the same way. There's so much truth in the saying, "Variety is the spice of life." I told this to a colleague last week as I preached my methods, and he walked right into my trap.

"You must have taught this course a hundred times. How many different ways can you lecture that the Declaration of Independence was signed on July 4th and that it says so and so?" he asked.

"I don't lecture. But I will handle it, at any given time, as many ways as there are students in my classes," I answered. He looked at me. "I'm not interested," I continued, "in when the Declaration was signed or what it says. The students can get that stuff out of the book or find out every July 4th. I am interested in letting them explore why it says what it says and what it means to them. Then, I have 60 possible routes to take in each class in each quarter."

"But you'll never know what discussion will pop up at any given time until it happens," he replied. "That's scary. Instead of one lecture, there is a possibility of any of 60 discussions generated by God knows how many relationships, experiences, and personalities of the students. My God, how do you handle that?"

"I stay alert, on my toes. But you're right. I can walk into class never knowing what's going to happen. I just let it happen and go with the flow. Sometimes, it does flow. Take the Declaration and Jefferson. One time, an African American female student became Abigail Adams by raising the issue of 'all men are' as opposed to 'all men and women' and got us into a knock-down-drag-out discussion about women's rights. At another time, some white students wanted to know how Jefferson could seriously use the word 'equal' during a time of slavery without being a hypocrite. 'Where were the Indians during all this?' a student once shouted out, and off we went into a discussion of cultural collisions. Once, a student wanted to know what do we do when two inalienable rights clash with each other. Better believe that prayer in school and abortion popped up. That one lasted two days. I've had discussions about what the Founding Fathers meant by 'life' and 'liberty' and 'happiness' and 'self-evident truth.' We've gotten into discussions, arguments, debates over matters about welfare, government, individual rights. Heck, once a student raised the question that, if the Founding Fathers disagreed on these things, how would we know just what they intended to happen? There's no end to the possibilities. I'll let them talk about anything, no matter how controversial or confrontational. That keeps the blood flowing in class. I just don't let anything get personal."

"You do that every day? That's too unmanageable for me. I'd rather avoid any controversy in my classes," my colleague replied in disbelief.

Not me. For me, teaching, then, is like my walking. I still walk; I still walk the same distance; I still walk the same distance at the same pace. I just always am prepared to change the way I do it. And as I do, I have a never-ending sense of revitalization. There are different sights, sounds, and experiences; the walk is awash with newness and unexpectedness and alertness and challenge and discovery. I have to be more alert now that I have to be tuned into my walk while I am tuned into myself. I can't take anything for granted. I have to keep on my toes, so to speak, for the unknown cracks, bumps, and potholes in the street, consciously think about the traffic patterns of those occasional cars and trucks and which side of which street to walk on, beware of what new turns to make, and plan new pacing strategies. It's now a bit of an adventure. And when I feel that sense waning, I will again change the route.

Have a good one.

Wednesday, 29 December 1993

EDUCATIONAL FAD 'N FASHION

*A*s I was walking this very brisk morning, I bumped into another early-morning bird looking for worms, a man in his mid-40s. As we went along for a short way, it was obvious that we weren't birds of the same feather. There I was in my ratty, drab, frayed, gray sweats that I had gotten at a discount store, my head covered by my Carolina-blue UNC knitted hat, and my hands protected by stained brown gloves. Eclectic to be sure. He was decked out in the latest, wondrously colorful running *haute couture*, obviously selected by Elsa Clinch, CNN's fashion reporter. Everything was color-matched: running tights, jacket, hat, gloves, and shoes. I looked like a wrung out rat pigeon waddling next to a strutting peacock in full feathery display. And when that rare car approached, he looked like a moving Jean Miro in its headlights while I resembled something like a lump of cement. He told me that he had started jogging a few weeks ago.

"You're pretty serious about this, aren't you?" I said.

"You bet. If I wasn't serious, you don't think I would have spent all this money on these clothes do you?" Then, he jokingly pronounced, "Hey, you're out of style in your clothes; no real jogger would be caught dead in your outfit."

"I like being out-of-step, you might say," I matter-of-factly replied.

After a few long blocks, our routes parted. But after he went on his way, I started thinking about two dirty words. They are words that none of you in education will like, but they've been creeping into my psyche and troubling me. They are such popular, unprofessional words. These words lack an air of intellectualism; they are words of whim and superficiality; they better belong among the giggly teenagers, macho beach surfers, and social snobs than among stable, thoughtful educators. But I think these words might be apt descriptions of what is regrettably taking place too often in our educational system as we rush and stumble to meet the growing demands by the public for educational accountability. *Fad* and *fashion*!!! Those are the words: fad and fashion.

That's how we so often talk about teaching and learning. It seems that educational ideas and concepts appear more often than not in the trendy, sporadic, short-life-expectancy way of fad and fashion: come and go; now it's here, now it's gone; it's the in thing this year, it's out the next; it's today's rage, it's yesterday's craze. They go by different cuts and styles, like hems and necklines traveling up and down in blurring speed. Everything is heralded as revolutionary. Everything is promoted as brand new. Everything has its own unique twist, its own name, its own initials, its own jargon, its own public relations campaign, its own publications, its own guru. Sometimes the progression of leaps and bounds smacks of a never-ending line of medicine men, hawking their patent educational cures from the back of their peddling wagons.

The problem with fads is that they so often have us all running about without any concerted direction, except maybe in circles. They create a bandwagon on which too many of us unthinkingly jump, a craze that lacks a sustaining concept, theory, technique, or approach. Proponents of each fad claim that theirs is different from everything else, a whole new and separate way of looking at education. Each theory, concept, technique, or approach is promoted as the instant cure from which we expect much too much. Too little time is given to settling in, adjustment, adaptation; so much time given to technique; so little time given to explanation and training; so little time given to the complex human factors of affected teachers, students, parents, administrators, and public officials. I sometimes get the feeling that supporters of these miraculous formulae don't trust anyone to understand the complexities and don't take the time to explain, to answer questions, to dispel confusions. I think the "common folk" are smarter than many of us "experts" think. They could understand, and might even support, new approaches to education if their concerns were addressed, if they were spoken *with* rather than *down to*, if we used plain language.

But sometimes I get the feeling that the attitude of the proponents of a given idea is all too often, "Don't ask questions. Trust us. We're the experts." And when expectations aren't met, we hear advocates proclaim in their own defense: "The concept would work if it wasn't for people." And after the public invests its time, monies, and confidence and the fad fails to produce almost immediately, we get despondent, abandon it, run for cover in an apparent display of a lack of commitment, and cry out in disappointment, "Back to the basic 3 Rs" — until another apparent craze, another wholesale solution comes upon us.

This ceaseless activity makes us look important, serious, prominent, and professional when we see our reflections in the mirror or converse with each other or read conference papers to each other. To the public, however, it's too often foul-tasting, ineffective, and maybe dangerous snake oil that has to be spat out before it kills. That helter-skelter progression may be one of the main sources of the public's distrust of us experts. It certainly erodes our credibility; it makes us suspect of being pompous, arrogant, cold, isolated, unrealistic, and groping amateurs disguised in caring professionals' clothing.

I am not sure I know why every new idea has to have a label and a jargon of its own, why we feel we need to make these self-proclaimed quantum leaps, these wholesale renovations. Why are we too often inclined to use the blare of imposed proclamation rather than the more substantial, subtle approaches of explanation, discussion, persuasion, and acceptance? Why isn't it sufficient to say quietly and humbly that our experiences and research are incremental, adding in step-by-step fashion to our body of knowledge about teaching and learning, nudging us to look differently at students and teachers, and suggesting that we think a bit differently about teaching and learning, understanding that the human equation is far more complex than a simple theory or technique would suggest? Nothing dramatic; nothing monumental; nothing cosmic; no "giant leap for mankind." Just small steps here and there by a person or two.

Maybe it's ego. Maybe it's a need to attract attention, to secure academic position, to secure grant support, to get an idea implemented. Maybe it's something in our culture that requires instant gratification, that our pronouncement be complete, perfect, and professional. I don't know. I do know that we do ourselves and society a disservice. These fads distract from the serious concerns many of us have about the state of education, from the serious acquisition of new insights or ways of thinking and talking about teaching and learning, and from the serious experimentation with thinking styles, learning styles, teaching styles, testing styles, and personality styles. Maybe we should just step back, take a deep breath, relax, and use our common sense before we trumpet the coming of the next supposed educational savior.

Have a good one.

Tuesday, 4 January 1994

THE MIND IS THE FUTURE'S FACTORY

I went out a bit later than usual this morning. Nevertheless, it was still miserable. It was cold, and after a night of wind and rain, it was biting out there. I was thinking about a comment someone made yesterday about my students' final exam presentations.

"High schoolish," this professor branded them in an obviously pejorative tone. "Void of any written critical thinking methods and signs of subject mastery."

"Why?" I asked myself. "Because my students chose not to express themselves verbally in the form of a ponderous essay? Is that the only mode by which perceptive understanding, resourceful creativity, analytical thinking, and penetrating reflection can be communicated? Who says so? Us? What makes our imposed, arbitrary standard, which demands demonstration of supposed competency by a single mode of expression, the only accurate criterion for achievement? How does this measuring straitjacket equate with the diverse perceptions, the diverse personalities, the diverse styles of learning, and the diverse forms and ranges of talent and ability that so often lie hidden within the students, condemned and suppressed by both our own myopic teaching practices and 'assessment' measures?"

No, to say that classroom performance must occur within only one medium does not necessarily reveal competency so much as the result may be false incompetency. You can't control the human imagination. You shouldn't. You should create an environment to let it flourish. The successful industries for tomorrow are becoming less and less the brick and steel buildings of old with their obedient mass production lines and air polluting smoke stacks. The successful factories of tomorrow, however, will not be the new technology or the human mind alone. I recall Thomas Edison's warning that whatever the mind of man creates, his heart and soul must control and guide. The single most valuable asset of tomorrow's industry will be the marriage of the human mind and human spirit. That union will determine the utilization of that technology: the human mind with its vast storehousing capacity, adventurous curiosity, unbounded imagination, and daring creativity; the guiding and energizing human spirit with its enthusiasm, confidence, courage, hopes, dreams, pride, integrity, honesty, confidence, and responsibility; the wedded mind and spirit of the "I wonder ... ," "What if ... ?" "Let's see ... ," "Maybe ... ," "Will it improve ... ?" "Can it help ... ?" "Could it be ... ?" "I'm sure I can ... ."

The state of this marriage affects the state of learning. Yet what do so many do in education? They still use "smokestack" readin', writin', 'rithmetic educational methods; they still concentrate more on the mental brawn of information transmission, acquisition, and collection. So many are still more inclined to practice educational crowd control, to herd students into impersonal and uncaring holding pens called large classrooms, to place students at a mass production belt, forcing them to engage in a string of meaningless, dull, stultifying, repetitive, parroting, memorizing routines: "Do it this way ... ," "Remember this ... ," "Memorize that ... ," "Think this way ... ," "Say or write it that way ... ," "These are the answers ... ." So many create, more often than not, an environment of copiers instead of creators, memorizers instead of thinkers, test-passers instead of learners, followers instead of leaders. They instill fear of trying by telling students that mistakes are sins rather than steps toward understanding. They inform rather than empower. They tailor student curiosity to fit test questions. They teach the test to students. They foster a non-productive competition in which there are winners and losers. It's a cold, unthinking, unreasoning, and too often destructive, immoral process of bland "whats"; it's not a warm, caring, supportive, encouraging, productive, creative, imaginative, and moral one of insightful and inspired "whys" and "purposes." What has regrettably been accepted so often as a process for the yesterdays and the remnants of today is not going to be worth much for tomorrow.

What, then, do we do, or should we do, beyond the dispensing of information? We should see teaching and learning as an adventure into the individual human mind, human spirit, human emotion, and human soul. It requires the daring, courage, and curiosity of an explorer who never really knows what lies beyond the podium but knows full well that beyond is where the journey goes. Teaching is not lecturing to a mass of nameless students; it is not talking down to them. Teaching is conversing intimately at the emotional level with individual students; it's helping, encouraging, and supporting each student to find for himself or herself that adventurous spirit within, to tap into it, and to use it to become a future adventurer.

Until we are adventurers in our classrooms, however — until we engage in a never-ending quest to see what's out there beyond the podium's horizons — we cannot produce adventurers. We cannot encourage our students to strike out beyond today's horizons into the unknowns of their imagination. We cannot guide the students to be what we aren't or no longer are; we cannot excite them or reasonably expect them to grasp life's visions and to reach for the stars of tomorrow when so many of us have taken so much life out of the subject, out of the class, and out of ourselves.

Have a good one.

Wednesday, 5 January 1994

J A N E

*L*ordy, it was miserably cold and breezy and cloudy out there today in the dawning morning. It was anything but inviting for a walk. To the blues of new winter walking grubbies, today you can add the red of my nose! But if the temperature outside me was icy, inside I was warmed by something that happened yesterday on that harried first day of class.

The first day is always tough for me. I go to class with a mixture of excitement, anticipation, anxiety, and expectation. Each class is a new adventure; in each class are 60 new adventures. There are the handouts of the syllabus, the metaphor exercises, the riddles, the introductions. I get sweaty-palmed and nervous, and I'm never sure if I'm sufficiently prepared to introduce, explain, and answer. I get that sinking feeling in my stomach as the students throw the questions at me with "Is he for real?" or "What did I get into?" stares: triads? journaling? tidbits? office in the hall? attitude and effort? no lectures? grades are unimportant?

I walked out of class drained and convinced that I had blown it, that I had been more confusing than usual, less ready than I needed to be, more unconvincing than normal. So there I was, behind my desk, asking myself in my daily journal why didn't I pick an easier way to do things. Then, like an apparition, my answer suddenly appeared. As if from nowhere, Jane (not her real name), a student from one of my last quarter's classes, out of breath and a bit harried, popped her head around the doorway. She had a nice smile on her face. There was a slight brightness in her eyes and a spring in her step. "Hi, I'm running to my English class. I just wanted to stop to tell you that I'm going to be OK. I'm on my way. Thanks. Talk with ya later." She pulled her head back and disappeared as quickly as she had materialized before I could say a word. I quietly pushed some papers aside on my cluttered desk, put my feet up, leaned back, took a very slow sip of coffee, put my feet down, straightened up and then wrote in my journal: "It *is* going to be OK. It's a very good day."

Let me tell you something about Jane. I want you to know about her. I want you to know that students are persons, that they are someone's child, brother or sister, husband or wife, father or mother. I want you to know the power a teacher, as a fellow human being, possesses to spark, to create, to inspire, to help, to guide, to rescue other people if inclined and willing to exert the effort, to endure the pain, and to have the compassion.

Jane is an 18-year-old first-year student from a small, impoverished north Florida county, the first female in her family to complete high school and the first person in her family to go on to college. On the first day of class last quarter, she caught my eye. I don't know why, but she did. Anyone who cared to look at her could see the unhappiness and fright that screamed out from her face. She would walk into class limp, almost painful. She would sit in class motionless and without expression. She looked like a storefront mannequin. It was obvious that distrust of herself and others isolated her from herself, from the members of her triad, and from the class as a whole. She wouldn't contribute during the weekly quizzes or to the class discussions. But during my regular study workshops for the students in the library, I saw her studying, off by herself, uninterested in interacting with the other students. She religiously did her share of the triad's daily and weekly written assignments. On her weekly self-evaluations she would write: "I'm a listener," "I don't like to talk," "I don't have anything important to contribute," "I'm not comfortable around people," and so on.

I spoke with her on several occasions, asking what I could do to help her. I made supportive and encouraging comments on her weekly self-evaluations. I told her that if she couldn't speak out in class, then work closely with the other members of her triad. Nothing. Then, I noticed that she listened closely and intently to the open and honest discussions the class had on racial and women's issues. It was the first time she had taken a visible interest in the class. On the next evaluation, about six or seven weeks into the course, she wrote — with words I remember to this day — on her evaluation: "I know I am not doing what I am capable of doing and I know I have issues that I can't face and I know there are issues so deep I need help to find them otherwise I ain't going nowhere." I took that as a signal. I asked her to talk with me in my "office" out on one of the campus benches.

"Jane," I said with a plea in my voice, "I know you want to be something."

"I try, but I'm not sure I can."

"Yes, you can. How can I help you?"

"You can't do nothing."

"Why?"

"Why you bothering with me?"

"Because you're worth it."

"No, I ain't."

"Yes you are, and don't let anyone tell you otherwise. I'll be damned if I am going to give up. One of us has to keep fighting for you."

"I ain't worth it."

"Why do you say that?"

"You wouldn't be worth it if you've been fucked by your father as much as I've been."

I went sheet white. My hands became stone-cold and clammy. I could feel a sweat breaking out. I started to shake. I felt a painful tightness in my gut. I mashed my teeth. My eyes glassed over. I was stunned, angry, sad, pained. I have read about it and heard about it, but it was in the flesh in front of me. After what seemed like an eternity of silence and paralysis, I told Jane that I couldn't help her. She looked at me with pain in her eyes as if I had betrayed her. I told her that I wanted to help her, but I didn't have the expertise. She had to talk with a professional.

"I'm not going to talk to no strangers about me."

"You're talking to me and I'm really a stranger."

"You're no stranger. You're a friend and you give a damn."

"Then trust me."

"I can't trust no one."

"Why are you here?"

"Honestly, to get away from my daddy."

"Do you want to stop running from your father and start coming to college for yourself?"

"I think so, but I don't know how."

"Trust me."

With an abrupt "no," Jane got up and started walking off. She hadn't gotten more than 10 feet when she stopped, turned around, and asked quietly, in almost a desperately pleading whisper, "Will you go with me?" I did. After I introduced her to the university psychologist, I went home. I could hardly walk that block and a half to my house. As soon as I went in, I had a stiff glass of wine, a real stiff glass, and slumped onto the couch, drained of every ounce of energy, thinking "I don't need this."

Two days later, without my asking, Jane told me that she had been referred to a local psychiatrist whom she was seeing twice a week. There seemed to be an aura of relief surrounding her. During the last three weeks of class, I noticed Jane starting to make a valiant attempt to participate in class discussions, a word, a phrase, an occasional sentence. It was as if just getting things out was a relief in itself. The other members of her triad commented positively in their evaluations on her activities within the triad and involvement with them. I noticed that she started contributing an answer or two during the last three weekly quizzes. She assumed the role of Dorothea Dix in her triad's final exam presentation. The other two members of her triad voluntarily came to me at the end of the quarter, assaulted my office, and fought — fought hard — on her behalf. "The hell with the first two-thirds of the quarter. Look at what she was doing by the end. ...

She told us some about herself, but that has nothing to do with it. ... She got the idea for the talk show and worked with us on it. ... In my book, that is worth a hell of a lot. ... If you're half the person we think you are, you'll pass her. ... If you don't give her a passing grade, and I mean a C, I'm going to pester you until you do!" Jane doesn't know they stood up for her. It was nice, very nice, to see students engaged in something other than selfish cutthroat competition. I was going to pass her anyway. It's that attitude and effort and performance stuff in which I believe.

Jane had sent me a holiday greeting card. In it she wrote this short message:

> You'll never know what a difference you made in my life.
> I'm still seeing someone and will keep seeing her until I don't
> have to. I think that might be for a long time, but I don't care.
> For the first time that I can remember, I am really starting to
> fight for me. It's hard, but you made it easier. You're the only
> one who cared enough to talk and listen. You're the only
> one I know who believed in me and showed me that there's
> something inside me worth looking for. If anyone tries to
> poor-mouth me again, I'll just think of the time when you
> said, "you're worth it." Lots of students say you're a mean
> son-of-a-bitch. I and lots of others know better. I'll come by
> and give you a 'hi.'

I have a simple idea, maybe simplistic. It's not even a new idea, but in collegiate classrooms, it is a generally ignored or avoided idea. Yet it has a profound impact on how I think about education, teaching, and learning, and how I act with students and those around me. My idea is that if students feel powerless inside and outside the class, they get resigned; if they are confused about themselves academically or emotionally, they get nervous. Anxiety and apathy are the two curses in the classroom that affect performance. We so compartmentalize students. We have the spotlighted intellectual and academic on one hand, segregated from the often separated and neglected emotional on the other. By such separation, the two are divorced. What we should do is connect the two and be concerned with both. Unless we are aware of and sensitive to, and unless we address, the underlying emotional distress that students carry around, it's very hard to motivate them to achieve.

My idea of teaching is to help students reach their inner strengths for development, put themselves at ease, feel true about themselves, feel more engaged — in the class and life in general — develop strategies, and operate more effectively in the class and in the world. What has helped me the most is to question whether the highest human function is the brain, whether the source of true "competency" and "mastery" lies in the brain.

I tend to think it is the soul, the soul in the Aristotelian sense, not in the ecclesiastical context. To speak of that word, "soul," that immeasurable essence of us all, might make some intellectuals uncomfortable. I'm sorry. I find that so many teachers are afraid of that word or its synonyms, "attitude," "character," "spirit," and "emotion." I like the word "soul." It's a much more accurate word than "spirit" or "emotion." To me, "soul" is the embracing, three-dimensional word that brings together and blends intimately and inseparably "mind," "body," and "emotion." That is what journaling, self-evaluations, and triads in my classes are all about. For me, everything starts with attitudes and feelings toward yourself.

Yes, Jane answered my journal question. Teaching is joy; it is happiness; it is accomplishment; it is meaning; it is purpose. Jane and others like her are the real reasons why I teach. Watching her and other students grow and transform is like walking at the moment a new day dawns, when those first rays of the sun begin to penetrate the darkness, when I feel the vibrant appearance of life. For me, nothing scholarly is as exciting, as enchanting, as loving, or as humbling as the appearance of new life. And when that happens, I live.

Have a good one.

Thursday, 13 January 1994

B A R B A R A

Hi there from dark, wet, cold "sunny, warm" south Georgia. Here I am dripping wet from the blasted rain that started coming down halfway through my walk. I felt like I was in an Iron Man marathon, walking one way and swimming back the other. Anyway, between the curses and the "Why me?" I was thinking about an exciting and insightful discussion ensuing on one of the e-mail lists concerning grades. It is a subject about which I have very strong feelings, even more so having just reread a holiday greeting I received a few weeks ago.

It's a lengthy letter from a student in one of my classes from last quarter. I'll call her "Barbara." All I will say is that, as far as a grade is concerned, she received a C. She did not have to write the letter. I guess she felt compelled to write it. She came into my office yesterday — maybe that's what prompted me to share this letter with you — gave me permission to share it, and said she wanted to do something to help my new students.

"What do you think you should do?" I asked.

"I'm not sure," she replied.

We talked and she was off to class. A couple of hours later, as I turned off the music with which I begin each class to get us in the mood to "get goin'," Barbara walked in and said, "Dr. Schmier, could you please sit down?" I looked at her, smiled, and, while everyone was wondering, "What the hell is going on?" I sat down. Barbara introduced herself as a veteran, a "Schmierite veteran." Her words told them about me, saying "He's for real." She went over the entire syllabus, always introducing a section with a "Did he tell you this?" intermixing her comments with "You ain't gonna be able to hide" or "Help each other" or "Think about the whys and don't memorize the whats" or "Come in prepared" or "Take a chance and do it," and ending a section with a "He means it. You're going to work your asses off." Then, she gave the class her address and telephone number, and strongly invited anyone who needed help to call or stop over at her room at any time of day or night. She also said she had talked and arranged with one or two other "Schmierite veterans" to be in the library each day at certain hours to help with the library reading assignment "or anything else that pops up. Use us," she urged. One student asked why she was doing all this. She answered, "Because I didn't get anything near out of the class what I am capable of getting and I don't want you to be as stupid as I was." From their journal entries, it would be an understatement to say that the students were impressed by Barbara and put at ease.

I am sharing this letter with you to cause us to reflect on our craft and to applaud and celebrate a very courageous — yes courageous — young lady:

> Happy holidays, Dr. Schmier. You are a son-of-a-bitch.
> You're putting me through hell here at home. Actually, I did
> it to myself. That C grade I got has made me do some talking
> with two very upset parents who aren't used to anything but
> As. Mom was upset that she couldn't brag on me anymore.
> I told her she could, but in a different and better way.
> Dad called you a son-of-a-bitch. I agreed, but I told him that
> you are a wonderful son-of-a-bitch!!!
>
> You put me through hell in your class. That wasn't supposed
> to happen. My parents couldn't understand why I had so
> much trouble. It was obvious to them that it was all your fault.
> After all, I was the valedictorian of my class, a straight A
> honors student. I was supposed to breeze through your class
> like I did in all my high school and my other college classes.
> All through school I was told that I was bright and smart and
> had a great future. I was told I was better than others. I was all
> this and all that. I really believed all that stuff and was really

taken with myself and looked down on others. I thought I was really some hot stuff. All because of my grades.

I didn't like it one bit when I came into your office that second week of class to impress you like I did the other professors and you weren't impressed one bit. I was also annoyed when you took me out of the room into your real "office" in the hall to sit down and talked about my background and talked about yours, how because of trouble with your son you had realized a few years ago that you had a strong streak of arrogance in you and that it was standing in your way of being a better person and teacher, of reaching what you called "your truer potential." You didn't say a damn thing about me like you were supposed to. You caught me off guard. A teacher bearing (sic) his soul to me, a student. I could have cared less about you because I was concerned about me. Later, too much later when it was too late, I wondered why you had told me that. I figured it out, but wouldn't tell you and wouldn't admit it until it was too late. I kept blaming you to everybody for my trouble. I wouldn't cooperate with my triad members and did just enough to get by. You were telling me that I was arrogant and that it was holding me back. I was and it did because I wouldn't be honest with myself. I think you said about yourself during that talk that no one is best because your best can always be better, no one is best in everything and there is always someone out there who is better than you were in something even teaching. By the time we finished, I was so mad I could have killed you. You were at the top of my shit list for a bunch of weeks and I wasn't going to do anything you said. But, you were right. Well, this class has started knocking that arrogance out of me. I'm not sure when it happened, maybe it was that piece you read to us about blue-berries, but Melinda said you were that one teacher for her and for a few others. Well, I had to write you that to tell you that I'm one of those others.

Now I know that all my teachers taught me was how to pass their tests and those others that everyone took including the SATs. They taught me how to memorize. I call it tell-memorize-test-forget kind of teaching. The only thing I really learned was how to forget very quickly after a test. My last year or so, I cruised on my reputation. Teachers gave me "As" I can now honestly say I didn't deserve. I once handed in a paper with some blank pages inside and got it back with no comments marked an "A." He never even read it! I think some

were afraid to be honest and give me less than an A because
it would reflect badly on them. I sure learned, not memorized,
a lot of history in this class, but not enough. Just
enough to pass. I'd like to take the class again and
really dig into it. I appreciate it now, but I think the
most important thing I learned was humility. There
were people in this class and in my triad who had lots
lower high school grades but knew how to think better than
I could, and I had to start learning from them! Now I know
what you mean when you say grades are worth shit. Everyone
says we have to have them, and I guess I still have to play the
stupid game, but now I know it's not the most important game
in town because they don't say a thing about what I know and
what I can know and what I am and what I can be and what I
will become. I know now that what's important is that journey
you always talked about in class, not the destination, that
whatever I do, like that fourth boy, I do honestly and fairly
and humbly while considering and helping others along the
way just like you did for me.

Yesterday, Barbara showed that she got more out of the class than she
thought. More than I thought. She became, in my eyes, a valedictorian
in life.

Have a good one.

Saturday, 15 January 1994
F O U R   B O Y S

Hi there from cold — very cold (down in the mid 20s) — south Georgia.
It's so cold the cockroaches decided to wear sweats rather than eat
them. Anyway, I thought I'd explain what Barbara meant by wanting to be
like "that fourth boy." She's referring to a sort of parable about the meaning
of grades that I tell each of my classes sometime in the early part of each
quarter. It goes like this:

Four boys enter a convenience store to purchase some munchies. The place
is a madhouse. Cars are lined up outside to pump gas; people are screaming
to have their pumps turned on. Inside, the place is jammed. Impatient
customers are crowding the counter, vocally demanding that the clerk
immediately check them out. Meanwhile, the harried clerk is nervously
eyeing a suspicious person in the back corner of the store. In the midst of

this bedlam, each boy brings a Coke and bag of chips to the counter and each hands the clerk a five-dollar bill. The distracted and frazzled clerk separately bags each purchase, takes the money from each boy, and returns to each boy five dollars in change. As the boys are about to leave the store, each realizes that he has received too much change. Each turns around and returns the money. Everyone applauds their actions; everyone praises them. "You all have earned an A in citizenship," the store owner announced as he patted each of them on the back. "You have proven that you are honest, upright young men." As a reward, he gives each of them a free bag of chips and a Coke. All the boys but one proceed to prance around in the store like proud peacocks, and then, like Little Jack Horner who just pulled out his thumb, rush out to tell the world what good boys they are. But did their performance tell the true story?

The first boy felt the clerk's mistake was his find. He was going to keep the money without a second thought if he could get away with it. "Hey," he said to himself, "this is a dog-eat-dog world. You have to get what you can, even if you have to climb over bodies. Everyone else would keep the money, so why shouldn't I? I'm no sucker!" As he opened the door to leave the store, however, he hesitated. "What if someone saw what happened and says something?" he asked himself. "Hell, there'll be another time." Then, with some disappointment with his cowardice, afraid that he would be stopped and charged with theft, he turned around. Was he truly an honest, upright young man?

The second boy also wanted to keep the money. He did not feel he had done anything wrong. "After all," he said to himself, "the clerk gave the money to me. It's not like I stuck a gun in his ribs and demanded it as if I were a common thief. I didn't rob anyone." But as he opened the door to leave the store, he hesitated and thought, "Hey, maybe I can get something bigger out of this for me than a few measly bucks. If I play my cards right, people will notice me. Maybe I'll even get a reward." So he turned around, ready to be praised and ready to publicly brag how honest a person he is. Was he truly an honest, upright young man?

The third boy immediately realized the clerk's mistake, but took the money anyway. He didn't feel there was an issue of stealing; it was just a stroke of good luck. "Hey," he convinced himself, "that's the throw of the dice. It's like the lottery. Someone has to win." But as he approached the door, he started feeling sorry for the clerk. And although he didn't feel any overriding obligation to return the money, he didn't want the clerk's salary to be docked for the mistake. "Damn," he cursed himself, "if the clerk wouldn't get hurt, I'd keep it. Anyway, I'll get some thanks." So he turned around. Did he deserve the A for citizenship?

The fourth boy, the quietest one of the four, turned around unhesitatingly, without a second thought, as soon as he realized the clerk had made a mistake, simply because it was the right and honest thing to do. He didn't feel he had done anything out of the ordinary and never said another word about it to anyone.

Does, then, as Polonious would tell Laertes, the "grade proclaim the person?"

Have a good one.

Sunday, 16 January 1994
REALLY RANDOM THOUGHTS

*M*y lord, it was cold out there this morning — really cold. My blue UNC hat got bluer from the chill. I came back from my walk and the dog was still frozen to a tree by a horizontal icicle! I'm talking about an eight-degree wind chill factor! In south Georgia! It took me a long while to thaw out because the flames in the fireplace are frozen. Unfortunately, weather like this down here seems so out of place. The pristine, quiet solitude of a blanket of snow, the strong, upright sticks of bared trees are missing. In their place, shriveling uncollected pecan nuts lie strewn about, semi-tropical plants are bent and shriveled, and there are the ever-present, messy pine needles.

Nevertheless, I was thinking about two sublime and reflective messages that I had read from Ray Rasmussen in Alberta and Len Van Roon in Manitoba. Isn't this electronic highway of communication marvelous? They generated a bunch of disjointed, really "random" thoughts that kept popping into my head like a series of exploding flashbulbs. Luckily, I found a ball point pen lying in the street. Call it kismet. By the time I came back from my walk, the palm and wrist of my frostbitten right hand looked like I had come out from a tattoo parlor. I'd like to share some of those thoughts as I try to translate my "writing-on-the walk" — contorting my right hand and peck-typing with my left:

> For a true evaluation of our classes and ourselves, we would be better to look into the eye of each student, read each of their faces, and watch the tempo of their walk.

> I love music and art and my flowers. I have found that playing the flute has helped me listen, which is different from

hearing; my very occasional dabbling in sculpture has helped teach me to see, which is different from looking; my flowers have taught me to be quiet and reflect and feel, which is different from talking and posturing.

How we connect with each other on the electronic information highway is a very technological thing. How we use that connection and react to it is a very human thing.

How many of us, by virtue of our position in the classroom, have conditioned ourselves to a form of human inequality?

There is a vast difference between the privileges of being professors and professors being privileged characters.

Maybe the students aren't "dumb"; it's their schools that are "dumb."

I know a lot of "dumb" people who come out of college, and I know a lot of smart people who didn't go to college.

What makes education is not its jargon, its format, its techniques, or its curriculum, but its goals and purposes.

I sometimes think that so many of us feel our educational system would be great if it weren't for the students.

Everyone thinks of changing education, but so few educators think of changing themselves.

Many of us give an up-front image for the students to break through rather than break through our own image and present our true selves to the students.

Before we wish to change anything in students or the educational system, we ought to first see if there's anything in ourselves that could be improved.

Why are so many of us troubled with feeling and so untroubled with thinking?

Human growth in our students does not stop at high school graduation. Human growth in professors does not stop with the receiving of the degree or the bestowal of the hood.

Why are so many of us professors more at ease presenting ourselves as fonts of knowledge and masters of our subject, and so uncomfortable with the perception that we are developing, fallible human beings?

I recall Kahlil Gibran saying that the true teacher doesn't give wisdom, but faith and lovingness.

It seems the more professionally renowned a professor is, the more professionally renowned that professor wants to be. The more books and articles a professor publishes, the more books and articles that professor wants to publish. The more conference papers that professor presents, the more conference papers that professor wants to present. The more grants a professor receives, the more grants that professor wants to receive. To achieve all this, that professor becomes more sensitive to what others think, and thus the more that professor loses his or her independence. Maybe the less a professor wants, the more that professor becomes.

Maybe we should care less in our classes about achieving the illusory goal of mastery of a subject and care more about instilling an appreciation and love of learning.

If we are to produce the leaders of tomorrow in our classes, should we not be concerned with what kind of leaders we are producing?

The truths in both my teaching and my life are only momentary perceptions of today which, if not constantly re-evaluated, can stagnate my potential as a growing teacher and human being.

Well, I thought I'd share these musings with you. I don't know about you, but I'm going to think and reflect hard and heavy on them. Thanks, Ray and Len.

Have a good one.

Friday, 28 January 1994

F E E L I N G S

*I*t was damp out there this morning. A light drizzle hung in the black, tepid morning air. I kept being splattered by drips from the overhanging tree limbs. Wish I had windshield wipers on my glasses. But as I splashed through the small puddles, I was thinking about late last night in my office.

It had been one of those days. Ever have "one of those days" when everything seemed to come crashing down in a never-ending avalanche? That was yesterday. It was one of those particularly long and hard days that everyone has nightmares about: not a walking day; a very early morning Minority Affairs Committee meeting — no doughnuts; a long, painful conversation in my "hall office" with a tearful student afraid to try to achieve for fear of failing to meet the expectations of unreasonably demand-ing parents, and a walk to the university psychologist; politicking to get extra funding from anywhere so that I could attend a teaching conference where I am supposed to present two workshops; quietly reading student journals and marveling at their insights, honesty, and reflections; tackled as I left the Dean's office with a refilled cup of coffee by an angry student who refused to work with the other members of his triad "who just aren't as good as I am," and discussing humility with him, asking him to think about how he would feel if I, as the professor, felt the same way toward him as the student; talking with a journal editor about two soon-to-be-published photo essays; preparing a weekly quiz; grading weekly tidbits; a walk with an African American student who doesn't know how to contend with the pressures of the "Oreo syndrome"; lively and emotional and substantative class discussions about an assigned article, "The Founding Fathers and Slavery"; a discussion with a student who is self-conscious about his accent and taking him to the College of Education's speech clinic; a confrontation in the Faculty Senate with the president of the university, conniving to undermine the Senate because he prefers the throne of Louis XIV to the chair of the Senate Head; a conversation with my younger son about giving it his best shot in everything he does; a walk back to the office to finish reading journals.

But when I slowly opened my office door, tired and drained, I unexpectedly found a letter slipped under the door. It was written by a non-traditional student who had been in my class last quarter. She is a 27-year-old mother of three who returned to get a college education 10 years after she graduated from high school: first in her family to attend college; wants to be a teacher; faced constant and vocal opposition from her husband's family about "my leaving my marrying duties"; always heard her own family's suspicion about "whether anything worthwhile can come of it." I'm not sure how long I sat at my cluttered desk reading this letter over and over again. Reading it rejuvenated me; it made me feel that it was all worth it. If someone had asked me yesterday morning why I teach, I might have said something philosophical about preparing students to live truer lives or to teach students to improve the world in which we live. Last night, I would simply have said: "Debbie is one reason I teach."

Here's what she wrote:

> Dr. Schmier:
>
> I'm not really sure what I want to say here, but I feel I must say something. I'll do my best. I believe that I'm already saying a lot just by writing you this. I could never have thought to do such a thing at the beginning of last quarter before I got "trapped" in your class. I'm letting you know that I worked to do my best in your, no, in MY history 200 class. I may not be able to rattle off history facts or remember all the so-called "important" dates, but I can get those facts in a book. Besides I don't remember all that stuff I once had memorized in high school. I learned much more than that in this class. You opened up my eyes and mind to why things happened and how they influenced the future and me instead of the dull when, who, what, or where.
>
> I learned how to work with people. If one of my triad members had a weakness in a particular area, say, tidbits, the other two of us used our strength in this area to help them learn how to get them right. I learned to rely upon others when we did our quizzes and trust them for the exams. I learned that I could be a leader.
>
> I learned how to work with me. I learned that I have weaknesses. That wasn't easy. I've always put up a strong and quiet front to hide them, but you know that. You saw through me somehow. I learned not to dwell on that anymore like I used to because I learned that I had strengths and could use them to overcome my weaknesses. I now try continually to improve myself and reach that unique potential you said each of us had. I don't do this now for others. I learned to do it for myself. I have learned that there are people that I will never satisfy. But, if I don't like something about myself, I will work to "fix" me so that I am the best that I can be. So, I just worry about me. As long as I like me and the things about me,

my ways, I don't have to worry about what you or anybody else thinks about me.

I am still kinda rusty from being out of school for such a long time. I am maybe a little slower for now than other students on picking up on things but I will catch up and probably pass. No, I will pass some of them.

It's kinda like something we learned in church. If you are doing something and God deals with you on it then you have discovered a fault that you have. Faults become sins when you still have the same ones year after year and you don't do anything about them. I guess your class has been like a church. It showed me my sins and has started cleansing me of them. I've tried in your class as I never have before, and that's a lot to me because at the beginning of last quarter, before taking your class, I would not have even tried. I believe that your teaching method has given me confidence that I did not have before. Who would have thought at the beginning of the quarter that I would help write an original song, stand up in front of the class and sing it with the others in the triads, and then take the risk of helping give you a jigsaw puzzle to solve for our final exam. Not I. I guess that when it really comes down to it, it didn't matter what grade you gave me at the end of the quarter. Why? Because that's your judgment of my performance, and in the long run it's MY opinion of my performance that really has come to matter to me. Well, I'd better quit writing now before I put you to sleep. I'd like to say thanks for all your time and advice and for being so hard on us all. I needed it. I got a real education in your class.

As I see it, a large part of my role is to teach the students something they need to know, something that will hopefully make them more interesting human beings. If our educational system is only about grades and grade-point averages, only about jamming subject matter down a student's throat to be vomited forth for a test, it's way off the mark in my grade book. I don't grade a product. I encourage process and progress and development within the classroom and for a lifetime beyond it. Isn't that the point of education?

Now, this is not a matter of being "student-oriented" or "subject-oriented," and it's not an issue of either process or content. It's about "both"; it's a matter of "and." It's an ever-changing balancing act: the subject matter, with its principles, concepts, and people about whom I teach, is balanced by my concern with the student's attitude. At the same time, attitude is a balance to subject content.

What I am trying to foster is courage, risk-taking, taking the plunge. I'm trying to bolster self-confidence and encourage growth. I am trying to promote knowledge of some principles. I am trying to develop critical thinking. I am trying to support the application of such skills, and I am trying to emphasize emotion or attitude. The competence demonstrated by a student should not be only a grasp of the subject, but the emergence of a greater self-assurance and self-confidence that would do him or her in good standing in the rest of the class, in other classes, and hopefully throughout life.

So many students come into most classes with a bunch of hidden, non-academic, non-intellectual factors that limit or prevent their success. Singularly or in combination, these factors cause anxiety, apathy, and/or chaos for many students. I just held an open evaluation in my classes. Do you know that few students doubted my authority or knowledge? Instead, they talked about whether I was fair, did I care about them as human beings, were they capable, did they have potential. The first reactions students exhibit in the class are not about whether the professor knows his or her stuff or not, not whether this is going to be a good course or not. They are about "Will the professor understand me?" "Does the professor care?" "In what ways can the professor connect this stuff to me and my issues?" And those issues, not necessarily conscious ones, are self-esteem, self-confidence, need for validation, and need for affirmation.

All I'm saying is that the emotions are there. If we truly care for the students, then we, as teachers, need to be more aware and less afraid of that dimension of our students *and* of *ourselves*. We must be more honest and more authentic in what we're doing. The purpose for recognizing, naming, and addressing tensions and emotions that exist within both the students and professors in the classroom is to help us become more comfortable with the spirit of inquiry and the joy of learning, become more aware of our intellectual powers. If a student believes he or she is mediocre, that is the best he or she will strive to become and will ever be. Fear and apathy have a debilitating impact on performance. The state of mind can affect the state of learning. It is manifest in the unquestioned self-descriptions of "I'm shy" or "I'm a listener" or "I can't write" or "I can't talk." And it's all too easy to let immediate "can'ts" evolve into prolonged "won'ts" that mire into eternal "don'ts."

Teaching to emotions or attitude is motivational. The emotion drives and gives direction to the intellect. It leads to academic performance and deepens understanding. It focuses on the student's attention, arouses interest, connects the student's world to learning, and, in my classes, builds a classroom community.

I acknowledge the world of feelings and take very seriously the role that emotions play in teaching and learning, in the professor and in the student. Call me a spiritual teacher. I make no bones about it. I make no apology for it. I take pride in it. I teach with passion and compassion. I struggle to warm the learning atmosphere in my classes.

What's the purpose of what I do? It's to deliver on some teaching goals: helping students learn skills, acquire an appreciation and/or knowledge of my discipline, and believe in themselves; helping them to possess a grasp of principles, concepts, formulas, axioms, and even facts; helping them to begin acquiring analytical skills, to begin learning to apply those skills, and, above all, to begin acquiring self-esteem, self-confidence, empowerment, integrity, honesty, humility, and the pursuit of excellence. It's the beginning of an acquisition of the appreciation of learning and the wonders of life.

A very long time ago, I once gave a take-home exam in a World Civilization freshman course. The question was fairly simple, yet demanding. I asked: "Assume you are Charlemagne. Write me a personal letter describing the world about you and your feelings about it." Two days later, in came the pile of completed answers. As I was going through them, I came across four dog-eared, unsigned blank pages. Well, that one didn't take too long to grade. I scrawled a huge F across the entire page and wrote, "Think you ought to crack a book?" By a process of elimination, I discovered to whom this "answer" belonged. She wasn't one of the better students in the class, and I thought, "What could I expect?"

The day after I handed the exams back, she popped her head into the office. Our conversation went something like this:

"Dr. Schmier, can I talk to you about my grade on the exam?"

"What about it?"

"I think I deserve a better grade."

"For handing in nothing but four blank pages?"

"Yes."

With a tone of slight curiosity in my voice, I asked, "What grade do you think you deserve?"

"An A."

"For four blank pages?"

"Yes. You told us to assume the identity of Charlemagne."

"Right, and you didn't."

"Charlemagne, creator of the Holy Roman Empire, originator of the feudal hierarchical system, admirer of Roman law and order and government, defender of Roman Christianity against the Arian heresy, introducer of learning in the early Middle Ages?"

"Yes, but you didn't write about any of that."

"I can't read or write. I'm illiterate, in spite of all my titles and what I've done!"

I sat there in stunned silence. And then, without hesitation, I changed that student's grade and gave her an A because it all boils down to what I, as a professor, wanted that student to get out of the class experience. It takes courage to challenge the professorial authority figure. Most of us professors won't even do that with our colleagues, much less with the administration. If this student bets on herself, bolsters herself, I'm not going to say, "Great idea. Good job. You've got a grasp of who Charlemagne was. You understand that being Holy Roman Emperor had nothing to do with education or intelligence. You took a risk and answered the question the way YOU thought it should be answered. Good job. You get an F." That's a mixed message. If I did that, then all she would do the next time is worry about "What does he want?" and seek to parrot me.

No, I think that this student and Debbie got the most important thing they seldom can get from books. I think maybe they started getting an appreciation not only for the subject, but, more importantly, for themselves and for the excitement of learning as a daring adventure. And that's the point of education: not so much to make sure the students "get it right," but to motivate them to aspire to their fullest potential, whatever that may be. If they do that, then they're getting it right.

Have a good one.

Saturday, 19 February 1994

C L A S S   S I Z E

*W*hat a strange walk this morning. The temperature was a balmy 55! While huge parts of the country lay buried in feet of snow, there I was, walking in my spring grubbies of shorts and torn short sleeve shirt. There was just enough chill that wisps of air prickled my skin. A heavy ground fog blanketed my route. As I walked, bushes and trees and lampposts eerily emerged from the thick mist like a ghostly parade of Flying Dutchmans. It was an overwhelming scene. Yet I wasn't in the rhythm of things this morning. I couldn't walk, to paraphrase Dylan Thomas, gentle in this good morning because I just couldn't stifle a quiet anger and fear that has been building for some time inside me.

It has been eight months since my campus graduated from a college to a university. With the school's "coming of age" have come inflated administrative egos, inflated faculty egos, inflated communal egos, and, worst of all, inflated class sizes. There are the never-ending public boasts by the administration that the leap to university status has resulted in an increased student enrollment of 10 percent for 1993-94, a 25 percent increase in applications, and a projected minimum additional 10 percent increase for 1994-95. Loud talk is being trumpeted around for all to hear that we are aiming for a student body of 10,000 in the very immediate future. Around here at VSU, it seems that an institution of higher learning is beginning to mean an institution with higher enrollment figures.

This growth, however, is loaded with disturbing contradictions. Our recruitment brochures continue to brag of small classes in which instruction is individualized. Administrative statements assure the public that the "average" size of classes has not increased. The public is assured that our newly acquired status will not endanger our reputation as an institution at which "all students retain their identity and don't get lost." Administrative statements pour out that say we have statistically only increased classes by one student per class. That may be true when they factor in such courses as individual directed study or directed thesis or goodness knows what else.

Yet the pressures are building that we figuratively bust out the walls of our classrooms and literally pack them wall to wall with students, as if we were laying a human carpet. My freshman classes have jumped already in size by 33 percent, from 45 to 60, and the administration has tried to exert pressure to increase the size of intro classes by another 33 percent. Only the physical limits imposed by the current classrooms and labs are preventing the administration from pressing to have its way. The administration asserts forcefully that any faculty member's resistance to an increase in the size of his or her class can only be construed as an act of selfishness and proof that he or she is not "a team player," and it has let it be known that it will not tolerate anyone interfering with administrative enrollment policies. It ignores the fact that enrollment and the size of future classes are as much academic issues as administrative ones.

We co-sponsor national conferences on excellence in college teaching, support on-campus workshops run by expensive consultants to develop faculty portfolios for the improvement of classroom teaching, and draw up departmental classroom teaching assessment statements. Yet we push up class sizes that increasingly undermine the quality of educational programs and make effective, personalized teaching practically impossible.

The president quite rightly talks of how important the first quarter is for ensuring first-year student retention. Yet we throw these students into ever-depersonalized classes that studies tell us are less able to attend to student needs, and thus increase the risk that students will be packing their bags by the end of the first quarter.

Yet I see or hear so little meaningful vocal and public opposition coming from the faculty. Individual muttering? Oh, yes. Private grumbling? To be sure. Quiet conversations? Certainly. I was in one of those hidden gripe sessions yesterday morning in the Student Union. These were student-oriented professors whom I highly respect. They were talking about cutting back on written assignments, class discussions, and essay exams; about instituting more lectures and replacing essay questions with less time-consuming and so-called objective tests, computer generated and graded, along with short-answer questions.

"With more students in our classes, we just can't do it. If that's what the administration wants, that's what they'll get," a friend angrily threatened.

"This doesn't make sense," I said.

The conversation continued in the same vein and ended when one of them sighed with depressed resignation, as the others looked down at the table and nodded in a supportive act of submission, "What can we do?"

"That's it?" I said to myself. "What can we do?" Then we all got up to go to class.

I kept saying that final sentence to myself over and over again as I walked to class and strolled among the 60 students in each of my two intro classes. Thankfully, it was weekly quiz day. I wasn't into it. They noticed that I was miles away. I couldn't get that haunting sentence out of my mind. It scared the hell out of me, and I raged.

I raged at a weakening of courage, a fading of vision, a compromising of integrity, and a declining of values in those people who would have me ignore my conscience and sacrifice the students' education as we blindly follow other institutions down that abysmal path of instructional mass production.

I see much silence, much cowering, much excusing, much finger-pointing, and much rationalizing. But I see so little admitted culpability. I see some shaking their heads in dismay as people sorrowfully utter a "tsch, tsch, tsch" and then go on as if they had done their moral duty merely by recognizing the immorality of the developing situation. But there is so much passivity, resignation, submission, and apparent surrender.

I am scared. Pressures are building that I, like my resigned colleagues, undergo a reverse Darwinism that would transform me from a beautiful butterfly of a mentor into an ugly worm of an uncaring talking head. I will not, I cannot idly stand by and let all that I am be drained away from my being for the sake of expediency and ego. We must acknowledge, tap, and encourage the wondrous diversity and mixture of experiences, talents, and expressions students bring with them onto our campuses. The pressures are building, however, that would mix this human palette of rich, distinctive colors into a bucket of drab putrid green, that would make this human symphony of distinctive instruments play a single off-key note. No, others may submit. But on this issue I cannot go gentle into the good night. I rage at the dimming of the educational light.

I have experienced, seen, and heard about the destination of the path we are walking on this campus. The class sizes on my campus pale compared with those on many other university campuses. Two hundred students in a class! Four hundred students in a class!! Eight hundred students in a class!!! Twelve hundred students in one class!!!! And we think "distance learning" is something new. No, it's been around here a long time in those large classes. Oh, it hasn't been involved with optic fibers, cameras, computers, or monitors, or with far-flung, off-campus classes scattered here, there, and everywhere. This distance learning in the classroom reduces students and professors to specks in each other's mind, heart, and eye. It so separates the professor, psychologically tethered to podium microphone, from the students that the two may as well be physically miles from each other. In classes of those proportions, students acquire an anonymity and cease to become individuals. The idea of a human relationship in education is trivialized. It is almost impossible for either student or professor to be alive, to be aware and be aware of, to touch and be touched, to move and be moved, to change and be changed, to see and be seen, to listen and be heard, to teach and be taught. What passes for teaching is more often than not a mere presentation that is sugar-coated with technique into performance. The truth, however, is that professors, whatever gimmicks and theatrics they may use in standing before such crowds, are no longer educators or teachers. They're at best performers, lecturers, professional speakers. They do more entertaining than teaching, offering more show than substance.

Now I know the howl that will arise as professors of such large classes defensively trot out their philosophies, attitudes, techniques, TAs, and student evaluations. I already know colleagues for whom such bravado is their chief defense. It's like someone who, when they start having chest pains, gets down on the floor and does push-ups to prove to himself or herself and others that nothing is wrong.

I think we're over-representing our resources and abilities and how well we're able to cope in these huge classes. We present it as if we had every-thing in hand and there aren't any big problems with big classes. No, we don't quite have it all in hand as much as we say. I'm feeling those same rationalizations creeping into my attitude toward my ability, and it's frightening. I say that I can handle a class of up to 75 without any adverse impact on my methods. But that is merely a self-deluding cushion. My "blueberries" are being pushed to the limit! I don't have a class of 60 students in hand as much as I did in a class of 40 students. I am not as effective. The students benefit less. I know that some students will always "fall through the cracks," but I am less able to fill in those cracks, and I think more students than I want to admit to are falling through. That prospect is giving me a flat, stiff, sick, empty kind of feeling.

I am scared, and I rage that I can't do much alone to fend off the impending deluge of bodies into my classes. Yet we don't really want to talk about it. Maybe it's our way of making it not real. You know, if we don't say any-thing, somehow it's not really happening. But if we're honest with ourselves, we know.

I was talking with a well-respected professor at a conference. He is renowned for his teaching. During a conversation, he told me how he taught a class of 400 students and how well the students received the class.

"How do you know if they understand the material?" I asked.

"Well, they are more afraid to admit they don't understand something in such a large class. I have a system. I place a green and red card in front of each seat. When I ask if they understand the material, those who understand hold a green card to their forehead and those who don't hold up a red one."

"How many would you say usually hold up a green card?"

"About 75 percent"

"Heck, you've only earned a C grade on your effectiveness, maybe less. What about those who admit they don't understand?"

"I tell them to come to my office and discuss their confusions."

"That's 100 students! You have enough office hours that allow you to talk with 100 students a day?"

"Well … ."

"Do you really think that a class of that size is on firm educational ground?"

"Well … ."

I think caring is good, effective education. Caring for students, having them understand that the professor really wants the best for them, opens up whole vistas. In these large classes, you cannot have connectedness; you cannot deal with the spirit. It's not enough to be competent in your field. You have to pay attention to the underlying relationship with the student; it's imperative to have that understanding, that skill. The large classes take that caring out of the educational equation.

I don't think that most of us want that to happen or like the situation or think it is educationally sound. Large classes are sterile and callous. They're like a concentration camp or a jail or a place that was created to mass service a need. They beat out of the professor a lot of compassion and empathy and a lot of willingness and ability to understand the student. Everyone talks about student overload. The pedantic portion of their teaching is beating them up. In the course of a week, for just two intro classes of 60 students each, I read 120 individual journals, read and comment on 120 individual self-evaluations, read and comment on 40 weekly triad written assignments, read and comment on 120 daily triad written assignments, prepare weekly quizzes, read the daily discussion assignment, prepare myself daily for whatever discussions might pop up in class, and mentor students for untold hours. And this does not include the work for my senior class or time involved with department and university committee work.

I am a great respecter of defenses. I have a hunch about what a lot of professors are going through in those huge classes. I really understand from whence they're coming. When they get into the classroom, they may develop the attitude that the student is the enemy. Or, as a colleague told me, "They're necessary nuisances." *They* waste our hard-earned expertise. *They* distract us from more important professional activities of research and publication. *They* take our scholarly renown and dash it on the rocks of anonymity. It's little wonder that these courses are palmed off on TAs who are there only because their fellowship says they must be and who are interested more in their own research and course work than in the students; or that these courses are taught by professors who so often denigrate them as "combat pay"; or that the courses are viewed in departments as service courses — "bread and butter courses" we call them — needed to provide the necessary class contact hours that would allow for the funding of smaller and more meaningful senior or graduate classes.

Universities should be places created for the service of students. We should be student-centered. We ought to deliver education as best we can within a very clear value system. I think we forget that. We become too busy, too concerned about other needs like budgets, financial aid, access, and a host of other distractions that we are all fighting. We spend a lot of time not satisfying students.

If you are going to be in the caregiver, mentor role, you must pay attention to the underlying relationship with your student. Is it any wonder that students don't take these classes seriously? As soon as they hit campus, whether they're motivated or not, they're told by word, deed, and manner that they don't count, that the courses they are taking — are forced to take — don't really count. It is little wonder that students feel cast adrift, lost, demeaned.

In our coffee conversation, I told a colleague that we should work on the principle that it's better to have students loom large in little classes than to diminish them in big classes. "Get real, Louis," was his quick retort. "Those large classes are cost-effective. The administration gets more professor for the buck."

"And we get less student," I replied with a sneer on my face, "while the students get less professor!"

Maybe that's what it's really all about. Not people, but money! Sad! If that is the case, then at least let's be totally honest. It is also about a contempt for and dismissal of students. It is also about a demeaning of ourselves as educators. It is also about an abandonment of our educational mission.

It is unfortunate that we cannot gather the educational equivalent of Somalia-like photographs to create a moral outrage.

Now, we can argue that it is something called the "educational establish-ment" that has let these students down. But let's be honest. With all of our self-proclaimed expert posturing, we, who should know better, have let the students down the most. Now, if you want to blame that ethereal entity called "society" or something more substantial like the state legislature, the board of trustees, the state regents, the administration, each other, and goodness knows who or what else, please feel free to do so. But in the process of pointing fingers of blame, let's blame ourselves for letting it happen. No, on this one, with so few exceptions, we all have gone too long, and far too gentle, into the good night.

Have a good one.

Friday, 11 March 1994
CHEATING/LEARNING

*D*ickens opens *A Tale of Two Cities* with: "It was the best of times; it was the worst of times." That's how I felt as I started my walk this morning. I thought a good walk would be soothing and cleansing. I was wrong because I felt the same way when I finished. It was a very strange walk. Very strange. I felt like there were two people inside me, each moving at a different pace along the darkened asphalt, side by side, each in a different dimension, distinct yet bound together. Because of the events of the last three days, it was as if each of those two people inside me was in Dickens' different time warps.

One of me was walking along crisply with excitement, thinking Monday had been the best of times. I had just returned from the four-day Lilly conference on college teaching. It was something else. The site at UCLA's conference center at Lake Arrowhead, 5,000 feet up in the San Bernardino mountains, was idyllic. The atmosphere at this altitude may have been thin, but in the conference lodge, it was densely relaxed, congenial, familial, and collegial. There were no stiff and stuffy formalities, no egos, and no professional posturing among the over 150 teaching faculty, staff, and administrators. Everyone, initial strangers and friends alike, was on an instant first-name basis and quickly started talking on a very personal level. Everyone really cared about teaching; everyone listened carefully to each other; everyone was truly interested in what each had to say and what each was doing; everyone was supportive and encouraging.

When the conference ended, it closed with warm hugs and sincere handshakes of camaraderie. For many of us, what had initially entered into our brains had traveled to our hearts and had become part of our spirits. I flew home Sunday physically tired, emotionally fulfilled, and intellectually exuberant. My brain was as stuffed by the flow of ideas as my stomach was by the unending servings of sumptuous food. I was thinking about all I had learned, about how I could introduce some ideas and techniques into my classes, and about how I could electrify some of my colleagues. And excite them I did. A professor in the English department was stirred by a service-learning concept. The head of developmental studies was enthusiastic about the idea of merging two developmental studies reading and writing classes with one of my intro history classes in order to offer the students something substantial and purposeful with which to learn reading and writing skills. The director of the university's struggling First-Year Experience program ate up the idea of creating an advisory body of concerned senior faculty to revive the program. The students in my two intro courses had demonstrated their responsibility and my trust in them by discussing their reading assignment on Thursday and taking their quiz on Friday without a hitch, without a monitor, and without me. Monday did, in fact, seem to be the best of times.

The other me seemed to walk slowly, finding each step was an agony, because Tuesday had been the worst of times. I had left campus Monday afternoon with a nagging feeling. I had asked one of the students in my first intro class how the quiz had gone. After a moment of silence and obvious hesitation, she quietly answered, "Fine." My "blueberry" sense said something was awry, but I chalked it up to her natural reluctance to talk in class.

Late that night, about 11:30, the telephone rang. At the other end of the line, an agonizing, nervous voice said, "Dr. Schmier, this is John (not his real name). Sorry to bother you so late, but I've got to tell you that there was widespread cheating in the class Friday. I left the room and didn't take the quiz because I refused to violate your trust. I wasn't in class today because I was afraid. But something won't let it go. I feel that if I didn't talk to you I would be violating your trust as well."

I felt like I had been hit by that proverbial ton of bricks. We talked for about an hour. As I nervously pranced around the living room, with a sinking feeling in my stomach, he told me what had happened. The students who had finished the test quickly pressured the student I had left in charge to go over the test so they could leave early; the students who had yet to finish the quiz were ignored or told to leave when they complained, and as the answers were read out, still others — many others — copied or changed answers. Finally, he asked for advice about what to do next.

I asked in return, "What do you think you should do?"

"I don't know," he replied. "I just don't want to accuse anyone. I don't even want an apology. I just want everyone to know that I felt that I was not given respect, and hope that they would realize what they had done to me and to themselves and to you."

"How are you going to do that?"

"I guess I have to tell them. But, hey, that's tough."

"The right things to do are never easy."

"I'm going to be in there alone with maybe one or two others."

"They're also lonely. I know. I'm where you are now in a confrontation with the president of the university over class sizes."

"Will you be in the class when I say something?"

"Of course. Do you want me to be there?"

"I do, but no. No one will be honest with you around. I don't know if I've got that much guts. I've got lots to think about tonight."

"You do whatever you think you have to do."

"Thanks. See ya tomorrow."

As I got back into bed, my wife asked, with quiet understanding, "What are you going to do tomorrow?"

"I don't know," I quietly answered with a heavy sigh. "I don't know, but I think I'm going to print up a sign: 'Caution. The Surgeon General says teaching can be dangerous to your health.'"

I fell into a troubled sleep that night, feeling betrayed, violated, raped. It hurt; it broke my heart. I won't deny that. The successes and joys are easy to handle and write about. It's the pain that offers the challenges. It's situations like this that remind me that teaching is easier to talk than walk, that assault my identity, that challenge my values, that heighten my sense of vulnerability, that put my outlook and philosophy to the test. After all, when I talk about teaching, I am talking about an "inner labor." A course, an approach, a technique, a concept, an assignment, a test, or a discussion is really me. That course and all of its parts are inside of me.

They're a part of my being, and if students do not respond to the spirit of the course, they are, in fact, jilting me.

Tuesday morning, I was having coffee with some colleagues and reluctantly told them of the situation. I was ready for a barrage of "I told you so's." I got some of the "What did you expect?" stuff. As for advice on what to do:

"Flunk them all for the entire course," advised a colleague with a callous firmness that was in the spirit of the Queen of Hearts screaming, "Off with their heads."

"You did your best. It's all their fault. I'd read them the riot act and ream their butts and give them all zeros," another asserted.

"You at least have to fail them on the quiz," a third suggested. "Technically, it's within your right to have them expelled."

"Right. But the administration wouldn't back you up. You have to make them an example. They screwed you good. If you don't want to give them all F's for the quarter, I'd give them a makeup and make it so hard they'd fail. At least they'd think you were being fair."

I went back to my office, closed the door, dimmed the lights, shut the computer off, and took the phone off the hook. For the next two hours, with my feet popped up on my messy desk, leaning back on my chair, occasionally sipping a quickly cooling cup of coffee, staring at the ceiling, sometimes closing my eyes, I just thought. Somehow it didn't seem right to spurn the students, to distance myself from them, to undo everything I'd striven for, to wield the power of the grade as retribution for being spurned at a time when they seemed to need guidance and support the most. That's almost always been the traditional academic knee-jerk reaction: blame the students, proclaim them intellectual invalids, declare them morally corrupt, pronounce punishment, wash your hands, and walk away. That seemed to be the safe thing to do, and so many of us do it. But I knew it would make me feel less of a teacher and a person.

I was facing a challenge. I knew when I started my triads and developed my character-based curriculum that not everything was going to be peaches and cream. There were risks. There were going to be setbacks. I knew there was a big risk in letting them run the class. There's no quick cure for the "Learning Dependency" that infects and debilitates so many of the students. If I want to teach well, I have to keep myself and my integrity exposed to both the joys and the pains. If I started being open only to the good experiences and shutting myself down to the possibility of having to taste less palatable ones, I would become isolated and my teaching would become defensive. My techniques might not change, but I would start walking the road of shutting myself off from all experiences, for fear they would be threatening and painful. That fear would forever destroy the possibility of creating the bond of trust between me and the student; it would cut the connectedness of intellect, emotion, attitude, and purpose between me, the student, and the subject. I knew that if that happened, I would stagnate. I would be so distanced, so shut down and shut off, so isolated in a personal ivory tower that I wouldn't feel either the joy or the pain of my craft. I felt like a doctor's needle was pricking the soles of my feet to see if there was feeling in my legs. The moment I stopped feeling, I'd stop caring, stop growing, and be dead!

Then I thought: Carpe diem! That's my life's motto. Seize the day! Realize that not every day is going to be sunny and warm. Not every lovemaking with my wife will be magnificent. Not every effort will succeed. But I believe I have to find something bright in even the darkest of days, because right now this is the only day I have. I'm not a Scarlet O'Hara thinking tomorrow is another day.

So I took my feet off my desk and went to class thinking about how to seize the day.

I slowly entered the classroom. There was no music this day. No joking with the students. Disappointment and pain were written all over my face. No smiles. No frowns. Just an emptiness. My movements around the classroom were slowed. I could see the students knew I knew. I stuttered a few words when John nervously stood up and asked me to leave the classroom so the students could talk. I sat on the steps in the hallway, deliberately sipping my coffee, concentrating on the liquid swirling my mouth as I tried to think about how to make this worst of times into a best of times. For the next 30 minutes, students came and went, stunned, hurting, angry. Some needed a smoke to calm down. Others needed a drink of water to wet their parched mouth. Still others just walked aimlessly around, tightly clutching themselves, trying to quickly recharge their batteries. Some didn't want to go back into the room. I quietly told them that they were part of the class and had to return. Each time the door was opened, I could hear the cacophony of voices, at times raised and at times deliberative. I didn't know whether the class would explode into smithereens or come together as a family in crisis. One young man just crunched down on the lower steps and sobbed. He turned to me and said tearfully, "I'm sorry."

"You hurt yourself as well as me," I quietly said. "I guess we've got to help each other now." As I said those words, I realized that if that sense of a supportive community was to be saved in the class, the students and

I would have to revive each other. As I came into the classroom, Wanda, one of the non-traditional students, was rising to speak.

> Before Dr. Schmier says anything, I have something to say.
> I've been listening to all of your excuses. I wasn't here Friday.
> If I had been, I would have tanned your selfish bottoms like
> I feel like doing now. You're nothing but selfish children!
> I wasn't here Friday because my 16-year-old daughter tried to
> commit suicide on the school bus while all her friends looked
> on. Not one had the guts to try to stop her because it was
> none of their affair. That's what they said. You who just
> looked on or the other way are just as guilty as the ones who
> cheated or violated the rights of some others. If you look on
> now and do nothing when your fellow students are cheating
> on an exam because it ain't your business, you will learn to
> look on and do nothing as you go on in life, convincing
> yourselves that nothing is your business. I know my
> daughter's friends could have stopped her if they had the
> guts to do more than look on.

In the few minutes left, I spoke to the students about helping each other. Classroom community can exist only if respect and the exercise of power — real power — is a two-way street. I asked them if they realized the power they wielded in the class, and said that when they use that power improperly, as they did, I can't help but get turned off. And I and my teaching and their learning suffer, just as when I use my power improperly, they and their learning and my teaching suffer. "Journals are due tomorrow. Let's all of us journal about this, and think about what consequences you should impose on yourselves," I said to close class.

The next day, Wednesday, we read our journals to each other, mine included. Here's a sample of the full range of what some of the 60 said:

> "I'm a whore. We're all whores, and damn cheap ones at that.
> I figured I sold myself out for .34 percent of my final grade. A
> drugged up whore downtown gets more than that for a lousy
> quickie! My honesty doesn't seem to be worth much of a f—!"

> "The real tough test Friday, the test of trust, we failed
> ourselves."

> "I'm here for myself. No one here is for me. If anyone wants
> some (sic) to care for them, let their mother enroll in class!
> I'll do whatever I have to do to pass. Read, study, discuss,
> cut a corner or two, whatever. I need the grade to get into the

nursing program! I don't see where anyone did anything wrong except get caught."

"When am I going to learn to work harder at learning rather than just working at making a grade? No one has ever taught me the difference except you. I thought I had that licked. Habits are hard to change. I've got to. But how do I get that to sink in? Really sink in. I'm really scared. No bullshit."

"I'm not guilty of cheating, but Wanda is right. I'm just as guilty because I didn't try to stop them from cheating."

"I've been cheating my way through all my school life to get the grades because it was easy. What you're asking me is tough."

"I just followed the crowd like I always have done all my life. I guess I have some growing up to do and need to speak up for what I feel is right and wrong. It's easy to write this in my journal. I don't know if I can do it outside these pages."

"I've always been content to sit in the shadows, but I think maybe that's not enough. I have to have the self-confidence and determination to stand up for what I believe. I am truly as disappointed in myself as you must be with us."

"I didn't cheat, but I should be punished because I looked the other way and didn't do what was right. I sure admire him (John) for taking on the class almost alone. I don't have those balls. I'm going to talk with him."

"All I'm going to write is that I think people who tattle on others are weaklings!"

"For 13 years I've been taught that grades were the most important thing on earth. Grades, grades, grades at any cost. I looked into your hurt eyes yesterday and now I wonder."

"I once wrote in my journal that you can't climb to the high ground if you settle on the middle ground. Who am I kidding. It's easier to climb down than up. I took the easy way. Now I have more to climb."

"I don't think what we did was all that bad since that quiz only counted for 1.5 percent of our final grade."

"I was just too much of a coward to do anything about it.
I'm tired of being a wimp, a nerd. Next time, I'll stand up for
what I know is right. I hope."

"I thought what we did was cool. I'm just sorry we got caught.
It's a dog-eat-dog world out here. We have to make our GPAs
and all that to graduate."

"How can you ever trust us again?"

"—— said in class what we were doing was cool. I thought so
too. That's chilling."

"You gave us 200 percent of yourself and we threw shit at you.
I guess it would serve us right if you threw us to the wolves.
The way I feel now, I think even they would spit us out."

The overwhelming majority of the class decided that everyone should get
a zero on the quiz.

I think that I and many of the students — not all — came out from this
experience beaten and bloodied, but, hopefully, being sufficiently
courageous to use this trying episode and to face those issues yet to come
and to keep growing into the kind of people my university and society so
badly need.

As I write this thought, I remember something one of my colleagues said
Tuesday morning. "Louis," she sympathetically said, "why do you get
yourself into these things? What you're doing is great, but you're at the end
of your career here. It's not going to make a difference because no one is
going to give you any pat on the back or awards or salary increases.
Just decide and have done with it, and stop torturing yourself. Relax."

For me, one lesson is that, in spite of the fact that teaching is not easy —
that it's frustrating, time-consuming, challenging, irritating, and, when
things go wrong, demoralizing — I remained undaunted. I felt the painful
prick of the doctor's needle on my sole that told me I cared and was alive.
I reaffirmed to myself that I don't care if anyone else knows what I did or
if I'm going to get some payoff or if it is going to make a difference in my
career. What I do has little to do with getting a salary increase. I'm a
tenured full professor with three years left to go for my 30 years at this
institution and retirement. I don't have to do it because it will look right
on my vitae or evaluation. I admit that there was a time when I did these
things to be important and look important. Now, I do what I do — I have
to do it — because it is important, because it is right and just, because

I have to try to do the right thing for no other reason than that. I'm not out to change the world. I can be satisfied with making a difference in the life of one person. That may sound self-righteous and idealistic. Maybe a bit preachy, but I've found this to be the most satisfying of all reasons for teaching.

When it goes right, there's nothing like it. No prize, award, recognition, promotion, or salary increase can match a student going out of his or her way to tell me that I had a significant influence on his or her life. The most wonderful returns I receive for teaching are those letters and conversations with students, some of which I have shared with you.

So I think my very best answer to my colleague and to myself is by example — to be me, to be what I profess, to fight the good fight in defense of the value of teaching, whoever may approve or disapprove.

You know, now that I look back on this entire week, it may just have been the best of times.

Have a good one.

Wednesday, 14 March 1994

C R A M M I N G

*W*hat a walk this morning. I went out a bit later than usual. The sun was up. The birds were singing. The temperature was an inviting 57 degrees. No humidity. The bugs haven't figured out that winter is over. I glided through the streets bare-chested in my grubby shorts. There was as much spring in my step as in the air. It felt great. I don't remember touching the pavement: not a heavy breath, not a feeling of the slightest muscle twinge. I felt like I was Mercury with wings on my feet. But if I thought I was fast, I was a tortoise compared with what's been happening on campus this past week.

It's the end of the quarter! That means it's sprint time! Off goes the academic regalia, on go the racing shorts and track shoes. Like Alice's hare, so many professors have been anxiously running and exclaiming, "I'm in a bind. I'm in a tight bind because I'm so far behind. No time to say hello, goodbye. I'm in a bind. I'm in a bind. I'm in a bind." For almost a week, so many have been in a panic, racing around at a blinding speed to finish the course: running from office to library to secretary to copier to class; making assign-ments in rapid-fire, "Read chapters 29 through 43 for tomorrow" fashion;

running between desks like Speedy Gonzales and throwing reams of hand-outs in the air while yelling, "Grab one. You need this for the test"; fanning textbook pages as they scream, "Ignore that paragraph, omit these pages, skip that chapter"; sliding transparencies on and off the overhead projectors so fast that they create motion pictures; scrawling on the blackboards in a blurring speed; lecturing at sixteenth note pace and sounding like a 78 record being played at 45. In fact, the whole place has been looking and sounding like a VCR on fast-forward.

Today is the last day of the quarter. I assure you that, when I leave campus this afternoon, the place will be sprawling with bent-over professors, painfully heaving as they hold on to their knees for dear life; with professors struggling for breath as they lay prostrate out on the grass in total exhaustion; with professors slumping over their desks, drained of all energy as their lungs cry out for air. But all of them are whispering, with great satisfaction between their heavy gasps, "Whew, I made it. I covered all the material. Am I good or am I good!" Then, with a great sense of dedication and accomplishment, their eyes roll, their heads sway erratically, and they faint dead away.

And we say students cram? Ah, but our cramming is so different. We can go to sleep comfortably thinking we have been academically honest because we have left nothing out. We have covered everything required. We have prepared the students to take our exam or the depart-ment's exam or to move on to the next course or to take the standardized exit or entrance exam. We have done our duty. We have offered them a mastery of the subject.

I don't think I'm being impish. I was in the English department Monday morning, sipping a cup of coffee and talking college basketball with some colleagues, when a junior faculty member quickly walked by muttering, "I'll never finish this course."

All this helter and skelter reminded me of a conversation I had with a professor last fall who had participated in one of my workshops at a conference. He asked me: "With all the time you spend in class on journal sharing, exercises to help the students learn how to critically think and study, to develop a sense of family, to do evaluations in class, how do you finish a course? If I did all that, I'd never cover all the material. As it is now, I'm always so far behind that I have to race to catch up at the end of the semester."

"I never finish a course and I don't try to," I assured him. "I'm always cutting stuff out during the course and changing the syllabus' calendar as the students get into prolonged discussions. During a 'good' quarter, I usually cover only about two-thirds of the stuff in the textbook, whatever that's worth."

"But," he replied nervously, "they won't learn everything they have to."

"They won't anyway, so why sweat it?"

"But that's history. This is microbiology. I've got to cover a certain amount of material because they need certain material to take the next course in the sequence."

"How much of that material do you think they remember afterwards?"

"I don't know. I'd guess about 80 or 85 percent."

"Not in your wildest dreams! Try somewhere around 30 percent to 40 percent — if you're lucky, real lucky, 50 percent."

"But they can't pass the next course without this content."

"Which is better — that your students learn twice as much material half as well or half as much material twice as well? Why not take time out and get them to appreciate the impact and influence of microbiology? Let them read articles about the moral issue of human genetic engineering and discuss it in class. Make the course an exciting, meaningful, and fun course. They'll remember more of it."

"That's asking a lot."

"Look, if you cover all that material just to say you've covered it, and little or none of it is retained in the first place, it's the same as if you never covered it at all. The only difference is that now when someone asks, 'Why are the students doing so poorly?' we can say, 'Hey, don't look at us. We covered all that material. It's not our fault they don't know it now. It's their fault for not learning it.' "

So in this academic Daytona 500, whom have we really served? It seems to me that we often cram all that stuff into our courses more for our bene-fit than that of the students. We seem to think that it is some dereliction of duty, some indictment of our ability, some demonstration of incompetence if we do otherwise. We seem to think, to paraphrase the Bard, that it is better for the professors to have said it than never to have said it at all; that it is better for the students to have heard it than never to have heard it at all. I sometimes get the feeling at this time of the quarter that professors lapse into the belief that all they have to do to teach is tell and all the students have to do to learn is hear; that professors mention it, the students get it, and if professors don't, the students won't.

But have the students really learned all that material we cram down their throats for any purpose other than vomiting it back to pass a test and get a course grade? Have they really retained the material in a way that is purposeful? Or have we merely perpetuated the talk-listen-memorize-test-forget patterns?

I once had a professor, Dr. Birdsall Viault, my mentor at Adelphi College, who set me on my course when I was adrift and who replied to a student protest that the class hadn't finished the textbook, and to the student who asked if omitted material would be on the final exam, "Mr. Schmier, only geniuses and fools finish the course. I can assure you without fear of contradiction that you and I are neither. But I can assure you that whatever we have covered, we have covered well."

"But," I continued in my subtle protest, "I'm taking the GRE next month. What if the material we didn't cover is on it?"

Dr. Viault replied, with a twinkle in his eye, "Mr. Schmier, I am confident you have the ability to learn that extra material on your own if you so wish."

Personally, taking my cue from Dr. Viault, I'd be happy if students really learn a few key concepts about history, get an appreciation for it, and maybe acquire an understanding for it. If they become history majors, they can get the finer details when they get sufficient background. If they become historians, they can rise to the level of sophistication where they can wrestle with the latest controversies in the field, grasp them, and see their ramifications. For now, I would much rather my students learn a lot about how to assume the responsibility for their own learning and how to learn on their own for the rest of their lives — and learn a lot about themselves. Whatever we cover, let's make sure we cover it well — and that it serves the student, rather than us, well.

Have a good one.

Thursday, 24 March 1994

G R A D E S

I slept in this morning and went out a bit later than usual. After all, it is the break between winter and spring quarters. It was very nice outside, a tad on the warm side, enough to break into a slight sweat. The entire route was lined by a sun-bathed nature, bragging with a dazzling display of fluttering yellow butterflies, azaleas blooming in a variety of colors, flowering white and pink dogwoods, beds of daffodils, and an amaryllis and bearded iris or two poking through here and there.

I walked this morning with a sense of hesitant and reflective relief. The Quarter is over. Grades are in. The Judgment Days are over. The weeklong dark and depressing period of senseless, life-threatening torture on campus, that contrasts with the surrounding beautiful reminders of renewed life, has come to an end. My mortality has returned. My cloak of supposedly divine infallibility, now wrinkled and tattered and stained, once again hangs in the closet; my reserved seat on Mount Sinai once again stands empty.

During the last week of class, many of my students had been making their final exam presentations, displaying that awe, wonder, curiosity, risk-taking, knowledge, and personal growth that education should be all about. Mickie, Eric, and Christy sang their original song, music and lyrics, on slavery and racism; Mike, Sarah, and Janice discussed their sculptured figures depicting their answer to the question, "What is an American?"; two triads ran an impressive bingo-type game called "Histo"; two other triads put together a takeoff on Hollywood Squares that they called "Schmier's Squares"; four triads presented a great *Jeopardy* show; Lamonica, Stacia, and Travis involved the class in a profoundly realistic role-playing skit that taught us what it was like being the brunt of prejudice and hatred as a minority throughout American history; Brad, Tim, and Mandy made a videotape of their original four-act pantomime play on the influence of religion in the American experience; Pat and Jaime presented their original interactive computer program on religion in American history; and two triads sent the class out on a scavenger hunt all over campus that required a knowledge of the religious experience in American history.

How to grade that? How to take all that exciting and daring creativity, imagination, understanding, and accomplishment and convert and compress it into an unexciting, impersonal, and inadequately revealing letter grade? My eyes still sting, my brain still hurts, my back still aches, my heart still tugs. I am mentally tired, emotionally drained, physically worn out, and just numb. It takes me a lot of time and effort and concentration to issue a final grade for a student. No computer grading programs for me! For six days, including a Monday all-nighter to meet the registrar's deadlines, for each of my 120 students, I have been struggling to "get a feel" for the "big picture," to see how far each student has come from where he or she was. I pored over their journals; pondered their weekly self-evaluations, final self-evaluations, and peer evaluations of each other; went over my daily class notations; reflected on the final exam presentations; recalled conversations with them; factored in both academic and character development during the *entire* quarter; balanced effort and performance; assessed just what it was that each student learned; juggled quiz grades and weekly written assignment evaluations; and thought about the nature of participation in daily class discussions and contributions to the triad. I pushed my "blueberries" perceptions to the edge. Then, second-guessing myself, I went through the tortuous process again. For more than a student or two or three, I called upon the "Schmier factor" for an adjustment here and there. "Progress," "development," "improvement," "growth," and "process" are words that reflect my guiding criteria for evaluation — not calculation or compilation.

I'd be dishonest if I didn't admit that there were times I was tempted to envy so many of my colleagues, who, with great ease, coldly, distantly, and quickly add, divide, calculate, record, hand in, and go off, or who let a mindless, heartless computer program do the calculations for them. It would be so easy to agree with those who comfortably argue that their grades reveal unbiased judgment, consistent standards, impartial evaluation. I could avoid all of my inner turmoil if I accepted the fact that grades represent precise instruments of evaluation, offer irrefutable evidence of performance, are scientifically arrived at, and provide absolute truth.

Each time, I realize that handling an arithmetical computation is so much simpler, easier, and safer than handling the unpredictable and extremely variable human equation. So many people place so much stock in something that is so arbitrary and means so little. They get so nervous thinking that there may exist things that are beyond standardized or absolute measure that they tend to measure only that which is measurable. I can't, however, in good conscience be intellectually or emotionally imprisoned, or be immobilized by numbers, or shirk my responsibility by hiding behind scores, or feign innocence by proclaiming, "I had no choice. The grades made me do it!"

Those kinds of grades don't say how far each student has come, with what they had to struggle, the barriers they had to overcome. I wish you all could read some of these students' journals. If you did, you'd be gripped by the sincerity of Robin saying:

I have never ever relied upon anyone else or trusted anyone for anything. What I have painstakingly come to realize is this: no one could possibly do everything themselves all the time. Sometimes one has to depend on others to help them accomplish their goals. To not trust others and depend only on myself was cheating the other members of my triad of their responsibility. I learned much about myself and others during my time in this class. I believe now that was, aside from learning history, the main purpose from the beginning.

When I grade Gary's performance, I factor in his growth. "I learned a lot of history," he wrote in one of his last journal entries. "But that was only because you showed me how to take chances, how to believe in myself, not to be average like everyone else, but be different and take the risks to be the best." Rebecca's grade is influenced by the fact that "grades mean a lot to me and I got a pretty good knowledge of history, but I think I learned that life is all about working for each other, learning to deal with people, to cooperate with them and respect their differences. That's almost as important a lesson as history." There's Wayland who wrote: "I learned to express my thoughts. ... I'm better or should I say I'm more at ease with myself. ... I've learned not only to explore history, but also my inner self." Carrie's words ring as I contemplate her grade: "I learned a lot about myself. It has helped me develop my learning ability and my sense of purpose. I didn't just learn history, I grew as a person in this class." You'd be amazed at Amy's realization: "It was like waking up from a social and education coma that I had been in for so long. I finally realized that getting by just gets you by, but going all out will get you anywhere you want to go." You'd be surprised at Angela's development: "I've learned not to be embarrassed of myself or so afraid of failing. I am not as easily intimidated. I've learned how to study the material. I no longer read words, I look for things behind the words." Or Kim's: "I have seen myself change. ... I am not afraid to voice my opinion anymore and it feels great. ... I have learned self-respect, to think for myself, to improve my study habits, as well as a lot of history."

And you'd be haunted by Alisha's unforgettable words:

> Thanks to this class I am starting to realize that education is not just taking tests and getting grades. It's about life and what each of us can accomplish on our own. It's like when we get in class, everyone is like a family who will stick up for each other and work with each other instead of stabbing each other in the back to impress you. When we walk into the room it's like we had a special bond that no one, no matter how hard they try, will ever forget. ... My ride is going to

leave me here Friday. But I've decided that no matter what it takes, I'll be in class at 9:30 a.m. sharp Monday. I'll find a way to get home. Having this class be disappointed in me by me not showing the respect I should toward them during their final presentations would hurt me and them. I'm not coming back to school next quarter, but I hope to God this class stays with me wherever I go and whatever I do.

Alisha was in class. I thanked her and asked if she had a ride home. When she replied that she didn't, I asked the class if anyone was heading down Florida way and had room for her. One girl answered that she was going to Florida for the break and if Alisha had felt that much obligation to the class and had made that kind of sacrifice, she could go a few miles out of her way and a take a few hours out from her vacation. She would make room for Alisha and drop her off in front of her house. Everyone applauded both of them.

I racked my brain trying to figure out how to quantify fairly the immeasurable, how to gauge a numerical or letter value for those ethereal feelings and those accomplishments. I despise having to take the human quotient of my class and reduce it to cold, impersonal numbers and letters. It's like sucking the spirit out of the students and reducing them to the proverbial $1.47 worth of chemicals. I will not accept the assignment of the role of an academic meat inspector staining the rumps of the students as they emerge from the class at the end of the quarter, like so many sides of beef coming out from a meat-packing plant with a purple stamp of approval segregating them into premium, choice, commercial.

I think that the personal growth the students take with them out from the classroom is far more important than the quizzes and tests they take and leave inside the classroom. The simple truth is that the more I get involved in the humanity of each of my students, the harder it is for me to ignore their humanity and the humanity of the classroom experience. And so I admit that a lot of non-measurable intuition goes into my evaluation, because a lot of what I think should be factored in defies the quantitative demands of the slide-rule. I just do what I tell my students to do. I take the risk, jump in, rely heavily upon my gut feeling — that "blueberry" sense, call it intuition — and issue a grade, swearing under my breath, "Never more, never more, never more."

Needless to say, I have been agonizing about grades on most of my walks this past week. I can't say that any of the walks were easy. The rhythmic beats of my feet touching the asphalt during each walk, however, have made me feel increasingly lyrical about the subject, a phrase here and a phrase there. This morning, about a mile from the house on the return leg of my walk, I felt it all coming together. I couldn't wait to finish. I gathered speed with increasing elation. A few blocks from the house, I started running. I rushed inside the house before the spirit left me. So here I am, with rivulets of sweat streaming down my body, in a very giddy, "'Poe'-etic" mood:

> Grades. Grades. Grades.
> The tintinnabulation of grades. grades, grades.
> Letter grades. Numerical grades. Pass/Fail grades.
> The student's chests are palpitating
> by the cold, inhuman calculating
> of passing grades, failing grades, average grades.
> From the juggling and the tinkering
> of professorial hankering
> with curved grades, sliding grades, adjusted grades.
> You can listen to the fuss
> over the minus and the plus
> of grades, grades, grades.
> Student spirits afluttering.
> Their tightened lips amuttering.
> Their tortured minds acluttering
> because of grades, grades, grades!
> Student moods are somber
> waiting for that number
> fighting for that letter
> that lets them think
> they're better.
> Just see their grades, grades, grades
> Telephones are ringing
> with the melancholy singing
> of desperate desire,
> rising higher, higher, higher.
>
> What a world of solemn thought
> these computations bade!
> What a tale of terror
> these recordings made!
>
> Hear muted voices groaning
> in their sleep amoaning.
> Their bodies tossing and turning,
> their fevered hearts aburning
> about grades, grades, grades.
> Bodies bolt upright
> in the middle of the night

    dripping drops of sweat
    wondering what they'll get
  with an awful cravin'
  for that assuring haven
    of a passing grade, grade, grade.
In the silence of the night,
  students shiver with cold fright
  of the coming light
    when the judgments on the door
     are posted
      of the ones the prof has hosted.
Through the halls the students ramble
  to see if they have won their gamble.
  Afraid of that fateful blow;
   yet, all wanting to know
"What have I made?" "What have I made?"
"What have I made?"

What a horror grades outpour,
  tho few can say what they're for.
There is nothing discerning
  that grades reveal any learning.
It truly is a wonder
  that no one thinks they blunder
  when they kill that glorious awe and wonder
With the drowning tintinnabulation of grades, grades, grades.

Have a good one.

Sunday, 27 March 1994

MORE ON GRADES

I went out for a late walk today because Passover is upon us and I had to help my wife prepare for the evening's seder. As I sweated along in the hot, late-morning spring sun, I was still thinking about grades — how, as some have indicated, the hiring bean counters in both business and government, contrary to what they say, for the sake of expediency or laziness or sloppiness, rely so heavily on the grade transcripts for their judgment of a prospective employee's abilities. How unfortunate.

The grade will not tell them how that student will perform in his or her future vocational, social, and personal lives. It does not even reveal what that person might have learned in class. I know all the components of "the system" demand grades. That's fine, as long as we recognize grades for the approximations that they are: subjective, relative, arbitrary, distorting, inconclusive, contrived, socially segregating, weeding out, thinning out, and educationally divisive instruments. But that's not the signal we send out to the students. And that started me thinking once again about Mary (not her real name) because I saw her last week on campus. She walked right by me without uttering a word, even refusing to acknowledge me, though I gave her a warm hello. She still is mad at me and refuses to talk to me. She is not one of the success stories in my class, and I hurt that I couldn't have done anything to have made it otherwise.

Mary, a third-quarter first-year student and an only child coming from a high-achieving and demanding family, was in my spring quarter class last year. She always came to class with a smile on her face and a cheery greeting in her voice in obvious attempts to warm up to me. But she barely did what she thought was minimally required. "I read the material," she would always say, "but I didn't study it." "I don't want to talk," she replied to my comments about her lack of class participation. "I'm not going to rely on anyone else for my grade" was her explanation for her lack of cooperation with the other members of her triad. But when it came time for the triad to take the weekly quizzes or to hand in the daily written assignment, she was more than willing to let the others do the work and share in the credit. I talked to her on more than one occasion, even offering her any alternative means of expressing what she was understanding and learning to that of class discussion. Nothing.

About five weeks into the quarter, she came to me at the beginning of class with a drop form in her hand. With the other students looking on, we had this conversation. I remember it like it was just an hour ago:

"This far into the quarter?"

"Yes, just sign where you are supposed to."

"See me after class and we'll talk."

"No, we'll talk now. I don't have time. Just sign."

"No 'please'?"

"Please! Just sign now."

"Why do you want to drop the course?"

"Well, I'm going to medical school and need to get all good grades."

"What's stopping you from making one? You certainly are capable. It's your attitude that's holding you back, not your intelligence."

"This course is too hard. It's not cool. There's too much work. I'll probably only get a C with you. That'll kill my chances of being a doctor. I'm going to wait to take an easier professor so that I can make sure I get an A. Are you going to sign?"

"Will you learn as much in that kind of class?"

"I don't care. I just want an A. Are you going to sign?"

"Well, I'll sign, but it will be with a failing."

"No, I want you to give a withdrawal with a passing."

"I'm sure you do, but you don't deserve it at this moment."

"I need a withdrawal with passing."

"Don't you need the signature of your advisor first?"

"He's the one who told me to drop your course so I can be guaranteed an A."

"Well, unless you want to drop with a WF on your transcript that's the same as an F, I'm not going to let you drop it. I don't think I'd be helping you one bit. I'd be hurting you if I let you tuck tail and run at the slightest challenge. I know you can do it if you want. What are you scared about?"

"I'm not scared and I don't want to."

"Well, I'm not going to sign. You now have a few choices to make. I suppose it's crunch time. You can stop coming to class and get an F; you can cruise like you've been doing and probably get a C; or you can rise to the challenge, do what you are capable of doing, and get that A."

"If I stay in the class and work, will you guarantee me an A?"

"I'm not going to guarantee anything. Only you can do that."

"I don't want to think or talk or do any of that stuff. I just want to read, take notes, memorize, and get my A!"

"That's the easy way. When are you going to start trying to do things the right way?"

"I've done all right through high school."

"Do you think that's good enough to get through med school? Will you only try the easy way in med school or when you become a doctor? You're going to have to use your judgment, analyze situations, and come to a decision. How are you going to develop those skills? When are you going to start?"

"I will."

"Do you really want to be a doctor?"

"Yes."

"Is that what you wrote in your journal?"

"My parents want me to. Will you sign?"

"What about the other members of your triad?"

"I don't care about them. I don't like working with other people. I like being alone. You going to sign?"

"What kind of doctor are you going to be?"

"A surgeon."

"And to be a surgeon you don't think you have to learn about getting along with people, with other doctors, with other nurses, with the patient, with the patient's family, and with God knows who else?"

"I'll learn."

"When?"

"I'll learn. Are you going to sign?"

"No! You have no choice. You're stuck with me. I'm not going to let you come into a class, dip your toe in the water for almost half of the quarter, and then decide you want out and that you're not going to take a swim. At least not in my class. That's a lousy habit to develop."

"I've done it before each quarter, and no one argued. I've done anything I had to to get that A."

"Well, this prof doesn't roll over and play dead. Does that include cutting corners?"

"That's the cool thing if you can get away with it. You going to sign?"

"I appreciate your honesty, but I told you, no. But remember this. If you want to do it, it can be done. And if it can be done, do whatever it takes to do it. And I'll be there to help you all I can in any way you wish."

"You can help me by signing this drop form!"

"Sorry, I care enough about you that I won't sign."

"If you really care, you'll sign. Or I'm going to your bosses, to the president, to force you to sign!"

"That's your right," I answered in the same quiet, calm voice I had used during our conversation. "But answer is still 'no.'"

Her voice had been getting ever louder and all the students were watching. With my last "no," she stormed out and I started class. I later found out from her acquaintances that Mary was ready to try to embarrass me into signing that drop form if I refused to do so voluntarily. It didn't work. I guess that was one reason she got increasingly annoyed as our public conversation progressed.

Anyway, a few hours later, I got a call from her advisor. "Louis, who do you think you are to refuse to let her drop?" he berated me in no uncertain terms. I think he used the words "obstinate," "arrogant," "pompous," and "self-righteous." Our conversation went something like this:

"Do you care about Mary?" I asked quietly.

"Of course I do."

"Tell me about her."

"Well ... ah ... I don't know that much. But she's a good student. I got her transcript in front of me. She got all A's in her high school and during her first two quarters here."

"Well, I know a lot about her from her self-evaluations and her journal. You ought to read her journal, if you were really interested. Ask her to show it to you. You might find it interesting. She knows she can do it. She's just scared to try for a whole variety of tough reasons. What do you think will happen to her in med school if you steer her only into the crib classes?"

"If she fails your course, there won't be any med school. It'll be your fault. Will you sign the drop form?"

"She won't come anywhere near failing it if she doesn't want to. Maybe if we work together we can help her get on track."

"I don't have that kind of time. Will you sign?"

"Well, I've got that kind of time. You sound like Mary. And I don't think so."

"I'm going to your department head and the dean."

"That's your right, but I'll tell you this. I won't sign even if they tell me, and they won't after I tell them what you said to Mary."

Well, to make a long story short, no one went to the department head or the dean except me. I let my department head, the other department head, and my dean know of my "displeasure" about this professor's attitude, not just toward me and my class but toward education and learning as a whole — and especially toward Mary. More importantly, Mary refused to rise to the occasion. I talked with her, still offered her any alternative means of expression she might wish to choose, asked the other members of her triad to help her when they came to me with complaints. Still, nothing. Out of spite, and I suppose for other reasons, she just would not bet on herself. She continued to perform minimally, received a C in the course, blamed me, and spread the word that I was a thoughtless son-of-a-bitch. I think of her often. It hurts, and I wonder what I could have done differently to help her.

As I was walking and thinking of Mary, as well as the comments about hiring practices, a word she kept using in the conversation, "cool," haunted me. I hear that word frequently uttered by students on my campus when it comes to grades; I see it reflected too often in their attitudes and actions. I think it is regrettable, but there are too many Marys and too many of the likes of her advisor on our campuses, receiving and sending signals that promote the idea of the self-centered purpose of getting good grades at any cost — and that grades are absolute indicators of achievement and success.

Well, I started feeling lyrical again. This time I was asking the question, "What students are considered the 'coolest' ones on campus by their fellow students?":

Mirror, mirror on the wall
who are the "coolest" students of them all?
Replied the Mirror,

an answer I can deliver
  without hesitation,
    reservation,
      equivocation,
        or the slightest quiver.

I can say
  without delay
    that it's the students who get an "A".
But not the students you might think.
    What I am about to say will make you shrink.
It's not the students, the so-called bookworms,
    the nerds,
      who in small herds
        roam the library throughout the terms.
It's not the students who do not cheat
    just to be in the academic elite;
      or who cut a corner
        to receive that collegiate honor.
It is not the students who could boast
    that they struggled to do the most;
      whose midnight candles always burn
        doing whatever it takes to learn,
      and whose light
        is always on late into the night.
It is not the students who could say
    that they received that "A"
    the hard and honest way.
Those students are not thought as coolish
    because everyone thinks they're foolish.
These are students who often feel ashamed,
    embarrassed,
      derided,
        emotionally maimed.
They are made to cry
    merely because they always try.
Each is labelled a silly jerk

just because they're dumb enough
  to do the work,
just because they wish to grow
  with the knowledge and experience
  an education can bestow.
No, no, no, no.
  It is not them other students laud;
    it's not their actions other students applaud.
  The students who are the envy of them all;
    who receive the academic game ball,
      are the students who are secretly sleazy
        and take the professors who were easy
          so that their elbows would not be greasy.
      Their noses have no hone
        'cause they never used a grindstone.
On their shelf lie some dusty books,
  uncracked,
  unmarked,
    and never given the slightest looks.
They will cut a corner here and there,
  and argue that no one will care
    how you got there,
      for in the rat race all is fair.
To seek the grade they resort to guile,
  as well as to a fraternity or sorority file.
They enjoy all the campus fun
  without regret for what they have done.
And contrary to what you might have thought,
  in the spirit of sport,
    they're the sort
      who are proud that they were never caught.
Oh, everyone thinks they're "coolish"
  for having made the system look so very foolish.
So, with slight remorse
  that they got little out of a course
    except the high grade
      that they made
        with its taste of honey
          as the sweet pipeline to job and money,
they will loudly boast
and raise their beer mugs in a toast
that they got away with the most.

Mirror, mirror on the wall
who are the "coolest" students of them all?

Replied the Mirror,
an answer I can deliver
  without hesitation,
   reservation,
    equivocation,
     or the slightest quiver.

I can sadly say
  without delay
   that it's the students who take the easy way,
    who do the least
     to get the A;
    who passed the test and
     ignored the rest,
    but graduate with a high GPA.

Have a good one.

Sunday, 10 April 1994

STUDENT TEACHING EVALUATIONS

Trick or treat! I'll bet you didn't know it is still Halloween. At least, it seems that way on our campuses. That realization came to me this rare but deliciously nippy April morning as I walked through a slight fog that cast a supernatural haze over the landscape.

I had left the house with what I thought was little on my mind, except anticipating the agonizing effects of a week's layoff because of a knee I had wrenched while gardening last weekend. Anyway, about a couple of blocks into my walk, I was startled momentarily, almost out of my grubbies. I stopped to catch my breath. My heart fluttered a bit. I dared to look across the street. On the curb was a darkened, irregularly shaped mass, ominously looming up from the ground. Its contorted shadows seemed to reveal concealed grotesque demons. As I approached it, I saw that it was the heaping results of what was obviously a weekend of robust spring cleaning. Then, I saw what had caught the corner of my eye. In this pile of shadowy garage sale rejects, reflecting the light from the street lamp across the street, shone a bright orange, plastic jack-o'-lantern. It was secretly peering out from under the slightly open lid of a city garbage container. Its two sharply angled black eyes were glaring at me with sinister mischievousness, as if it had been lying in ambush for some innocent to pass by and now was about to jump out at me to rip out my throat. I chuckled and started off again.

But as I regained my pace, I began to think mischievous thoughts about that pumpkin and how so many faculty would love to place it at their door to ward off a particular hobgoblin that is haunting the halls of ivy. Its presence makes so many faculty jittery. They walk nervously about, constantly glancing over their shoulders, their ears sharpened for its slightest sound, their eyes roaming to detect its slightest movement. They are ever on the alert for the presence of this phantom, ready to make a mad dash for their lives should it suddenly appear. They sit tensely at their desks, behind the protection of heavily barricaded doors. They stand behind the lectern, casting nervous glances at the door, fearful that it will enter their classrooms when they least expect it and they are the most exposed. Their blood turns ice-cold at the thought of confronting its twisted, snarled, gargoyle features. They shake with uncontrollable fright as the eerie sound of its ghoulish moaning and groaning reminds them that it never rests in its quest for fresh victims.

The hobgoblin's minions, disguised to look like normal students and administrators, are everywhere, ready to betray the presence of the weakest soul. They're running about knocking on every door. They dance tauntingly about any faculty member who dares to travel the campus. They teasingly wave wads of questionnaires, computerized answer sheets, portfolio models, grade surveys, student grapevine sheets, enrollment figures, salary endorsements, and promotion and tenure recommendations in the sweating faces of the harassed faculty. Their high-pitched cackling betrays the sadistic glee they get out of their torment.

With fearful resignation, professors know that there is no place to hide from this dreaded phantom. Ultimately, they know they will fall prey to it. When it has them in its clutches, they fear it will pluck out their hearts, tear them limb from limb, and condemn their souls to torturous purgatory. Oh, it is a fearsome creature, a heinous gremlin, a merciless ghoul, a profane demon, a pernicious fiend. Its very name strikes terror in their hearts. It is called the "student teaching evaluation."

To protect themselves, the faculty offer magical incantations to banish this monster and its serving hordes from the campuses. "Nobody really knows what good teaching is, so how can anyone measure it?" they chant. They supplicate, "There is little to teaching beyond knowing the subject." "Student evaluations are worthless," they sing, "because they're related to the grades the students receive." They cry out, "Students do not know what's best for them." "We have to keep the amateurs, the politicians, and administrators out of the classroom," they wail in anguish.

We can be facetious and smirk about the irony of professors being so nervous about being evaluated when they always are saying that they are in the business of evaluating the performance of others. I think, however, that there is something to be said about questioning the validity of the measuring instrument; about being skeptical of any call for student evaluations of teaching, when all the other signals on our campuses seem to indicate a general administrative disinterest in both classroom teaching and the creation of the campus as a learning community; about being anxious about its misuse and abuse; and about being suspicious of the true and hidden purpose of it all. But I think there is more to this issue of evaluation of faculty than meets the eye.

All that skepticism, cynicism, and anger about evaluations hides fear, a fear of being judged for something that most faculty do not think they are. For the truth is that few professors identify themselves as teachers in the first place. "It's a case of mistaken identity," they protest. They are not teachers of this or of that. They are scholars in this or that field; they are professors of this or that discipline. They find themselves in the classroom, but feel far more comfortable in an archive researching this or in a lab experimenting on that, or writing this, or presenting that, or consulting on this or that. Their sense of purpose, accomplishment, and success has little to do with the classroom. Few were hired for their classroom mastery. All too many of them cringe at being evaluated for doing something about which few of them know very much, other than writing an essay called a lecture, standing up in front of a class, and talking. They're being measured on something for which they were not trained, about which they seldom reflect, and about which they seldom articulate.

Let's face it. Almost all learning about teaching takes place on the job, often at the expense of students. With few, if any, alternative classroom models, and without any training, most professors fall back on their own experiences as students and base their own teaching on the model of their lecturing professors. "Hey, that's the way I was taught," they proclaim. "And Dr. So-and-So was a damn good teacher. He knew what he was doing. Look how much I learned. And if it was good enough for me, it's good enough for them."

Faculty know how to comb archives or run experiments in labs or draw up surveys. They can analyze a document or the results of a lab experiment or the outcome of a clinical study. They were trained to present conference papers, publish scholarly articles and books, and talk in a professional jargon. They were educated to reflect on the sophisticated issues associated with their disciplines. They were not trained to articulate a philosophy of education.

They were not trained in the processes of learning. They were not taught how to use the tools of teaching. They were taught so little that would allow them to make intelligent choices about teaching, about ways to introduce a variety of instruction methods other than lecturing, about involving students in a variety of roles other than as passive note-takers, about evaluating students, about using new technologies, about doing so much more in the classroom other than lecture. The future scholars were not shown how to be future teachers; they were not shown how to communicate their knowledge to those who are not knowledgeable; they were not shown how to find the intellectual, attitudinal, and emotional passageways into the students' hearts, souls, and minds.

It's little wonder that faculty are far more secure talking about their discipline. They have the virtually unassailable control of the expert and they have a greater sense of who they are. In effect, it seems to them that amateurish outsiders are doing more than just changing the rules of engagement on them without a protective grandfather clause. They are challenging beloved values, altering priorities, stripping away control, exposing weaknesses, ripping away masks, revealing amateurishness, eroding authority, questioning identity, challenging purpose, and establishing new goals. They are threatening the very souls of the professor. They are attacking the meaning of professors' existence.

All that skepticism, cynicism, and anger about evaluations hides fear, a fear of being judged by the students. Can you imagine resting your salary, your promotion, your tenure, your future on the opinion of some teenage kid or some older, uninformed adult whom you don't know and who doesn't know you? One of my colleagues phrased it this way: "If they know so much about what should be going on in the classroom, why aren't they teaching the course? Who's the professor here? I mean, if they know so much about what's good for them and what I am supposed to do, what am I here for?"

For those professors who don't care about the students, who don't want to know them, who don't even want to learn their names, who are not going to be "touchy-feely" with the students — for those professors who exercise power over students rather than be in a state of mutuality with them; for those professors who meekly stand by without protest as classes grow in size while they and the students become faint specks on the horizon to each other; for those professors who do not forge bonds of trust with their students or create learning communities in their classrooms; for those professors who see no need to reconstruct one-way dictation into two-way communication; for those professors who have little mutuality and relatedness with the students — for all those professors, such anonymity and distance is coming back to haunt them. They don't know who is evaluating them any more than they believe that those who are evaluating them know them. They see it as an intolerable situation of inept, suspicious strangers judging knowledgeable, suspicious strangers.

But at the heart of it all, all that skepticism, cynicism, and anger about evaluations hides fear, a fear of looking at themselves in a mirror, a fear of how their professional and personal lives might be changed or have to be changed if the world talks back. Professors say they are agents of change in society and the classroom, but they are fearful of changing themselves; they talk so much about that world out there, but cringe at attempts to understand the world inside themselves. Evaluation, in its highest form, is not so much about subject knowledge or technical competence of classroom delivery as it is about inner drives and desires — a reminder that an education is, as I have said so often, an inward journey. We academics have so arrogantly, so long promoted the myth of objectivity — that accurate judgments can only be made disengaged from afar, that truth can be attained only if it is untainted by personal bias, that only by using a form of personal and professional distance learning, only from faraway, can we truly evaluate and accurately know things. For "things" read not only subject matter, but students as well. We have so distorted our view of life by believing that we can easily remove ourselves from ourselves and students.

We live, however, in a world of subjectivity, and I think that scares a lot of us, because subjectivity makes demands on our personal lives. It requires that we acknowledge our involvement with the world around us, that we recognize that we are frail humans no less than are the students. I think so often we forget that our humanity and subjectivity were not erased with the bestowal of the hood.

And so evaluations make us address the detached, impersonal, inanimate "teach-talk" that we are fond of unconsciously using. In this professional jargon, one human being becomes a separated lifeless thing called "teacher." Another becomes a faceless image called "student." It's like we walk through a wax museum. We disengage from ourselves; we stand apart and look at ourselves and students as something else, a place outside of us and them where education supposedly takes place. When we teach-talk, we lose our connection with ourselves, our humanity, our past, present, and future; we lose our connection with others. Evaluations can have the uncomfortable impact of proclaiming that learning, education, teaching is a human, personal experience of living that takes place within both the teacher and the student. What happens in the classroom happens to a *me*, to a *him* or a *her*, not to an *it* or a *something*. And when we evaluate teaching, we are evaluating what goes on inside of us, our being, not something out there. The evaluation forces us to confront the need to surrender power over the students and create a mutuality with them. We are in charge of our classes. Whether we use that responsibility

creatively and productively to foster a relatedness to them is
another matter.

Imagine how much our lives would be changed if we let the students
talk back to us and establish a relatedness which either has hitherto been
lost or never has existed. I will repeat that I believe teachers are caregivers.
To be a caregiver, however, you must trust; to trust, you must understand;
to understand, you must listen; to listen, you must hear. You must
understand, listen to, and hear yourself; you must understand, listen to,
and hear others. If we do not, we cannot care for ourselves; if we cannot
care for ourselves, we cannot care for others.

Teaching, I think, is a vulnerable act of "spilling your guts," by which the
personal becomes public. For me to properly teach, I have to reveal things
about which I feel very deeply. Sometimes that means even the intimate
details of my personal life, but more often it means issues I find crucial and
compelling that have helped shape who I am. Such vulnerability requires a
lot of courage to exercise among strangers. To do that, I risk the judgment
that comes with the exposure of my passions to public scrutiny.

I like to hear from students. I want to hear from students. I think that is
important. Too many of us professors talk too much. Too many of us listen
too little. I think there are two general categories of teachers. There are
those who are very much taken with themselves and are the same with
everyone and are, therefore, oblivious to the human diversity with which
they deal. There are others who are concerned about those with whom
they deal and are different with different students and vary themselves to
meet the needs of the students. In a caring environment, you must listen.
If you listen, you're groping to find out what students need and what they
say about their current education. I'm a better teacher if I am informed.
I encourage students to be open and honest in their comments, to be
frank with me about their feelings, their angers, their fears, and their
disappointments. It's part of the process of learning who we are in our
professional lives. I have found deep insights in students' comments —
if I have the courage to listen.

So I think we should welcome such evaluations. I don't see them as
tormenting gremlins and threatening hobgoblins to be combatted. I greet
them as soothing angels of renewal. I have found that the sense of
defenseless exposure wanes proportionally to the growing strength of a
trust bond in the classroom. For an effective and honest evaluation, faculty
have to draw students into community with them. I work very hard to
establish a bond of trust in my classes. It's the life's blood of the learning
community that emerges. I spend the whole first week or two of class with
personal introductory, trust, and bonding exercises in which I also partake.

During that time, we have, as one student insightfully commented in her journal, "started stripping away our fears, defenses, and excuses for not doing things because we've started to know and trust each other and feel relaxed about things."

I guess that's one reason I'm not afraid of evaluations, and why my students almost always demand that they sign them. To the contrary, I welcome my students' comments. I have confidence in their judgment because I know them and they know me. I respect them and they respect me. I trust them and they trust me. My classes are one big ongoing evaluation: weekly evaluations, weekly journals, daily personal discussions, open-class evaluations, final evaluations, and unsolicited personal letters. I'm constantly asking my students, "How's this working?" "What do you think?" "Should we adjust this, drop that, add this?" "How do you feel?" "Am I doing my job?" I find that it's marvelous, uneasy, exciting, exhilarating, nerve-racking, adventurous, and uncomfortable to let the world talk back to me.

No, the evaluations are not the hobgoblin out there. The real hobgoblin is here inside us. I need that evaluation to help me avoid stagnation. It helps me to forever climb my mountain. It helps me to change and to grow and to help nurture the new that is coming behind me. I need that evaluation, that feedback, that assessment, whatever you want to call it, to help me teach and live both fully and well. I need that evaluation to help me reflect on how I label myself, how that labeling affects how I perceive myself, how I expect myself to behave, how I label students, how I perceive them, and how I expect them to behave. I need that evaluation to help me assess my skills in getting to both myself and the students. I need that evaluation to help me see if I know how to use those skills, if I have the courage to use them, and what I have to do to improve them. Evaluations help me understand my own inner drives and desires — why I do what I do. Evaluations help prevent me from removing myself from both myself and the students, and to stay in a state of relatedness with both.

Then, and only then, can I create that bond of trust among students and between the students and myself that I believe is so essential to true learning. Only then can I create an authentic learning community with my students, my own spirit, my subject, and, hopefully, my fellow teachers.

Have a good one.

Saturday, 16 April 1994

A P O L O G Y

*I*t was a delightful walk this morning. It had just rained and the air smelled clean and sweet. The flowers were glistening in the moonlight of the clearing, pre-dawn sky. Reflections from the drops of water that clung to their petals sent off a multitude of micro-bursts of light, as if they were saluting me as I passed by. As I passed a batch of twinkling, trumpeting amaryllis, without thinking, I turned my head, slightly nodded, winked my left eye, and briefly raised my left forefinger as a returning gesture of appreciation. Actually, it was I who I was saluting. I felt good. I felt clean and sweet. I felt relaxed, relieved, satisfied, and at peace with myself. And I still do. I flew over the asphalt like a bird that had just left the edge of a cliff and was soaring high and free. I can honestly say to myself that Monday will be the first time I will feel at ease, truly at ease, with one of my classes since the first day of the quarter two weeks ago.

That's curious because my classes had been going very well. In fact, devoting the first week of the quarter to introductory bonding, trust, and critical thinking exercises was successful beyond my wildest hopes. There is a greater sense of a learning community in the classes than at this time in past quarters. Most of the students have a greater sense of trust and openness with themselves, with the other members of their triads, and with the entire class than in previous classes at this point in the quarter. Most of them are seriously journaling. Most of them are already struggling to assume responsibility for each other's success. We've already had some good, honest, heated, and respectful debates and discussions about early slavery and racial prejudice, the contributing role of religion in the early American experience, the position of women in developing American culture, and whether the rebelling colonists were unreasonable extremists. Some of the students are starting to make discoveries about the subject — and about themselves. Many of them are taking those first uncomfortable steps to come face to face with their prejudices about gender, race — and themselves. They should be pleased with their progress, their development, their discovery, their growth. I am.

Yet there was something that had been nagging me in one of my intro classes. I always felt slightly unfocused in the room. The sharpness of my "blueberries" was ever so slightly dull. Every time I walked into that class, I felt slightly off-balance, on the defensive. That didn't make sense. I always looked forward to that class with great anticipation, wondering, "What will they come up with next?" This is the class in which one student got up to share an article she had read that discussed an accepted tale in one Southern family of how one of their innocent young belles during the Civil

War had gotten unintentionally pregnant after a Union sniper's mini-ball had pierced her sweetheart's scrotum while they were out walking in the woods, had ricocheted off a tree trunk, and had entered her uterus! You can imagine the wild discussion that started about sexual mores and practices in both past and contemporary American society.

Yet, every time I passed over the threshold, I felt slightly ill at ease. What it was, I didn't know, but it was there. I swept it aside, saying to myself that "it's just the adjustment jitters of getting used to each other." Deep inside me, though, I knew it was more than that. But I tried to ignore it.

Then, two days ago, I had a discussion with James (not his real name). He obviously had not been prepared for class and had not participated in the discussion to the extent I felt he was capable. He wasn't challenging himself to reach for his best. His facial expressions betrayed the fact that he was in another world. When he told me that he had not been journaling, I told him we had to talk. So, after class, in the hope I could encourage him, we sat on the steps. We talked for about an hour. He told me that he had a lot on his mind because a lot of responsibility had been dumped unexpectedly on his shoulders when he became treasurer of his fraternity. "It's so damn distracting. I can't get this stuff out of my mind," he said, annoyed. There were federal tax problems, serious issues of incompetent leadership, and "now it's my job to figure out a way to throw a brother out of the house who refuses to leave because he was caught taking a class for another person."

But he assured me that he should have his act together by the weekend and asked if I could bear with him. I told him that I understood. "Yeah, I know," I said sympathetically. "Sometimes, shit happens and you can't do anything about it except slog through." I went on to tell him how, when my youngest son was at risk, it was almost impossible for me to keep my mind on my work. I explained how in class I always had one ear cocked for the secretary coming through the door with a message that Robby was in trouble; in my office I was always snatching secretive glances at the telephone, waiting for its ominous ring. I gave him a few suggestions, like talking with the other members of his triad and asking for their support, studying in the library instead of at the frat house, drawing up a weekly calendar and setting aside 45 hours for all school work, getting together with his triad to study, and dropping by just to talk and suck on Tootsie Pops anytime he felt he needed to.

Toward the end of the conversation, James said, "Doc, you're pretty cool. After your comment to Bill (not his real name) the first day of class, I was really pissed with you. I was ready to drop the class. I thought you hated all Greeks. Even when we talked later in the hall and you explained yourself, I thought you were bullshitting me and just covering your ass. Now, I really know differently. Thanks." We shook hands. As James walked away, it hit me like a revelation.

James was absolutely right. I think by now the students know that I take great joy in bringing excitement and enthusiasm into my classes. I play an eclectic selection of music at the beginning of class to set the mood, to tell everyone, "I'm ready. Let's go!" I find that humor is an antidote to stress, an ice-breaker, an instant respite, a simple introduction, an entryway, an image-destroyer. But they didn't know that on the first day.

So there I am taking roll, first names only, starting a bonding process of familiarity and comfort, and I come to Bill. Bill was wearing a ——— fraternity shirt. The last quarter, his fraternity, whose reputation was not the highest on campus in the first place, had been involved in a scandal involving alcohol at a frat-sponsored event, a DUI, traffic accident, and serious injuries. Consequently, it had been placed on indefinite social probation, and its members have to perform untold hours of social service. When I called Bill's name and he responded, I looked up. Seeing his shirt, and trying to be humorous, I said, "You sober today?"

As soon as I uttered those words, I tightened my stomach, quietly mashed my teeth, tightened my lips, and screamed silently to myself, among other things, "Oh, shit!! Are you stupid." I had inadvertently stepped over the line and I immediately knew it. There's an old saying about sticks and stones breaking bones, but names never harming. Of course, that is not true. Words can harm if they are hurled intentionally or otherwise as weapons. What I said, I knew instantly, wasn't witty. It was a wounding weapon. At best, it was embarrassing, probably a humiliating dart. I so desperately wanted to lunge forward and grab those words before they reached anyone's ears and stuff them back into my careless mouth. Bill nervously chuckled. What else could he do? Although I was prepared to accept any response in kind with good humor, laughter, ribbing, and jokes, he didn't know that at the time. He could not have known he could retort in kind. It was too early. We didn't know each other; we didn't trust each other. I was Dr. Schmier, THE PROF! He only knew that I was weird: dressed in jeans, sucking on a Tootsie Pop, sipping a cup of coffee, playing music in a history class, and bantering with the students. But I was still THE PROF, one of those "hungry wolves," the bestower of the grade who had their future in my hands. And for all he knew, the grapevine was right — I was a mean, evil, demanding son-of-a-bitch of a professor. Besides, all that didn't matter because what I said was inappropriate and I was wrong. Period. No argument. End of discussion.

Instead of stopping and apologizing, I whizzed through the roll, almost like running away from the scene of an accident, hoping against hope that no one had noticed or that everyone would have a sudden attack of amnesia or that the saying about being out of sight, out of mind was true. That was my first mistake. Immediately, after I took roll, we settled into an introductory biographical exercise. About halfway through the class, as I walked around, I said, "OK, this is about getting to know each other. Here I am. What do you want to know about me? I'll tell you anything." They asked me about my family, my religion, my background, my dog. Some of the questions got personal, but I answered them honestly. Then, James asked, "Is it true you're anti-Greek?" My "blueberries" caught the signal, but I ignored it. That was my second mistake. I instantly convinced myself that I could deal satisfactorily with what I had done by the indirect, · safe, and hidden way, by talking about my belief that fraternities and sororities had their place in campus life, though academics had a higher priority. I was afraid that if I were honest, if I admitted my mistake, the students wouldn't understand and my credibility would suffer. After class, I apologized to Bill and explained myself. The next day, as Bill came into class, I asked, "Are we cool?" "Yeah," he nonchalantly answered, "no sweat."

Six days later, journals came in. As I sat on the floor of my office, listening to some music, tapping my pen to the rhythm, sucking on a Tootsie Pop, I read James' journal. Those words on the first day of class came back to the surface to haunt me. In it, he wrote how angry he was with my comments toward Bill and that he was ready to drop the course because obviously I was anti-Greek. The only reason he didn't was because something about me, my honesty in answering personal biographical questions, the "turn-on" I brought into the class, told him to give me another chance. Besides, he had gone up to Bill the next day and had talked to him about it. Bill had told him that he and I had talked and everything was OK. He accepted Bill's assurances and he figured everything was settled. Again, I didn't act on that signal. I merely talked privately to James in the hall. Mistake number three. I had convinced myself that it had been a small matter that had been settled, but it weighed heavily on my soul because my conscience knew better. It knew that explaining and apologizing privately to both Bill and James was inadequate, unacceptable, and safe.

This last conversation with James, however, pricked my conscience once again and there was no laying it to rest. I could no longer ignore it. No, I knew I had to step up and do what had to be done or be a hypocrite — be like one of those "do as I say, not as I do" people. It was another mountain to climb. I knew I had to get past the inertia of caution, ego, image, and authority. I thought how painful it is when I hear students say in their metaphor exercises or during conversations that they feel that professors are often irrelevant to their education, that they're irritants, the enemy, the obstacles to an education. Yet though I pride myself on being none of these, I may have given the impression, however subtle, that I was in those ranks, that my style was not substantive. I knew that if I didn't act on my conscience, and not worry about my status, that I would remain one of those unacceptable "closed books" or one of those "mothers with dried up breasts."

I had a restless sleep. I went walking Thursday morning, real early, to sort things out. The black, thick fog helped envelop me in my own deep thoughts. I started taking an inventory of my personal teaching philosophy. So what was it that I believed, I asked myself as I roamed the streets. I answered that I believe it is more important to ask if the student learned than to ask if I taught. I believe that no subject matter is more sacred to me than a student's growth. I believe that teaching and learning are an act of human relationship, the cornerstone of which must be an honest bond of trust between teacher and student, and to forge that bond I need to share with the students not just my subject, but me and the truth of my life. I believe that the student, the whole student, is my prime subject. In handling the situation, I realized that I had submerged the more vulnerable side of myself. I had used my authority somewhat subtly and abusively. And I realized that to be a truly meaningful teacher, I had to face the students with that truth. I had to expect to struggle and share my growth in the same way I asked of my students. There are always going to be mountains out there that need to be climbed. The question was whether I had the humility to take James' subtle criticisms deeply to heart and the courage to heed them. I guess I realized that if I wanted to be that spiritual teacher, I would have to be prepared once again not only to reap the unimaginable rewards, but to endure the arduous and painful demands and costs of dealing with the truth about myself, my commitment, my abilities, and my life.

As my walk came to an end and I rounded the last corner, I knew that my imbalance was the result of seeing Bill in his chair every time I walked into class and being subliminally reminded of what I had to do but feared doing. Now, I knew what I had to do. More importantly, it was what I wanted to do. It must have been about 5 a.m. when I came in from my walk. I sat down and wrote.

I walked into class about three hours later, quiz in my hand, smile on my face, the sound of Meatloaf resonating throughout the room from the boom box, nervousness in my heart, and a little weakness in my legs. I wondered how the students would react to what I was about to say. Would they respect me or think I was a jerk? Would I make a fool out of myself or a hero? No matter, it was important what I thought. I needed to say it for

myself. Then I turned off the boom box and said, "Before I hand out
the quiz, I want to share something with you that I wrote this morning."
I didn't read what I had written. I spoke it, but this is what I wrote:

> Something about this class has been nagging me, tugging at
> my conscience, since we began two weeks ago. Unlike my
> other class, every time I walked in here, I felt something was
> wrong. I didn't know why. I didn't know what it was, but I
> knew it was something. Well, actually deep down I did know,
> but I chose not to know it, maybe hide it from myself.
> Yesterday, James showed me what it was. It wasn't any of you.
> It was me.
>
> You know, life in general would be so simple, and being
> a teacher would be so much easier, if you don't make any
> mistakes when you try to do the right thing and if all sins were
> caused by fiends who delighted in hurting people. But we all
> have clay feet and none of us has earned a gold medal in
> the sport of surface water-walking. Whenever you try to do
> something, there's a risk that someone will not benefit. That
> goes with the territory of trying. There are always going to be
> those times when you will unintentionally make mistakes,
> when you will hurt someone. The first day of class was one of
> those times, and I made one of those mistakes. I think you
> know by now that I like us to joke with each other about
> ourselves and each other. That way we don't take ourselves
> or each other so seriously. But on the first day in the class,
> however sensitive I am, I inadvertently screwed up and
> momentarily forgot to take seriously the unequal relationship
> that exists between me and you when I made the comment
> about Bill and his fraternity. Just for a second, I forgot that my
> words as a professor weighed a heck of lot more than yours as
> student. I don't like it, but that's reality. However I struggle
> to change that relationship, it's still there. However I try to
> diminish the weight of it's presence, I cannot totally succeed so
> quickly. You always talk about my authority in different ways:
> "You're the prof!" "Is this going to be on the test?" "Will it
> affect my grade?" "What do you want?" "Will this be
> acceptable?" You showed your distrust of professors in your
> metaphor exercise at the beginning of the quarter. And on that
> first day, I regretfully showed you that you might be right.
>
> Everyone tells you that there are limits placed on you students
> by your status as students and by the authority granted to me
> as a professor. It doesn't matter if we recognize that fact or not;

it's there. I knew it. I just momentarily forgot about it.
My awareness, honesty, and sensitivity about our relationship
are an important part of my teaching. Common courtesy and
respect is never out of place. On that first day, I was out of
place. I have to pay at least as much attention to what I say
and how I say it as to what I do. We can use a word here or
there. But this classroom is not a saloon. It's not a rowdy party.
It's not a company picnic. It's not a matter of infringing on free
speech that should allow me as the professor to say whatever I
wish. I do not say certain things in class because I'm afraid one
of you is going to sue me. I am not sensitive because I'm afraid
that you will complain, that your parents will call, or that one
of my bosses will ask me to explain. It's not even a matter of
being politically correct. It's simply a matter of decency and of
respect. It's a judgment call. And, on that first day I accidently
used bad judgment and I was disrespectful to Bill.

I've told you that I see my mission is to teach to both your
mind and your character. To see each of you as a person,
not just as a student. That means being understanding,
demanding, fair, civil, and sensitive. I've already said that
when we have discussions in class, when I use an innovative
teaching technique, when we attempt to bond, it is not an
excuse to 'get personal' and belittle each other's status, beliefs,
or associations. I ignored my own warning on that first day.
Even though I realized what I had done and privately talked
with both Bill, and later to James when he courageously, yes
courageously, confronted me and told me how angry he was
with my comment, and everything is cool with them, it's not
cool with my conscience. My conscience tells me that the
insult was made publicly and so the apology has to be made
publicly. The right thing to do is to read this entry to you and
publicly admit what I had inadvertently done, apologize to
Bill, and demand that, if ever that happens again, you have
my permission to pin my tail to the wall.

I then said to both Bill and James, with a tone of deepest sincerity, "I'm
sorry for having offended you. My only excuse is momentary stupidity.
In this case, Ph.D. does mean 'piled higher and deeper.' And if you told
others about my comments, please either convey to them my sincere
apologies or, if you wish, I will come to the frat houses and personally
apologize. Your call."

After a few minutes of silence, I then continued in a perked-up voice,
"Now, clear the decks. We have a quiz to take." As I passed out the

quizzes, I danced around the class as if the shackles had been taken off my feet and a weight lifted from my soul.

I don't think it's unhealthy and dangerous for faculty to risk being open with their students and each other. Acknowledging a mistake is not a sign of weakness, and I found that my status among the students was anything but weakened. It's merely treating the students with the respect and dignity to which they are entitled. We're professors, but we're not finally formed individuals. I admit that it's personally threatening though — to review constantly a lifetime of work and a sense of commitment. But now, as I think about it, if I and those people in my classes are ever to find the place in class, in any class, in life for that matter, where we can march onward hand in hand in supporting cooperation rather than engage in fierce, back-stabbing competition, where we can create rather than merely uncover, where we can transform rather than improve, I have the responsibility to serve as a role model, a facilitator if you will, for insight and self-discovery, not only of the subject, but of themselves as well. I must be concerned not only with the logic of the mind, but the illogic of the heart. I am an agent of the personal, as well as the intellectual, development of my students. I think the impact I may have on a student's academic growth is but a small part of my contribution to the total person. I know, after having read student journals, that my essential mission as an educator is to attempt to be that person for whom so many students are looking, who can show them the way to becoming the whole person they are capable of developing into.

After class, I went back to my office, dropped the quizzes on the floor, and closed my door. An unusual act, but I wanted to be alone for the hour until my next class. I walked over to my desk, leaned back in my chair, propped my feet up on the desk, unwrapped an orange Tootsie Pop, stuck it in my mouth, put my intertwined hands behind my head, and closed my eyes. I felt like I was floating just above my chair. My senses were alive. I twirled the Pop very slowly in my mouth. As my tongue felt every irregularity on its surface and savored the taste of every molecule of the tart juices swirling in my mouth, I relived the feeling of those opening moments of that class. I think we became a learning community at that moment. I hope we did. Maybe I'll find out when I read their journals.

I know there will be more mountains to climb, more thresholds to cross over, more mistakes to face, more failures with which to contend. But as I learn to deal with each as it comes, those that are to follow will be less difficult to face because teaching, learning, discovering, and transforming my life and those of others are a bit more a part of my life. Anyway, on this day I feel good.

Have a good one

Saturday, 23 April 1994

THE APOLOGY AND JULISSA

*W*ell, it's Saturday. What a fabulous walk today. It was over before it started. Though it was a "cold" 56 degrees and the air was clammy because of yesterday's rain, nothing could chill or dampen my spirits. I have been on a high all week because of Julissa. I haven't been able to stop thinking about her. I want to share with you — in celebration of her success at facing and successfully meeting a personal challenge — the appearance of joy in her heart, a growing confidence in herself, an increase in her performance, and my pride for her.

Julissa is one of those students who come to our campus thinking they're not bright, who find the path difficult, who become unnecessarily discouraged, who come into class believing that they're destined for lesser things, and who play out that constricting role. If those same students, however, are encouraged to face and overcome difficult challenges, to see the potential that lies within each of them, they can become confident, productive, and fulfilled people. They can become filled with that awe and wonder. Julissa has started on that road.

I suppose the story starts with my apology to the class a week ago Friday. I had received an inkling of how some students felt as I handed out the quiz and roamed about the room for the rest of the class time. James had said to me as I passed by, "Nice going, Doc. That was really smooth." Bill had stopped his argument over an answer to a question long enough to catch my arm with his hand, press it, and say, "I really appreciate what you did." Karrie, with a surprised admiration in her face, whispered as I passed by, "That was something else." There was a glance here and a smile there, a slight nod, a thumbs up. And finally, Eleanor came up to me at the end of the class and said, "You've earned yourself a Tootsie Pop."

The students handed in their journals on Wednesday. About 45 of the 60 students had written something about that day. Here's a sampling:

> "That was pretty cool. … I was pretty leery about this triad stuff, but now I'm going give it a chance. No, I'm going to do more than that."

> "What Doc did to own up to a mistake was neat. Maybe that will give me help to do better in class."

> "Wish other profs had the same amount of guts. Maybe I can find the same stuff inside me."

"Boy, is the grapevine ever wrong. No son of bitch of a professor who didn't care for students would have done something like he did."

"Dr. Schmier apologized for accidently poor-mouthing a student on the first day of class. Interesting. That was more than show."

"I know I should say something more than 'Wow,' but that's all I can think of right now. Now, I am going to try to wow him like he did to me."

"Hell, I'll work my ass off for that guy now except I know if I tell him that he'll say I should work it off for me."

"Talk about a lesson in eating humble pie. Who would have thought a prof had it in him. Their (sic) never able to admit to anything except that they're right."

"That'll be one I'll long remember. I bet I'll never see another teacher do that."

"Dr. Schmier apologized in front of the class. He didn't have to do that. No one forced him. He just wanted to. I'm really impressed. I told my folks about it. They were surprised. I told them that I'm going to give it everything I've got in this class."

"I was really surprised. It proved to me that he really cares about us. I now know he wants me to care about me enough to make the effort to do my best."

"I wish more professors were as personable and caring. I truly admire what he did today. He showed tremendous respect for us."

"To have that kind of trust in us students, no other professor or teacher has ever shown me that he thinks I am worth that much. I don't think I can let him down now."

"I was really moved. Now I am going to start moving myself."

"I guess I owe it to myself to be just as dedicated and give 110 percent to this class and myself as he does to himself and to us."

"I really respect the Doc for what he did."

"Today the prof apologized for saying some remarks to students. That was real big of him. Most teachers I've had are so small."

"Most teachers won't admit when they are wrong. I didn't think until today that anyone of them knew that the word existed much less what the word meant. Dr. Schmier does."

"That was the most sensitive and kind thing I have ever seen a professor do. It makes me feel I can trust him."

"Damn, he's for real."

"He puts his heart where his mouth is. Now it's my turn."

"I'm going to buy him a bag of Tootsie Pops before this quarter is over."

"I didn't know professors had a conscience. Well, Dr. Schmier sure as hell does. He's got heart. I wonder if he really is a student disguised as a professor."

"Personally, I think he is quite brave and very admirable. If he can do that, maybe I can face my fear of talking in class like Julissa did."

"The doc gave Julissa courage by showing his."

As I read those journal entries, I remembered something a friend, a philosopher at the University of Alabama-Birmingham, once told me and often is said by my wife. They both say that Eric Segal was wrong. Love is often having to say you are sorry, and meaning it. I had thought that saying you are sorry to students would be just as easy as it is for me to say to my wife and children. I was wrong. It still is not as easy as it should be. As I look back, the need for the apology in class was obvious; and I thought the apology would not have been that big a deal for me. I guess I still have a ways to go before I am able to see easily what has to be done. My friend reminded me that, for me, it is still not easy to make saying I'm sorry easy to do, and that it is still not easy to pursue truth, goodness, and beauty, and to share publicly that pursuit with others, aside from my wife and children, without fear or embarrassment. I think it is important for students, and for professors or anyone else for that matter, in the midst of forming themselves — as we all are — to see that struggle in themselves so they can embrace it instead of ignoring or dismissing it.

It was important for Julissa. Julissa is an exchange student from Honduras. She is a conscientious student. But until Monday, she was quiet. She never talked during the discussions. She always had a look of insecurity. She seldom contributed to the triad during the quizzes. I almost got the sense she wanted to contribute, but was afraid to try. She reminded me of one of those students who would prefer to hide in the back of the classroom. But I noticed that she always came to class prepared. She had done her share of the chapter write-ups, her share of the outside reading assignments. As I roamed about, I noticed the highlighting in her textbook. I knew she had at least read the material. Once, I called upon her during a discussion. She became momentarily paralyzed. She stammered to say something, but nothing came out. A look of fright overcame her face as her lips tightened, her eyes bulged open, and the muscles in her neck became taut. There was a look of disappointment with herself.

Monday, just before I entered class, Julissa stopped me. I had just turned on the boom box. It was very softly playing "A Hard Rain's Gonna Fall" from the soundtrack to *Born On The Fourth of July*. The meat of our conversation went something like this:

"Dr. Schmier, can I talk with you for just a second?" she asked with great concern.

"Sure, what's up?" I answered.

"I have a great problem," she said with nervous hesitation. "I was afraid to come to you before because I thought you would think I was dumb, but not after what you did Friday."

"Why don't you tell me about it?" I answered.

"I'm from Honduras," she explained. "I only finished with my English lessons last year. I don't speak English so well. It is hard for me to read the book. It is slow. I sometimes read it two or three times. I use a dictionary a lot. I don't understand everything."

"Neither do I or anyone else in the class. Maybe you should ask questions in class, or at least ask the others in your triad for help. If you want, I'll answer your questions outside class. We'll get together and I'll give you some tips on how to study."

"I would like that, but I am afraid to speak up in class because of my poor English."

"Your English sounds fine to me," I softly and reassuringly replied. "But you won't learn to speak better unless you practice it. Start with talking about things with Jason and Flynn."

"But I get embarrassed. I'm not very good with English."

"You got up and sang on the first day of class, didn't you?" I reminded her.

"Yes."

"Well, nothing can be more embarrassing than that in this class. And you did it. What does that tell you about you? Once you did that, what else could be more embarrassing? Be honest with yourself. What's really troubling you?"

She hesitated and then said reluctantly, "I am afraid I am not good enough. I am afraid I will make a mistake and say the wrong word and the others will think I am stupid. I don't know what to do. When we talked about women, I wanted so much to say something about how women are treated in Honduras. But I was so afraid. I couldn't. The same thing happened when we were talking about the Indians and slaves in Latin America. I so much wanted to say something, but I was so afraid."

"You had a lot to contribute to the class and you could have taught the others. But until you stop worrying about what others will think about you, you're just like the colonial slaves. You have to trust yourself and trust the others. Believe in yourself. You have the ability, but it's not important that I believe it. You must believe it. Take the risk. Raise your hand and speak, or don't wait and just blurt out what you want to say. You have nothing to lose and everything to gain. And you can help the others by sharing your experiences."

"But what if I say something silly?"

"You know that, at least in this class, there is no such thing."

"I have another professor who makes fun of people who ask questions or say the wrong things."

"I'm not that professor. I guess you have to trust me, too. Has anyone been made fun of in this class for attempting to improve himself or herself?"

"No."

"Have we ridiculed anyone when they made a mistake?"

"No."

"When Chris told me that he stuttered, what did I do?"

"After Chris said it was all right, you told the class and asked them to understand and help him. But what if I look stupid?"

"To whom? It's not what you say that is important right now. It's that you make the effort, that you meet the challenge and see for yourself how able you are."

"What should I do?"

"What do you really want this class to be for you?"

"I want it to help me learn to do my best and be a good person."

"Then let it. Do you believe in yourself?"

"Yes. I think."

"Then act on your belief. Remember what I always say, 'You can't learn how to climb mountains as long as you practice on mole hills.' This is your first attempt at the mountain. I can't tell you what to do. I am me and I know what I would do. I can't tell you to be me. I can help you to climb. I can show you how to climb. I can even tell you that you have the ability to climb. But you have to decide whether to climb."

"What should I do?"

"I think you know the answer. That's why you wanted to talk with me. You just wanted me to reassure you. Well, I am. You can do it."

And decide she did. We went into class. I turned up the boom box. As I was seeing who was in class, I saw Julissa talking with the other members of her triad. They were making shoving motions. I then asked the class, "OK, chapter 3 today. What are the issues you want to bring up?" A few hands went up just as Julissa hesitantly rose from her chair and asked, "Dr. Schmier, can I talk to the class?" I gave her the floor. "She's going to do what I hoped against hope she would decide on her own to do," I thought to myself. I felt a sudden rush of excitement. Flynn pressed her arm in an act of encouraging faith. As Jason looked on with great support and admiration in his eyes, Julissa continued, "I am very nervous. I am not sure I can do this." She stopped and looked at me. I didn't say a word. I just made an encouraging nod. But I was screaming in silence, "Go, go, go!" Taking a deep breath, she straightened up and went on:

> But I think if Dr. Schmier could say Friday that he is sorry for something he said to the entire class, I think I can stand up and ask for you to understand me. I am Julissa and I am from Honduras and I only finished my English training last year. I am not sure about my English. I need your help. I want to talk with you in class and learn from all of you, but I will make mistakes with the words. I need you to correct me if I do and to tell me the right words.

Then, with a smile beaming from ear to ear, she ended, "I feel good and I will talk more in class now. I promise." She sat down to the applause and whistles of the class. A few stood up as they clapped. I even heard a "Bravo!" The other members of her triad grabbed and hugged her. She had such a feeling of relief and self-satisfaction. I was on the side of the room. I felt a lump in my throat thinking what courage she had just displayed. She looked in my direction. I nodded my head approvingly, smiled admiringly, raised my right arm, and made a fist as an expression of my pride in her. I said, "Julissa, that was a true act of courage that set an example for all of us. We'll all be here if you need us." From various parts of the class came a supporting "You bet," "Show us what you got, Julissa," "We'll help," and "We need you."

During the discussion on slavery in colonial America that followed, a student asked why didn't the slaves just get up and revolt. Julissa hesitantly raised her hand. With anxiety written all over her face, she answered the question with one phrase: "Didn't believe in themselves." That was great. The ice was broken and the river flowed. You could see a nourishing sense of satisfaction flooding into every cell of her body. A few minutes later, as the discussion continued, she raised her hand and spoke a sentence. A few minutes after that, she asked a question. I said to myself, "Julissa, today, this is your class." By the end of the class, Julissa was taking a position and making a lengthy statement. I was so proud for Julissa. As she left the class, she turned to me and said, "Thank you." I replied, "No, thank you."

Each day this past week, she came into class a bit stronger, a bit more relaxed. Her face had more of a soft glow where once there was a pallor of fear. Her lips curled upward with a smile more often, where once they had continually dipped with a frown. Her confidence grew stronger each day as her inhibition grew weaker. She participated in the class discussion every day. On Wednesday and Thursday, I watched her take an active role, a leadership role, in developing a triad symbol, motto, and name that is part of an in-quarter bonding exercise I have instituted.

I marvel at how deeply inhibited most students are. I ask them to show their true selves to others in a variety of ways. This is tough for most of them because they've been told that if they don't excel in everything, they are nothing; if they don't conform to someone else's ideal, they're not ideal. Here was an instance when I witnessed the awesome power of humility. Once Julissa confronted and overcame her groundless fear, trusted herself, and trusted the other members of the class, she started to learn to appreciate herself and her own uniqueness, and she started to truly learn.

I think that, in one respect, the classroom is a microcosm of life. We all have choices of being productive in a stressful situation or laying back and watching life go by. I don't think anxiety in the classroom comes from what professors do or don't do, or from what students do or don't do. It comes from how we each react to what we and the others do. I think the classroom is a stressful place not because it is a stressful place, but because the support system seldom exists wherein everyone is concerned for and cares about everyone else, wherein everyone assumes the responsibility for the success of each other.

The essence of teaching is in making the visceral connection with the students. The challenge, then, is to make teaching so powerful, so dynamic, so passionate, so alluring, so purposeful that it touches the students' emotions. For my part, at my son's school I learned that, if I am to make a serious commitment to the students, I must make a serious commitment to the truth, to recognize the value of being honest with myself, of being honest with them, of sharing my strengths and weaknesses, my visions and emotions, and surrendering the images of myself and of them that keep both me and them from being genuine.

I was reminded by a conscientious high school teacher that in our conservation-conscious society, we discuss ways to cut down on our energy usage. The electric and gas companies have come out to my house, taken an energy inventory, and have offered me cash incentives to become "energy-wise." Their motto is "more efficient, costs less." That may be true for using our fossil fuel resources. It is not applicable to the utilization of our human resources. Human growth is not energy-efficient. Nor can the assistance in this growth be energy-wise. In terms of an energy investment by both the student and professor, it is so expensive. But in the long run, it makes for both good sense and good cents.

In her journal, Julissa wrote, "Everything I did I owe to my professor." She's wrong. She owes it to herself, to believing in herself, to trusting herself and her classmates, to wanting to develop the character necessary to bring out her potential, and to doing whatever it took to start striving for that goal. I am so proud for her. If I must evaluate Julissa and give her a grade, as I must, I will measure her and the other students more by the number of challenges they confront and struggle to overcome than by the grades on their assignments and tests.

On Tuesday, I gave Julissa the highest grade at my disposal as both acknowledgement and encouragement. At the beginning of class, I approached her, knelt next to her chair, and quietly said, "This is for you for being so courageous in meeting your challenge." Her eyes lit up with a confident pride and joy that I do not expect will disappear. I quietly handed her an orange Tootsie Pop.

Have a good one.

Saturday, 30 April 1994
LEARNING COMMUNITY

I went out walking late, real late. My son had a party at the house last night. And while the music was delightful, there was no chance of getting any sleep. So there I was out walking, with the temperature as high as the coming south Georgia summer noon sun. As sweat poured off me in a network of small streams, I was in deep reflection about a bunch of things that have occurred during the past two weeks.

I was thinking very humbly about Julissa using me as the subject of an English composition class essay on the most influential professor she has had at the university. I thought of Tom, bravely standing before the class on Thursday to tell them about how he failed last quarter and decided to challenge himself to repeat the class, challenging others in the class to risk challenging themselves and offering his assistance in that effort. He got a Tootsie Pop on Friday. The picture of Kirk popped into my mind. During the quiz on Friday, normally quiet, shy Kirk had called me over to ask me what the word "volatile" meant. "Don't ask me," I replied. "Stand up and ask the others." He hesitated. The other members of his triad encouraged him. Despite feeling self-conscious, he stood up and asked. He got his answer. Seeing that it was not an embarrassment to ask for help, it was just a few minutes later that another student stood up to ask about the word "sanction." Then, a few minutes after that, still another without hesitation stood and asked about "tacit." I went over to Kirk and whispered, "See what you started?" He'll get a Tootsie Pop on Monday.

There was Ray, a non-traditional student who had spoken with me in my "office" one afternoon to explain how a discussion we had in class about slavery had a profound effect on him, and how much he owed to Yemenja — an African American, non-traditional, Muslim student — for her impassioned comments during that discussion. "Don't tell me," I told him. "Tell her." He did. As I was passing out the quiz, he asked if I could stop because he had something he wanted the class to hear. He got up and explained that he had never thought about the cultural amnesia that the slaves and subsequent generations of African Americans had to suffer, and the damaging impact that it had and still has on the African American psyche. "I went home that night and had a long conversation with my wife," he said. "I will see to it that my daughter will understand that. It's not much, but it's a step. And I want to profoundly thank you, Yemenja, for that understanding. You opened my eyes, and I hope I can help open other eyes." Across the room, tears swelled up in Yemenja's eyes. I noticed that hers were not the only watery eyes. After class, Ray came to me and said, "Was that OK? I sort of fumbled around and rambled." I quietly replied, "It was deeply sincere. You can't ask any more than that of yourself."

Then, there is Mark, an 18-year-old, first-generation college student. Mark had come to me about 10 days ago to talk. He wanted to tell me that the reason he didn't engage in discussions during class was that he had been brought up to listen respectfully to adults. "It's not considered proper in my family," he explained at one point, "for the kids to say anything or interrupt or join in when the adults were talking." I replied, "I can understand that, but you told me that you're 18. When are you going to start becoming an adult? When are you going to start talking so the children listen?" He was quiet for a minute and said, "I never thought about that."

Well, Friday I told Mark that he hadn't handed in his journal for the week. In reply, Mark said he wanted to talk with me after class. "Dr. Schmier," he started the conversation as we sat on the steps, "I've been wondering what a college education is really for. I mean, I know a lot of people who are making a lot of money who never went to college. If a college education is so important, it has to mean more than a job and money. I've been trying to write about that in my journal. What will it do for me as a person?"

Boy, talk about being caught off guard. I thought he was merely going to give me some lame excuse for not having handed in his journal or having missed class on Thursday. Now, I saw he had happened upon the "right" question to ask. I suddenly focused in on every word he said, every gesture he made. My "blueberries" were on full alert. We talked on those steps for over an hour. In the course of our conversation, we talked about him getting out of a college education what he puts into it and about what he wants out of an education and thinks he should want out of it. I told him not to ask what a college education would do for him, but what will he do with a college education. We talked about how, ideally, a college education can provide him new horizons, new flexibilities, new options; about how, ideally, it could teach him how to live, how to grow as a human being, and how to learn; about how, if he wanted a real college education, he could have experiences rather than get grades. At the end of our talk, he asked, "Could I hand in my journal on Monday? I have a lot to think about and write about." I told him to hand in the journal at the regular time on Wednesday. As he got up and said, "Yeah, you've given me a lot to think about and write about," I sat there for a minute or two, a bit stunned, wondering if I was witnessing a creation, thinking to myself, "When the heck did all this happen? How does it happen?"

Mark is not in Julissa's class; nor are Ray or Yemenja or Tom. Maybe the "stuff" project had some catalyzing effect I hadn't anticipated. "Stuff" is a bonding and self-development project. I got the idea while attending a conference on teaching. I had introduced it as closure at the end of class last quarter. The students went wild for it, but strongly suggested that I start using it about four weeks into the quarter to help the triads bond. So, to the surprise of this quarter's students, I had walked into class last week carrying a large roll of butcher paper on one shoulder and a box of color markers under the other arm. "We're going to do 'stuff' today," I proclaimed. I told them that each triad had to design a "family" symbol or crest and come up with both a motto and name that would express the collective personality of their triad. They stared at me. From the stunned expressions on their faces, I could tell they were thinking, "Where did he come up with this one?" Then, the whole place quickly exploded into a mass of fervent movement and zealous excitement. Some cut a sheet of paper and rushed out of the class.

With coffee in hand and swirling a Tootsie Pop in my mouth, I watched the students spread out all over the floor of the class, out in the surrounding hallways, and outside on the entrance sidewalk to the building as they hovered and crowded around large pieces of butcher paper. They were lying prone, leaning, kneeling, sitting. In the classroom, chairs were pushed aside and even piled on top of each other. Color markers were scattered about. All sound was drowned out by the din of laughter, discussion, small talk, argument, and joking. Bodies were hopping about, hands were moving all directions, heads were bobbing and nodding, brows were wrinkling, eyes were staring. The students were pushing each other in friendly banter. Everywhere, splotches of color were appearing in psychedelic delight on the paper.

The place was oozing with concentration, imagination, reflection, hesitation, creativity, adventure, discovery, and innovation as the students struggled to find those common bonds. They were having fun exchanging, analyzing, searching, evaluating, and deciding with each other, about each other, and about themselves. They discussed, argued, and pondered as they grappled to design a crest and come up with both a motto and name that would best express their triad. As they worked feverishly and vocally, faculty and students passed by, stepped over, and walked about. Most gave them strange looks. A few even stopped and talked. The students thought it was interesting. The faculty who passed by thought it was "cute" or "silly."

One colleague from another department, however, asked with a scornful smirk on his face, "Schmier, not again. What's it this time? Looks like kindergarten." Not appreciating his comment, a couple of the students gave him hidden scornful glances in return.

"No," I answered with great enthusiasm. "It's a bonding exercise to create a feeling of family and to help strengthen the sense that the class is a mutually supporting learning community. They're getting to understand each other better and to get closer so they can work with each other and help each other better."

"You're crazy as hell," he laughed with obvious suspicion about my sanity. "I thought you taught history."

"I teach students," I proudly informed him.

"You're no professor. You're a teacher." I took that as a compliment. I don't think from his tone of voice and body language that he had meant it as one. "Maybe when you retire you ought to go to the elementary school."

He didn't get it. But the students did, and that was more important. As I wandered about, I saw normally quiet, unsure, frightened students smiling and participating. I saw students ever so slightly opening that door and getting a peek at their inner potential. I saw students who "don't like to rely on others for their grade" relying on and coordinating with others. I saw cooperation and compromise as triad members trusted each other and divided up the responsibility — one coming up with a motto, another with the name, a third with the design, and all of them modifying and adjusting their suggestions. I saw teamwork as students listened to each other and respected each other. Followers became leaders; leaders were told to lay off and, as one student forcefully told another in her triad, "Trust us and give us a chance to show off what we can do."

After two days of working on this project, to cheers, applause, and whistles each triad presented its "heraldry" before the class. No list of their names or mottos, no verbal description of their crests, can do justice to their creations, but take my word that they were something else. I can say, from the reactions in class and comments written in journals, that the class experienced a growth in camaraderie and respect, a sense of closeness, community, family, and a sense of mutual responsibility. Few thought in terms of less creative, or more artistic, or more this or more that; few thought in terms of competition. They were surprised that they had put so much effort into something that was not graded. The students themselves felt that the class took a great leap forward, and the subsequent discussions and openness seemed to indicate they were right. At least, for the moment.

It has been a powerful two weeks in class. I think that seeking the acquisition of information is important. But "book history," as one of my students called it, is not ultimately the most important thing. At least not for me. I'm not sure I know why what happens happens. I do know things happen, and I stand back amazed that they do. I wonder about it constantly. I'm not sure I want to analyze it, break it down into charts and statistics, rip it apart into its components. Dissecting any living entity merely gives you access to the structure, but it destroys the living spirit in the process. I much prefer the excitement of the unexpected, wondering what will or might happen on any given day. I think the spirit would be dampened by a predictability. Maybe it's that unknown that gives me a sense of adventure. I think that these events occur only as the students become aware of or feel the appearance of a sense of community — a "learning community," as it is called — in the class that is both mutually supporting and larger than themselves. As the class evolves, students begin to share their fears, their weaknesses, the murky part of them, their strengths, their light, who they are. Certainly this is not true for all the students. As for me, I have to constantly be reminded by the serenity prayer of the struggle to change the things that I can, to accept what I cannot change, and to know the difference. Nevertheless, a few, or some, or many — it varies from class to class, from quarter to quarter — seize the opportunity to start becoming whole. That's a healing experience for them. Except for those occasional visits from students and unsolicited letters, except for their journals, except for the personal and confidential conversations, I can't prove it; it's something I feel and experience. I can only share what that experience has been and what that feeling is.

I do, however, work hard to create whatever it is that is created. We are each a gift to each other. As my son was to me, I am hopefully to them, they to me, and they to each other. We are human beings, and to separate and isolate the students in the traditional asocial atmosphere and setting of the class, I think, is unnatural. Because of them, I have a much greater sense of the value of life and of what life can be, and of the role an education, as I understand it, plays. I only hope that whatever it is I am doing for them and whatever they are doing for each other is as deep and lasting as what they are doing for me.

Have a good one.

Wednesday, 5 May 1994
TEACHING STYLE

*N*o walking today. It was raining like cats and dogs. Nevertheless, I was thinking about Julissa and Mark. I know what they think about the style of the class. That got me to wondering once again about what my old professors at Adelphi, St. John's, and UNC — those who taught me 27 to 36 years ago — might have thought of my less than traditional teaching style.

Standing there in their suits, sport coats, and ties, what questions would have raced through their minds as they saw me bounce into class in my less than professorial attire, a blaring boom box in one hand, no folder of lecture notes to be seen, sucking on a Tootsie Pop, bantering with the students on a first name basis. Would they have thought it "kindergarten-ish," like my colleague, to have the students create triad crests? Would they have thought it even more childish if they heard the students say to me, "Where's your symbol? You're part of this class. You've got to make one," and if they saw me go into my office, get a piece of butcher paper, and get down on the floor with it to create a crest depicting the entire class? (By the way, the name for the class that I came up with was the "Tootsie Pops." My motto was "Many flavors: all sweet.") I wonder if they would have judged it "rinky-dink" when they saw my upraised arm as a "quiet signal"? Would they have thought it "hokey" as they looked on during the first days of the quarter watching each student and me stand up to sing solo a few bars of their choice of a song as an opening ice-breaker, or to take biographies of each other and introduce each other to the class? I wonder if they would have shaken their heads in bewilderment watching blindfolded students being led through an obstacle course of chairs by other students, or diving off the desk into the arms of waiting students, or falling back into the arms of waiting students in a series of trust-forming exercises. I wonder if they would have raised their eyebrows in astonishment if they saw that I didn't hand out the course syllabus until the fifth day of class or didn't hear any discussion of history until after an entire week had passed? What would their reactions have been to the grouping of the students into triads and watching them taking the quizzes in open discussion and working on assignments collaboratively and getting common grades? What would they have said and done as they watched triads of students jointly presenting to the class a painting, a piece of sculpture, an original song, a game, or a poem as the "answer" to a final exam, rather than a traditional essay or short-answer questions? I'm not sure they would have understood the place and purpose of student journaling, weekly student self-evaluations, and open-class evaluations of me and each other. I think they would have been skeptical of my declarations to the students that "we're all responsible for each other's success" and "it's your class." Most would have been uncomfortable with my practice of letting the students alter the course curriculum.

I think some would have been, to say the least, certainly disappointed in the belief that I had gone astray. Some would have been outraged and would have branded me a traitor to my academic culture. Most would have turned and walked away from what surely would have seemed to them as "unprofessional" shenanigans or "high-schoolish" antics. A few might have stayed to ask a ton of questions, out of curiosity to see where I went wrong, but I don't think any would have given themselves a whirl at a style of teaching so unlike their own. I don't think they would have been prepared to explore beyond the traditional, to experience questioning of their professional values, and to experience possible personal uprooting. I think they would have been content to remain entrenched in their traditional, formal, lecturing ways.

As a defense, I think, most of them would have asserted that to teach, all they needed to know was their subject, and that there was not much to know about teaching techniques beyond being expert in the subject. Most probably would have proclaimed what good teachers they were by unrolling their professional résumés, replete with lists of publications, conference papers, consultantships, awards, and grants. Most would have been content to lock the door to exciting new worlds by saying that the non-traditional styles of teaching "don't fit my personality," "are not my cup of tea," "are not me." Most would have branded anyone using common language, rather than jargon, as "popular," "non-professional," or "pop" this or that. I don't think most could have found common ground with anyone who didn't lecture. Most would have been unsure of my celebration of "learning and teaching" rather than or as equal to any promotion of research and publication. A few would have thought me a pariah because I much prefer to call myself a teacher rather than a professor, to use my title "Dr." only when I can get a discount rather than to distinguish myself. Almost all would have rejected the idea that some of my teaching methods, used in the "lower" K-8 world of the "teacher," might have something to teach them about teaching in the "higher" collegiate world of the "professor." Most would have believed that I couldn't cut a proper authority figure or get proper respect without the proper attire of coat and tie. I think most would have been extremely nervous about the "real world" of the lay person invading the higher and adored order of the academicians' ivory tower. Most would have been horrified at the prospect of an erosion of the distinction between the two. Most would have been offended by what they deemed a corruption of the traditional academic ethos. Their customs, rituals, ceremonies, outlook, titles, language, dress, and style, like any tribe, were important to these members of a proud and aged intellectual culture.

But teaching, like everything else, is not so much about style as it is substance. Style in itself is merely physical appearance that you can walk into a class and see: a lecture, a seating arrangement, a method of testing, a discussion, a technique here, a technique there, a technological aide. Substance is process. It's the reasons, purpose, and direction behind the goings-on. It's the attitude and the spirit that permeate the air from which the style derives its drive and energy. It's not as obvious as the structural. You have to look hard for all that and feel it. It's those essential, intangible things: caring, bonding, trusting, learning, changing, growing, transforming, and sincerity.

We should make sure, however, that any style be more than stylish. It must be more than another way of talking, another way of moving, another way of moving things around, another way of assessment. It's an extension and reflection of a way of thinking and feeling about our craft, as well as a way of perceiving ourselves and the students. As I see it, techniques I am currently using are at best a skeleton that gives form to a personal value system and a deeper process of learning and growth that emanates from my soul and hopefully will resonate in the student.

After deep reflection on myself, as a person and a professional, I have chosen a style of teaching that I hope creates more of an environment of learning for the student than an ease of presentation for me; that is more fitted to the diverse learning styles of the students than to my teaching habits; that is more suited to the distinctive personalities of the students than to my disposition; that is more concerned with the question, "Did the student learn anything?" rather than with the statement, "I taught him or her." I recently read a profound statement from a teacher. "When teaching a five-year-old," he said, "get down on his level and see how it will look to him." It's no different with a college student.

Whatever style is used, there should be solid reasons for its adoption. We should ask questions about the processes of learning, about the various ways of instruction, about our teaching, and about ourselves. Who are we? Why do we do what we do? Why do we use one approach over another?

Why do we think one technique works with some students at some time and not with others at another? Why do we think one strategy will suit us and not another? What's the goal and purpose of it all? Whose class is it or whose should it be? And above all, who are the students the strategy is to help?

We should ask these questions with honesty, sincerity, authenticity, and deep reflection. We should not be superficial, going through the motions with the fullest intention of operating in a business-as-usual manner, merely asking these questions because some pronouncing administrator or interfering legislator told us that they must be asked, or because we don't want some "amateur" invading our campus, trespassing on our turf and intruding into the classroom to ask for us. We should not select a style because we think it will profit us in terms of higher student evaluations or earlier bestowal of tenure or greater salary increases. We should not select a style because it protects us from the accusation of being out of step with the times, sedentary, or old-fashioned. We should not select a style because we just want to look good. We should not select a style just because someone told us we should. We should not select a style thinking it, in and of itself, is teaching. If we do, as my metaphor exercise indicates, the students will spot the counterfeit and pin us for uncaring, educational obstructionists.

When we re-examine an old-and-tried style or explore a new and untested one, we must explore our own feelings and values. We must examine our own need to grow. We must challenge ourselves to grow and move on to another place. When we open new vistas for the students, we must open whole new dimensions for ourselves. We have to convince ourselves that we want to get deeper into the process of learning; we have to find the courage to face the exciting and frightening journey of exploration into our minds, souls, and practices; we have to muster the energy demanded by the task. Otherwise, we'll forget how to move on. Instead, we'll succumb to the comfort and familiarity of routine, tediousness, and desensitivity. And in so doing, we'll threaten ourselves with losing our edge — with sinking into the morass of stagnation, letting our notes yellow, letting ourselves become dull and boring, and, like the pre-historic creatures of old in the tar pits, becoming fossils.

We should select a style, then, that is challenging for both us and the students, in which we believe and trust, with which we become one, which becomes us, which serves the students, and which merges with them. We should select a style because we truly want students to be the best learners they can be, be the best human beings they can be, rather than because we are the faddists of today or the entrenched, self-serving defenders of yesterday. We should select a style because we care about making the class-room for the student an unending adventure in learning, a discovery of self, a cradle of creation. And we should select a style because we want the classroom to be for ourselves an adventure in learning, a discovery of self, a cradle of creation.

Have a good one.

Thursday, 12 May 1994
S T U D E N T   B L O O P E R S

*W*ell, it happened again this morning, and my blood started bubbling with annoyance. "This has to be the stupidest thing I ever heard," a colleague from the English department said as he stopped and cornered me in the hall. "Listen to this: 'Blacks couldn't become cowboy heroes in the movies because they weren't allowed to ride white horses.' And you think all students belong in college?"

"Hey, we made those same mistakes when we were students."

"We were different students back then."

"Maybe, but so would that student be if you used that statement to help him to learn how to express himself accurately instead of making fun of him to me."

Not appreciating my unwillingness to laugh with him or my less than subtle jab, he exclaimed with some exasperation, "Boy, you're a spoilsport! I read it to the class along with some others and we all had a good chuckle. No one saw anything wrong in them. We all thought they were funny. And you don't. Lighten up! Get a sense of humor!"

Ignoring him, I answered, "I bet the student that wrote it must have been rolling in the aisle."

"I do this all the time in order to teach them what not to do next time."

I thought to myself, "Where have I heard that before?" Out loud I asked, "Do you really think that that is what the students think? It's not exactly a confidence builder. I can think of more understanding and less embarrassing ways to teach."

"What would you do?" he asked with some annoyance.

"Whatever I would do, I wouldn't do it in public like that."

"I didn't use anyone's name. Hey, I know better than that."

"Does that matter? Anyway, I would treat that statement as a 'magnificent mistake,' turn it into something positive, and use it as one of those 'teaching moments.' I'd talk to the students privately. Ask them if they understood what they wrote and is it what they wanted to say. Ask them what they really meant to say. See what their train of thought was. Ask them to think of another way of saying what they wanted to say. If necessary, show them how to tighten up their thinking and language. Let them rewrite it. You could do a whole bunch of constructive things to teach them how to improve their skills."

Well, the conversation continued on for a while, and as he left, I thought of a donnybrook I had been involved in earlier with some professors on e-mail that was over the same issue of student bloopers. I think it wound up with me against the vocal members of the list after I responded to examples of student bloopers on exams in a manner similar to my conversation with my colleague.

It started when I wrote about a brief conversation in which I was partially involved that took place in the History department a couple of years ago. It went something like this:

"Hey, listen to this one," one of my colleagues proclaimed, as he came out of his office into the department reception area with a huge smile on his face. I was at the copy machine. Two other colleagues were getting their mail. There was the secretary and two student assistants. "This one is funny," he said as he read from a student's exam. "Did you all know that 'Jay Gould was a famous captain of industry because he invented Goulden Mustard?' Ha, where do they get this dumb stuff from?"

"That *is* a pretty good one," one of my colleagues snickered. He then unsympathetically sighed, "That's what we have to put up with. Oh, well."

"It's really pathetic," said another colleague. "I sometimes wonder if they really belong here."

"Don't you think that's funny?" my colleague thoughtlessly asked the students.

"Yeah, it's pretty good," they answered as they nervously snickered.

"Schmier, you're not laughing," he said to me.

I turned around and said, "I don't think it's funny."

"Damn, you can be such a tight-ass at times. Lighten up!"

I didn't answer. Knowing him as I did, I decided it would have been futile to have attempted. Immediately after my colleagues left the area, I overheard one of the students whisper, "Who does he think he is, makin' fun of us? He's the ass."

So I ask about the humor of what I consider "put-down" student bloopers. To whom are they funny? Now, I am not an avid supporter of political correctness. One person's humor, however, is another's hurt. As I see it, the deprecating blooper humor about students is just another variation of that kind of gallows humor that denigrates rather than elevates, boos rather than applauds, bemoans rather than exalts, ridicules rather than praises, and spotlights weakness rather than celebrates strength, and ignores the advice of the 1940s song by accentuating the negative while eliminating the positive. It's in the same category of, thankfully, now unacceptable ethnic, gender, and disability jokes.

I wonder what you women out there *really* feel about those supposedly "harmless" girl jokes or dumb blonde jokes bantered about by the men. I wonder how you of noble Polish ancestry *really* react inside to those supposedly "loosen up" Polish jokes. I wonder what you of Jewish or Catholic or Muslim persuasion *really* feel others are thinking when you hear the "Jew," "papist," or "Arab" jokes labeled as "light-hearted" humor. I wonder how you with Italian blood running in your veins truly judge the value of those "meaningless" Italian jokes. I wonder how you African Americans and Hispanics *honestly* react to the "Where's your sense of humor?" racial jokes. I wonder how much pride you special people *really* feel when you hear "good-natured" people telling those "spastic" or "retard" or "blind" jokes. I wonder how all of you who, individually or as a group, have been the object of such "nothing is meant by it" humor feel. And I wonder how many of you out there *really* felt when, as students, you were the target of such professorial "it doesn't mean anything" fooling around. My, some of us have short and selected memories.

I remember, and I remember I didn't feel like laughing. The truth is that everyone now recognizes that those jokes, however consciously or otherwise intended, display a prejudice of varied intensity, propagate denigrating stereotypes, perpetuate a divisiveness, deprecate the individual, promote a disrespect, and reinforce inequities. I am sorry. I don't think a display of humor at someone else's expense is funny. And I'm not sure that my colleague or anyone else can explain the educational value, the character-building purpose, or the psychological benefit of such humor, to either himself or the student.

The problem is that such bloopers always play to the student's weaknesses, always remind us that we are on a higher plane and they are on the lower one. I don't see respect, sensitivity, caring, and decency in publicly or privately disseminating these bloopers.

And when such humor is displayed, so many of us are quick to defend ourselves with a bunch of poor rationalizations, lame excuses, weak explanations, and a horde of unsatisfactory "I think's" and "I'm sure's." I have been told by professors that "I would not survive if I did not laugh at some of the things that my students say and do," or "I laugh at some of the things that my students do because otherwise I would be depressed and/or angry at them," or "I do it to survive the doom and gloom that I have to face." The one I like the best is the self-righteous, "I do not resent my colleagues laughing when I say something or do something that they find funny." Well, I know a lot of professors with onion-thin skins who would and do.

I think that any professor who uses student blooper humor has to remember that he or she is in a particular authority relationship with the student. We're not some bunch of entertaining comedians on a stage. Our classroom is not some silly television show. The student is at best, to use the theatrical analogy, a captive audience who, except under unique circumstances, does not feel empowered and safe enough to challenge or object to such poking. To the contrary, such "fun" is a reminder to the student, and subtly to the professor as well, of who wields the power and who is the subject of such wielding. The response of the student is so often that silent response of the powerless or the feigned laugh of the intimidated. But I can tell you from reading student journals and talking with students from other classes where blooper humor is commonplace that the overwhelming majority do not think it's funny. It's fear-inducing, paralyzing, confidence-destroying, and demeaning.

We may think that we're laughing with the students, when, in fact, we're laughing at the students. We may think they are laughing with us when in fact they are thinking that "he's laughing at me" or "she's making fun of me" or "he made me feel so stupid" or "we didn't think that was funny." This kind of humor segregates the students into false categories of superior and inferior: "He didn't ridicule me, so I guess I'm better," or "She made fun of me, so I guess I'm not that good." It doesn't matter whether we specifically name the students or talk in general terms — the students feel you're talking to each of them.

No, I don't see how spotlighting a student's omission in such a manner does anything assuring or constructive for the student. Maybe we ought to think and reflect on what signals such "fun" *really* sends to the students. Maybe we ought to wonder, before we act, whether such "fun" is just another indication to the students that we professors are "the enemy," waiting out there to pounce and to pour salt into the intellectual wounds and inflict emotional hurt. Maybe we ought to wonder if such humor freezes a student's ability to continue trying. Maybe we ought to reflect upon what the use and acceptance of such "blooper humor," such "put-down" humor, says about us, our attitudes, our perspective about the relationship between us and the students, and our consequent actions.

Now, I'm no saint. I once used blooper humor. In fact, for 10 years, I collected those bloopers. I had amassed about 180 typed pages worth. I once was toying with the idea of publishing a "History According to Freshmen." Well, about three years ago, I picked up the manuscript, thumbed the pages, read some of it, and thought about it. I remember that day well.

It was right after I had returned from a week of self-examining challenge sessions at my son's school in Maine, and a few weeks before I was to climb that cliff. I had spent an entire week asking questions of myself. You know, we teachers know the importance of asking questions. Our mission is to teach students how to ask their own questions. But we so seldom turn important questions on ourselves. Not the questions in search of knowledge, but the questions in search of meaning and purpose about who we are and what we do. Now, the more I thought about that manuscript in front of me, the harder I held it, and the more I didn't like what I heard. I was suddenly overcome by a very uncomfortable feeling. I realized that this collection of bloopers was not talking about the students. It was talking about me and of the need to reflect on, examine, and evaluate my personal educational values, attitudes, and priorities. It talked of my prejudices toward myself as a professor and toward the students, my subtle arrogance, my unrecognized aloofness, and my separation from the students. This collection of bloopers did not reflect a professor who has faith in his students and holds them in high esteem. It did not reflect a professor who has visions of success for the students, who sees teaching not just as employment but his life's work, who cares for the students, who affirms the strengths and beings of the students, who gives a high priority to benefiting them, who has a love for the students, who has a faith in them, and who treats them with respect and dignity. I came to the conclusion that my use of and association with this kind of humor, however harmless my intentions may have been, did not help to create or maintain a classroom learning community. This was a way of my life, one outlook, I no longer wanted to be part of me, or to affect my teaching and the students' learning.

After thumbing through that manuscript some more, I picked it up, carried it out into the hall, and, with a gesture of finality, threw it — no, slammed it — into the recycle bin. At least it did some good. I kept one page. It's hanging on my office wall as a reminder of who I once was and as a warning of who not to become again.

Now, some of you may say that I am making a big deal out of something so little. Maybe I am taking it too seriously. Maybe I am overreacting, like the reformed alcoholic does to the use of liquor or the reformed smoker to cigarettes or the erstwhile addict to drug use. But I'll take that risk, because my gut tells me that when we rationalize the use of student blooper humor, we're making something dangerously little and harmless out of something that is potentially big and harmful.

Have a good one.

Thursday, 23 June 1994

T O   B E   A   T E A C H E R

*W*ell, I just went out for a pre-dawn walk. After being spoiled by 10 idyllic days of walking the cool, inviting, gnatless, mosquitoless environs of Seattle's streets and Vancouver's Stanley Park, my body seemed to know what torture it was about to endure. I had started sweating before my hand was on the door knob. It is hot down here! It is humid down here! It was like slogging through a paved rain forest. And the sun hasn't even come up yet!

Anyway, as I was hoping against hope that the heated asphalt wouldn't fry the soles of my feet before I finished my route, I was thinking about a question raised by a student in my class yesterday morning. I think he and the others were intrigued by the four days scheduled in the syllabus for what I call "stuff," those bonding and trusting exercises with which I begin all my classes. It's my way of starting to replace what I think is the strangling atmosphere of isolating, destructive classroom competitiveness with the sweet-smelling air of a mutually supportive and cooperative learning community. He wanted to know what I thought it took to be a collegiate history teacher. I told him that I would have to reflect on that question and would bring in an answer today.

I'm sure he and the others are expecting me to talk mundanely about techniques, courses to take, areas in which to major, advanced degrees to acquire, research in which to engage, stuff to publish, and so on. But I don't think I will, because I don't think the essence of teaching lies in the "doing" — that is, I don't think teaching begins with, is, and ends with technique. Nor do I think that the seminal issue of teaching lies in the "knowing" — that is, having a grasp of the subject and the subject content of the course. Certainly both technique and subject are important, but I think that teaching, and learning for that matter, ultimately rests on "self." I think the essence of teaching and learning lies in the "feeling" and the "being," the spirit that surrounds each of us, brings life and meaning and purpose into the learning experience, and creates that critical common bond of humanity among the students as well as between them and the teacher.

So here is what I am going to tell the students about what I think it takes to be not just a collegiate history teacher, but a teacher of anything at any level:

If you want to be a teacher, you first have to learn how to play hopscotch, jump rope, and hide-and-seek, learn other children's games, learn how to watch a snail crawl, blow bubbles, read *Yertle the Turtle*, and watch "Bullwinkle." If you want to be a teacher, you have to sing "she loves me, she loves me not" as you blow at a dandelion or pull the individual petals of a daisy. If you want to be a teacher, you have to stop and watch a rainbow, listen to a distant train, wiggle your toes in the mud and let it ooze through them, stomp in rain puddles, look up and watch an airplane, and be humbled by the majesty of a mountain. If you want to be a teacher, you have to fall in love each day. If you want to be a teacher, you have to paddle a canoe, take a hike, or just get out. If you want to be a teacher, you have to watch intently the artistry of a spider weaving its web. If you want to be a teacher, you have to fly a kite or throw a frisbee, skip stones in a lake or brook, make sand castles, and love people. If you want to be a teacher, you have to listen intently to the rustle of the leaves, to the murmur of the brook, to the pitter-patter of the rain, and to the whisper of the breeze. If you want to be a teacher, you have to dream dreams, play games, talk to the flowers, catch fire flies, admire a weed, walk barefoot, hold a worm, and see what is yet to be. If you want to be a teacher, you have to think silly thoughts, have a water gun fight, have a pillow fight, swirl a Tootsie Pop in your mouth, burn sparklers at night, and see in a tree more than a mass of atoms or so many board feet of lumber or something that's in the way. If you want to be a teacher, you have to skip as you walk, laugh at yourself, smile at others, hang loose, always have an eraser handy, and concoct an original recipe. If you want to be a teacher, you have to be inspired and inspire. If you want to be a teacher, you have to fix a bird's broken wing, pinch the neck of a deflating balloon and play a tune, do zany things, play with a yo-yo, and lose yourself in the quiet scenery to find yourself. If you want to be a teacher, you have to feed the pigeons or squirrels, sing in the shower or tub, smell the flowers, play with finger paints, and do a belly flop in a pool. If you want to be a teacher, you have to bring joy into everything, watch in awe a sunset or sunrise, ride on a swing, slide down a slide, bump on a seesaw, and respect even a cockroach as a miracle of life. If you want to be a teacher, you have to ride a bicycle or roller skate or ice skate, and live today. If you want to be a teacher, make all those marvelous feelings and images an intimate part of you and bring them into the classroom with you and share them. If you want to be a teacher, as Carl Jung advised, you have to put aside your formal theories and intellectual constructs and axioms and statistics and charts when you reach out to touch that miracle called the individual human being.

That's what I'm going to tell my students about what it will take to be a teacher.

Have a good one.

Tuesday, 28 June 1994

M O R E   O N   T O   B E   A   T E A C H E R

*W*hen I wrote that little piece about what it takes to be a teacher, I wasn't talking about past childhood experiences. I am talking about a contemporary and continuous, joyous, adventurous, caring, and humble outlook on life that lightens up everything a person does, that floods the classroom with infectious caring, discovery, adventure, excitement, enthusiasm, electricity, awe, and wonder. Of course, I have to know about my subject. But résumés of publications and degrees acquired and books read and papers presented in themselves don't have much to do with teaching, except in the most euphemistic of ways. I have always maintained that teaching or whatever I do is a reflection of and an extension of me — "a baring of one's soul," as Bill Hunter at the University of Calgary so aptly phrases it. It's the spirit within myself — my attitudes and character, if you will — that ultimately determines the spirit that I bring into and flood the classroom with, the goals and purposes of what I do, what I do with what I know, how I relate to the students, and how I communicate with them.

We all have an outlook on life that impacts on everything we do, think, feel, and dream, including the way we teach. It includes how we relate to our-selves and the people with whom we personally, socially, and professionally associate. I do not believe that a person who sees little joy in life can be joyous in the classroom; that a person who is bored with himself or herself can be exciting and electrifying in the classroom; that a person who has a lack of self-confidence can relinquish control in the classroom; that a person who is self-centered, self-righteous, and/or arrogant can respect students; that a person who lacks a sense of adventure can cut new paths or chart new waters in the classroom. But a person who listens to the train in the distance can hear the individual student; a person who cries at a sad movie can be compassionate about the worrisome burdens carried by students; the person who gives milk to a scrawny, stray cat sees potential in each and every student; the person who can watch a snail crawl can have patience with the struggles of a student; the person who looks at the dew on a spider's web can see the individual student in the class.

We just had a torrential rainstorm. It was fun watching the ballet of raindrops dancing toward the house along the telephone line and then dripping rhythmically onto the bushes below. So often we get all of those youthful visions beaten out, educated out, spanked out, talked out, drummed out, and walked out of us. I remember that once, as high school students, we had to take one of those silly, insidious, predicting "what you should become" tests that we took in the '50s. When mine came back, one of my teachers told me that I had answered some of the questions wrong. The one that stands out in my mind was the one that asked if, given a choice, would I prefer to do voluntary work at a hospital, go to a museum, see a baseball game, or go to an opera. At 15, I wouldn't want to be caught dead languishing in a musty museum, or be lulled to sleep listening for an hour to the main character's extended death gasps, or smell the foreboding antiseptic odors of a hospital. My honest answer was to see a baseball game. That teacher talked to me about not having the right attitude, how I should have wanted to do volunteer work if I wanted to become a doctor. I remember vividly her saying something to the effect that I will become nothing if I waste my time watching baseball rather than getting some culture or helping others.

It seems that from a tender age, through graduate school, and on into academia, people are always trying to put us on the straight and narrow. They're telling us to be responsible, grow up, act our age, be prim and proper, know what we want to do, shape up, get serious, play the game, be political, be professional.

I was just at a teaching conference. While everyone was interested in teaching, there was a strong and distracting underlying current of anxiety about budget cuts, tenure, promotion, salary, publications, imposing administrations, antagonistic colleagues, etc., etc. One junior professor came up to me to ask some advice from "an old-timer like you" (I did not take that as a kind description) about how to maintain an emphasis on teaching in an institution that talks teaching but walks grants and research and publication. What could I tell him? The truth is that institutions of higher education are more about power than the noble pursuit of learning. Most of its members are more interested in the personal or institutional prestige, renown, money, and power that come with research grants and publications than in being silent promoters of dreams. So many of us are very good at denial. One of our greatest sins is to remain passive and defensive in the face of that truth. Authoritarianism against students or faculty destroys dreams; disinterest destroys dreams; arrogance destroys dreams.

So what was my advice? I first told him that I had learned to pick my battles and know my "adversaries." Isn't it tragic to describe colleagues and administrators in such confrontational and combative terms? I also told him that I constantly ask myself a series of simple, yet difficult and profound, questions that often require courageous answers: How much faith do I have in my institution and profession? How much can I remain or strive to be my true self? How much do I have to sell out to remain academically and professionally alive? Do I have a right to be whole?

I hate the idea that you have to surrender yourself and become, as a colleague described herself, "an idealist who crashed" in order to survive the power politics of academia.

But you know, I sometimes believe that all the people who try to "straighten" others out or who try to keep others acting and looking so "professional" are the Jacob Marleys and Ebeneezer Scrooges of academia. They have lost their youth and abandoned their dreams. Their lecture notes have yellowed. Their classes have become stale. They're bored with their classes, they have little respect for their students, and they are taken with themselves. They look at those who still retain their youthful charm and vim as foolish Bob Cratchetts and scream, "Bah, humbug!" But I think they feel jealous, saddened, or threatened because they see what they never were or once were and long to be, but cannot or will not or are afraid to be. In the face of what life has thrown in their professional way — promotion, salary, tenure, research, publication — they have lost their way, compromised themselves, and lost their spirit.

I refuse to believe that you have to lose your sense of youth — that ability to dream, to believe in magic, in ghosts, and in Santa Claus, to ride a carousel, to stop and watch a rainbow — as you age in years, acquire degrees, enter a profession, and acquire a reputation. Life is too short to take ourselves and what we do so seriously that we allow our spirits to become as brittle as aged bones, our values to atrophy like unused muscles, and our energy to be so sapped that we become old fossils. That so many of us do so is one of the greatest crimes of academia. I believe we have to retain or rediscover the innocence, daring, and vigor of youth. I don't believe that the belief and enjoyment in clicking your heels twice or wishing upon a star or believing you can fly or a bit of innocent mischievousness should be abandoned. They're not signs of ignorance, immaturity, or amateurism. They are what make me real, let me find the fun in what I do, allow me to take risks, make those farfetched ideas come true, allow me to laugh at my own mistakes, make me sensitive to the needs of students, challenge me to move on, and encourage me to do what I want to do.

You know, I'm 53. I have acquired a long scholarly résumé. I am approaching retirement here at the university. But I still can't believe that I am old enough to have a son of 25. I have a bottle of bubbles in my office. I suck on Tootsie Pops, wear bermuda shorts to class in the summer, just had a "finger paint date" with my wife, and always talk with my flowers. I often wonder what it is that allows me to make contact with my students. I don't think it's simply the fact that I know my subject. I think it is my sense of humanity, but I think it's also that I still hold frogs up to my nose and look at them cross-eyed, refuse to stop believing in Peter Pan, refuse to "act my age," refuse to be "professorial," enjoy what I do, and have toys in my office.

Have a good one.

Tuesday, 5 July 1994

TEACHING AND CARING

*L*ordy!! Have you ever gone out power walking four miles before the sun rose, felt your shoes filling with the water that's pouring off your body, and watched your skin turn green with mildew? That will give you some idea of the weather this morning. In fact, it's been raining every day for the last two weeks, and it hasn't even cooled off!

As I was "water skiing" along the streets through this south Georgia sweat bath, just after the 218th birthday weekend of a country that sanctifies the nobility of the individual, I started thinking about how students have a right to be treated on campuses no less as the individuals that they are off campus, that all too many professors — more than most of us want to acknowledge — are so quick to proclaim, "I am student-oriented." They give lip-service to the individuality of the students and yet coldly see and treat them as the faceless and nameless in a crowd. It wasn't, however, just that it was the day after watching the rocket's red glare that got me thinking about this. It was also a conversation I had last week with a non-traditional student — a conversation that has popped into my head once again, as it has almost every day for the last week or so.

It was the third day of class. I was sitting in a soft chair in the library. I was waiting for Maria (not her real name), who had come up to me at the end of the class and had said she wanted to talk with me after her next class. We agreed to meet in the library, my "office" for that day. I didn't know what it was all about. I thought she had a scheduling problem or wanted some help with the class library assignments or needed some reassurance about my unique approach to teaching. When she arrived, she was very nervous. She quickly sat down.

"What can I help you with?" I asked. She hesitated. Looking around anxiously to see if anyone was listening, she started talking. It was not what I expected.

"You touched me when you talked about your son in class and how what you went through with him changed your outlook on life, your attitude about yourself and people around you, and how you ran the class."

My "blueberries" came into play. I sat up. I quickly riveted on every word and gesture. All the surrounding sounds stilled and the surrounding movements froze into a silent tableau. The background scenery faded into a darkness, as if she were in a bright spotlight. She tearfully told me about her endless struggles with her ADD teenage son, her bouts with waves of guilt as a parent, her fears for her son's future, her fights with a less than supporting husband, her terror at a possibly impending divorce, her anger at unsupporting local medical and educational systems, and her combat with self-doubt and weak self-confidence. For over an hour she poured out her soul to me. For over an hour she did most of the talking and I did most of the listening. As I focused on her facial expressions and body language, tears periodically formed in my eyes, my breath occasionally shortened, silent cries swelled in my throat. My heart ached. The cushioned chair could not cushion the hurt within her, betrayed by her voice and face. "I can't get away from it or stop thinking about it," she said with a quivering voice. "I can't sleep. I can't concentrate. I can't study. It's consuming me. What can I do? How did you handle it?"

Without hesitation, I told about the road through hell each member of my family traveled together and separately: the misdiagnosis, the mistreatment, the indifference, the uncooperative schools, the accusations, the poor treatment, the daily wars, the family dysfunction, the trouble with the law, the failing grades, the frustration and anger, the attempts at escaping, the ostracism, the depression, the inability to think or feel, the isolation, the loneliness, the confusion, the doubt, the second-guessing, the drinking, the running away, the phone calls in the middle of the night, the climbing the walls at the sound of a siren, the tensing up at the ring of the telephone, being at each other's throats, blaming everyone, cursing everyone, screaming at God, yelling at each other, and the desperation. Then came the finding of a very special school, sacrificing our retirement nest egg, enduring virtual bankruptcy, the retreats, the challenge groups, the uncomfortable inward journey into ourselves, facing the hard truth about ourselves and each other, changing our values and outlooks, saving our son and ourselves, and beginning to find peace.

"I'm no fairy godfather with a magic wand that can turn your pumpkin into a coach," I told her. "Forget the quick and easy cures that everyone will throw at you. There are none. But I discovered that if you walk the hard road and ask yourself the hard questions about yourself and not rest until you start getting honest answers, when it's all over you will have started entering into another world. You'll have found something no one can give you. You'll have the knowledge that you are stronger and worthier inside than you ever thought you were. And you can apply that understanding to everything you do. I know. I've been there."

Finally, I asked her, "Why did you tell me all these personal things? After all, we've known each other for only the three hours of class time. We're strangers."

She answered something like, "I don't somehow feel you are. I don't know. I just felt that I could trust you with me, and that you cared, really cared. You could understand. You were honest about yourself with us. I thought I could be honest with you about me. When one of the others asked why you teach the way you teach so differently from everyone else, you didn't come up with some cockeyed, high-sounding bullshit we would expect from a professor. You respected us enough to be honest and open. A bunch of us talked after class and none of us have ever seen a professor be human enough to bare his soul to the students. It really impressed us."

"Thank you, but I'm sorry I couldn't really help you," I apologized.

"You helped me a great deal," she answered.

"What did I do?" I asked.

"You're the first one who cared enough to listen, just really listen, and let me get it out. I think I see what I have to do. If you could deal with it and find some peace, I think I can too. I just have to find the courage. You made me feel so much better and hopeful and confident."

I'm glad she did. I went home emotionally drained and physically exhausted.

I believe with all my heart and soul that caring, not technology or technique or subject mastery, is the most powerful teaching tool at our disposal. If we can put the student at ease and let the student know we care, we'll have a better relationship. Now, don't confuse sympathy and understanding with slacking off. To the contrary, caring about each individual student makes teaching far less casual and cavalier than blindly lecturing about a subject to an amassed class and giving a standardized test that the computer grades. It's a struggle to balance understanding with being reasonably demanding of each individual student. But if we care — if we stop talking enough to learn how to listen — no matter what we demand, the student is more likely to trust us and do what we're asking. I have seen over and over and over again that to be acutely sensitive to and understanding of students is the hammer and saw of teaching, that caring more about how they feel and think outside the classroom than how they answer a question or what they got on a quiz at times almost has a healing effect.

I think part of the public dismay with education is the almost total loss of close human contact. Professors are almost totally concerned with asking of the student, "What do you know?" So rarely do they care enough to ask, "Who are you?" The students are more than what they do. They are more than an I.D. number, a name on a seating chart or in a roll book, a tuition payment, or an entry on a grade sheet or transcript. There's heart and soul and personality. They come into class with distracting and debilitating economic, social, psychological, and spiritual issues.

Nothing proclaims this louder than an exercise I run about the second or third day of each class. It's part of the introductory bonding and trusting "stuff" I do for about a week or more at the beginning of each class. It's a simple exercise. I have the students draw two intersecting, perpendicular lines on a sheet of paper. At each point of the compass, they write a word that expresses how they feel at that particular moment. Next, I ask them to list five personal concerns they have in their lives at the moment, marking the most urgent of the five. Finally, I ask them to write a few-sentence statement about what they were thinking about at that moment. Then, they discuss the words and the reasons for these words with the members of their groups. Finally, I ask them to voluntarily share with the rest of the class. And many do it.

This exercise usually offers one of the most heart-rending insights into the students. For the past few days, I've been thinking about the meaning of the results of this exercise as well as the first journal entries as I work to get to know my students on a personal level. I will not deny that they have made me sigh forlornly more than once or brought a tug to my heart and a tear to my eyes.

Of the 43 students in the class, 38 wrote two or more words associated with depression, stress, or tension! They wrote words like: sad, concerned, confused, distrustful, anxious, stressed out, melancholy, frightened, angry, scared, worried, depressed, nervous, lazy, homesick, lonely, tense, apprehensive, impatient, lost, worthless, unsure, incapable, uncertain, hurting, worn, hollow, weak, helpless, limited, doubt, distracted, and shallow.

Of those 43 students, 33 had three or more immediate non-academic concerns: pregnancy, parents, girlfriends, boyfriends, wives, husbands, children, housing, finances, illness, and jobs.

But listen to what's going on in these students' lives and what's weighing heavily, like the proverbial rock, on their hearts and souls:

"I wonder if my folks know how to encourage anyone?"

"I was always told I couldn't get anything right."

"Everyone is telling me what's good for me and what to do. No one trusts me to make my own decisions."

"My husband is in Korea and I can't stop thinking and worrying about him."

"My folks and I just plain and simple hate each other, and I don't know what I did to deserve such shitty treatment."

"My father, the holier-than-thou preacher, disowned me and kicked me out of the house because I'm dating an African American. So much for Christian love and charity."

"I am battling my fear of speaking with strangers. I've got to overcome this anxiety if I'm going to be a teacher."

"If I try to get ahead, all my so-called friends call me a whitey. If I lay back, I'm called a dumb nigger. It's a constant bitch."

"All I've been taught is to distrust people. I guess I am anti-social, but I don't want to be. It's affecting everything. My classes, my job, and my relationship with my boyfriend.

I'm afraid I'm going to lose him and everything else if I don't find someone to help change me."

"I am frustrated trying to be a mother, go to school, be a wife, clean the house, cook the meals, be at my husband's sexual beckoning. It's just too much, but I want to make something of myself and stop being everyone else's slave and getting no support doesn't help."

"My husband is jealous and scared that if I get a degree, I'll be smarter than he is and will leave him. I have to constantly reassure him. It's a tough distraction."

"I just pure and simple don't like myself and that makes everything suffer."

"I have a speech impediment. It's an endless battle. I've been reserved for years because of this. I feel so self-conscious about what others will think."

"I have a neat, safe bubble. I want out. But I'm so afraid to pop it and expose myself."

"I am struggling with the memories of a dysfunctional family with a father who was a weekend drunk and who tried to commit incest with all his daughters while my mom didn't do a damn thing about it. I'm 49 and I still feel so dirty and guilty after all these years."

"I'm homesick and miss my daddy and mommy."

"These days are especially hard. I just found out my dad is not my real father. Having my mother lie to me all my life has ruined my ability to believe and trust anyone."

"Our refrigerator is broke. We desperately need one. We have a new baby that my husband cares for while I'm at school. But we don't have no money."

"Things are rough at home because my husband doesn't enjoy his job and he brings his irritations into the house and takes it out on us and the kids."

"I don't want to become the drunken, doped-up person I was at FSU. This is my chance and I'm afraid I will screw up again."

"I'm so afraid my dad will die. He has diabetes real bad and is going down hill real fast, but he wants me here to better myself. I am so scared I am shaking."

"I'm 21. I'm diabetic, but my attitude sucks. I don't care what happens. I really do because I just married a wonderful guy, but I'm just pissed at God for doing this to me."

"My mind is everywhere but here. I just found out that my boyfriend has been f—g my best friend behind my back. It really hurts. What did I do to deserve this? I'm so depressed. I can't go two minutes without thinking about it."

"I've been out of school for 20 years. I don't know if I can cope."

"I'm going through my parents' divorce. It's shattering, and killing my brother and sister. Can't think of anything else."

"My back is killing me a lot. I got hit by a DUI, am six months pregnant, can't take anything for the pain, just have to suffer through it."

"I want so much for this baby to improve things between me and my husband. I am so afraid that even after I have the baby I'll get divorced and be alone."

"I'm a single mom and my ex is trying to get the kids away from me."

"I've got to stop being down on myself and build up some self-esteem."

"Everyone tells me to act like an adult and they treat me like a child. I'm not sure what that means or how to do it."

"I worry, worry, worry, so much, I think too much, about grades. I don't have time to learn, but I need them to get into law school."

"I am the first in my family to go to college. Everyone has such high expectations of me. I am so afraid of failing them."

"My best friend just got killed by a damn DUI. Cut down by some drunken, redneck asshole. He was going to be an engineer. I just helped bury him. He ain't going to engineer nothing anymore. Why should I give a shit about anything? What's all this stuff for anyhow?"

"I'm a struggling Christian. I have been reborn, but I have a heavy heart that my heart is not pure. I don't think I am worthy of my Savior."

How could anyone not be touched by these struggles? Here are 33 students out of 43 who have expressed their inner feelings on the second day of class. The things they have talked about are about their personal experiences. They are very powerful. They're common, daily experiences. That's heavy stuff — real heavy. The kind of anxiety these students have expressed preys on them, distracts them, quiets them, stunts them, wilts them.

So many students are from dysfunctional families and dysfunctional school systems. It's humble and frightening to think that sometimes the compassionate teacher is the closest they have come to having some kind of support. Yet if we're deaf to what the students are saying about themselves, with word or gesture or even silence, we become blind to why they do what they do. And when we become blind, we become uninvolved, cold, cynical, and callous.

If you talk to the students who sit in the classes, and listen, you'll hear that the number one concern is something like "my professor is not the kind of person I want a teacher to be." I hear and read all the time such comments like: "She doesn't listen to me," "He doesn't give a damn if I'm there or not," "I'm just a number or a name," "She doesn't even know who I am," "He never treats me as a person," "He just talks and ignores us," "None of us get any respect in the class."

What students do, or don't do, should not be a trigger merely to say coldly, "They don't know" or "They can't do it" or "They don't belong." It should be a trip wire to ask, "What's going on in your life?" It should be a clue to ask that unusual question of "Who are you?" and then to say, "Tell me about yourself." I think "touch" and "feel" are education's real professional secrets. To ignore this truth is educational neglect. We just can't lecture, not lift up our eyes, treat students as background to our profession, listen to their questions and comments as if they were static that interferes with our brilliant oration, and walk out of the room. So many of us haven't made the time to listen to their fears. We've been too busy talking, working on our committees, researching and writing, and deliberately avoiding. We must take the time to get to know the students, how those students live, what their values are, and what their social support is like. If I don't know that a student is worried about her father's health and he may die, I will be less effective in teaching her and she will be less likely to learn.

I probe the students as if each was a mystery. I'm not, however, a Sherlock Holmes or an Ellery Queen who can solve every riddle. But I do want to recognize them and understand them as best I can because my understanding, perception, and imagination will affect the way I relate to the students. It's so easy for us to say what a student knows and describe what a student does or does not do. We all can do that blindfolded, with one hand tied behind our backs while standing on our heads. All too many of us merely look at a lack of information and a lack of skills and ignore what the student feels. It's the difference between merely observing that "Johnny can't read" and realizing that "Everyone is telling Johnny he is not smart enough to read." The problem is not that Johnny can't read — it's that he believes what everyone is telling him and doesn't try to see how much he really can read.

I think we have grossly underestimated the attitudes with which students confront themselves, their lives, and their education. We have consequently grossly ignored the impact such attitudes have on how students do in a class or during their entire college career, not to mention their lives. What kind of person they are and what they are feeling about themselves and others filters what they read and hear and do.

All of this, then, raises the question for all of us. Do we want to get into the soul and heart, as well as the head, of the student? Do we have the generosity to do this, the desire to do this, the patience to do this, the strength to do this? If we don't, maybe we ought to sell shoes!

Have a good one.

Thursday, 8 September 1994

ON EDUCATION

*N*ursery rhymes. That's what I was thinking about as I glided through the streets of Valdosta late this morning in the delightful cool air. I was thinking about one particular rhyme. I modified it so that it goes like this: "The five little kittens had worn the wrong mittens and they began to cry. 'Oh, mommy dear. Oh, mommy dear, the wrong mittens we have worn.' 'What? Worn the wrong mittens? You naughty kittens! Change them or you shall not get any pie!'"

As I repeated that verse over and over like a metronome, I started getting hotter and hotter. The five little kittens were five teachers in a Texas school system that treats all its teachers like little dependent children, and whose teachers apparently act like meek kittens rather than the professionals that they are. The system has a dress code for its teachers. Well, for you who don't know the story, it seems that five of them broke the code and they were sent to the principal's office. I can see him now: sitting pompously upright behind his desk. On the other side of the desk, sitting shoulder to shoulder, hands clasped in their tight laps, are five frightened teachers. He leans over and starts shaking his head and wagging his finger at them and lecturing them about how the "proper" clothing makes them better teachers, how they have to set the "proper" example of behavior and decorum. Why, if they wore the wrong clothes, who knows what moral decay could erupt among the students! Law and order in the halls would deteriorate into anarchy. Classroom discipline would disintegrate.

To avoid such predictions of chaos of "biblical proportions," the principal then sent the teachers home to their mommies and daddies, no doubt accompanied by a note, for a change of clothing. And the teachers, for fear that they would lose their pie, like dutiful children meekly went home to change. I wonder if such mindless obedience qualifies them for merit pay in that system. I couldn't believe my ears, any more than could the head-shaking Tom Brokaw believe what he was reading. And I wondered, how could these teachers now teach anything in their classes but control, order, and submissiveness? How could they help the students to learn self-worth when they have stripped themselves of it? How could they demand anything other than conformity when they have succumbed to it? How can they promote individual creativity and imagination when they have surrendered their individuality? How can they command respect from their students or even respect their students or even respect themselves if they not only are treated as half adults and half children, but allow themselves to be treated in such undignified manner?

Now, this may be too harsh of a judgment, and there may be more to the story. But when this story hit the national news services, I thought about what people must think about teachers and the superficial concerns of our educational system. All over Tom Brokaw's face was written ridicule. "With all of education's ills," his smirk said, "this is all they have time to bother with? This silly stuff is the best they can do?" It is little wonder that so many people have diminished respect for teachers and the credibility of education has fallen so low.

Now, this may be an extreme case, but I think it is symptomatic of the state of education and indicative of many of the attitudes at all levels — from K through university — that play as obvious and subtle varieties on this theme. I'm wondering what so many of those involved with education — parents, members of boards of education, administrators, teachers — ask of themselves and other people. They say they offer guidance, but do they have courage to lead? They say they offer enrichment, but do they have the courage to grow? They say they offer new horizons, but do they have the mettle to challenge? They say they offer growth, but do they take risks? They say they offer expertise, but do they have vision? They say they deal with people, but do they make time for a single person? They say they're preparing the future leaders, but do they relinquish control?

Confusion reigns in our ranks because we are guilty of committing the sins of redefinition. We define standardized scores and called it "intelligence"; we define classroom performance and call it "potential"; we define grades and call it "achievement"; we define awards and honors and call it "wisdom"; we define tests and call it "learning"; we define majors and call it "professional"; we define GPAs and call it "worth."

It is customary to blame society for the ills of education. We say that society's judgment of education is determined by budgets, test scores, grades, and job-getting. We say that society interprets education myopically in terms of acquisition of facts and display of skills. Yet what do so many of us say in reply? In our rush to gain respectability in this age of measurement and accountability, we prance around as social scientists, "jargonizing" our speech, talking in lifeless bookish scholarship, displaying test scores, and imposing dress codes for teachers. We expunge the poetry and celebration of our craft as well as the faith in our students, ourselves, and our colleagues. We dress out the body of education so that we strip its bones of the intimate flesh that proclaims that education is a human activity involving intriguing and complex real people with real names having real hopes and dreams and strengths and fears and frailties. And we are left with an education that is so skeletal, so institutionalized, so pedagogical, so guarded, so submissive. On the whole, students do not think that education is an exciting event or an expanding experience or an enjoyable occurrence. That is more than a shame; it's a tragedy. But don't blame society. So many educators grovel at society's feet, begging for pittances, patronizing the writers of checks, and saying whatever we think society wants to hear rather than what it should hear.

It would be more honest to blame education for its own ills. Education is on the defensive because it has become so dull, fossilized, oppressive, insipid, and, at times, irrelevant. There is no surrogate for commitment, no substitute for a sense of mission, no alternative to love. I am always hurt and stunned by the almost universal surprise students display when a teacher cares for them and respects them as individual human beings. When love of learning is replaced by habit of presentation, when reverence for the craft is replaced by pedagogy, when calling is replaced by dogma, when mission is replaced by discipline, when feeling is replaced by structure, when education loses the vitality of a living fountain, and when educators speak to students and to each other in the name of authority rather than with the voice of support, understanding, and compassion, the message and purpose of education become confusing and shallow, if not meaningless, and certainly not respectful.

Education has lost sight of the person of the teacher as well as the person of the student. It has become an impersonal affair, an imbalanced intellectual endeavor, an institutional discipline, a business operation, a fractious loyalty to a discipline rather than a unifying commitment to a craft, and simply a vocational training ground for a job. Education can no longer handle teaching and learning that is compatible with the truth and wholesomeness of the human being. It operates and survives on the noisy and visible level of activities and instant evaluation rather than in the shrouded stillness of commitment and long-term growth. Education means what is done intellectually rather than what comes about spiritually and emotionally. The chief virtue is performance rather than conviction. Inwardness is ignored. Attitude is cast aside. The values of humility, honesty, pride, integrity, and excellence are suborned. The spirit is a myth. The students and teacher treat themselves and each other as if they were spiritless machines.

We are too concerned with things and appearances. It is not buildings that are important; it is what goes on inside of them that is. It is not classrooms that are important; it is what goes on inside of them that is; it is not what teachers do or wear in the classroom that is important; it is what goes on inside of the teachers that is. Education without caring, without a soul, without spirit, without purpose beyond subject matter is as viable as a person with a brain but without a heart. Pedagogy, technology, and techniques are no substitute for love and caring. Scores, budgets, and grades are no substitute for meaning and purpose. But who is proclaiming this to the public? To the contrary, education has fallen as a willing victim to the belief that the real is only that which is capable of being seen and measured: SAT, ACT, LSAT, GMAT, IOWA, heavier content courses, longer school days, longer school terms, and dress codes.

Yet the failure, as grossly evidenced in Texas, to realize the fallacy of such substitution seems to be common in our educational institutions. We will not reform education because we don't address the essence of education. Education is not a rearrangement of chairs; it's not the introduction to new technologies; it's not more standardized tests; it's not more of the teach-to-the-test syndrome; it's not a grab bag of presentation tricks. Maybe this is the more urgent challenge and task facing us educators: to recognize, acknowledge, and save the inner person of the student and teacher — to remind ourselves that we are a duality of mysterious grandeur and a mass of measurable, self-righteous dirt, both of which should be served by education, neither of which can be ignored. Education is as much a soul craft as a brain craft. I have always said, and will constantly repeat, that education is an inward journey, not a classroom performance. It's about changing character, behavior, and attitude; it's about growing and changing, not just performing. Teach students to become principled and purposeful, and meaningful achievement, not just passing a test or getting a grade, will follow. High grades and test scores do not generate excellent professionals, good citizens, and caring people. There are a lot of good people around without good grades. Honors students are not necessarily honors people. Just look at the Keatings and Boeskys of this country. Look at those physicians who tamper with data in breast cancer studies. Look at the cadets involved in the recent cheating scandal at the Naval Academy. Look at those involved in Watergate, Contragate, Irangate, and any other gate you can think of. They were not dummies. They were bright students, achievers, graduates in the top of their classes. The people involved in these scandals were not high school dropouts. But they were character dropouts.

This is my most important thought as a teacher. Our education must depend upon our appreciation of the reality of the splendor of thought, of the dignity of wonder, and of the reverence of the individual. We each have a stake in the life of each and every student as well as in each other as human beings. The true meaning of an education is outside the classroom, beyond the campus, aside from the job; its purpose lies in every facet of a person's life, throughout that person's life. We have a stake not in teaching students more information, but to ensure that they learn to live truer lives; we have a stake not just to teach them to succeed materially in the world, but to see that they learn how to make it a better world.

The difficulty is that this idea does not offer a Band-Aid remedy. It is not a quick fix. It's not presented by Speedy Alka Seltzer with educational fast, fast, fast relief. It's not glitzy; it's not politically "sexy." It can't be preached, and it cannot be imposed from the outside by others. It has to come from within. It has to be lived by each of us. It has to be discovered by each of us. It must be experienced. And having a dress code for teachers won't do it for us, or for the students, or, ultimately, for society.

Have a good one.

Monday, 19 September 1994

TEACHING PORTFOLIOS

A lot of people would describe this morning as the beginning of a warm, ugly, and dreary yukker of a day. Though I sing like a frog, I am somewhat like Gene Kelly. I love to walk in the rain, especially this quiet, almost lazy rain in which drops of water seem to want to forever float in the air and are forever reluctant to fall and end their journey. It's a rain that is somewhere between an indecisive quiet drizzle and a determined noisy downpour. This kind of rain has a subtle rejuvenating quality. It brings a sense of freshness and cleanliness to the air as it softly washes away yesterday's dust and grime. It has a muted music of the raindrops faintly hitting surfaces that makes a person want to think afresh.

To tell you the truth, I have been thinking afresh for nearly the last two weeks, as we of the Jewish faith have worshipped during what we call the Days of Awe, the eight days that begin with the Jewish New Year, Rosh Hashana, and end with the Day of Atonement, Yom Kippur. Not being religious in the sense of being a ritualist or ceremonialist, I always find myself approaching these holidays somewhat like an unprepared passive participant, coming to read the words and enjoy the music and surprisingly emerging in a deeply involved reflective mood. Without getting theological, this time is a period of spiritual and moral self-reflection, self-examination, recognition, acknowledgement, resolution, and, hopefully, subsequent action.

As I walked this morning, I slowly found myself making a connection between this time of reviewing my spiritual and moral portfolio in synagogue and the reviewing and revision of my teaching portfolio in my office. I think it was partly because the beginning of the quarter next week is on my mind. I am anxious, expectant, and excited about that first day of class, when I and the students meet each other for the first time and size each other up. My heart pounds and the juices start to flow quicker at this time, as they do every time I go into class. Without that tension that creates an alertness and sensitivity to those around me, my teaching would be controlled, predictable — and flat. In anticipation of dealing with new challenges, I have been psyching myself up, reviewing my experiences of the past year, rereading student journals, and going over my teaching portfolio and updating it.

I think this connection between my worship and teaching was also triggered by something that was said at the introductory faculty meeting of the College of Arts & Sciences last week. One of the passing items on the agenda was a slight push to urge faculty to voluntarily create their own teaching portfolios. The limited emphasis was the purpose that a portfolio would serve to strengthen the applications for promotion and/or tenure. As the assistant to the vice president of academic affairs was talking, I started to think of a nursery rhyme. The inference was that the teaching portfolio was a way for faculty to become academic Little Jack Horners. As a counterpart to the scholarly résumé, the portfolio would be a Christmas pie into which a professor could put his or her thumb, pull out a plum, and proclaim to the department and college promotion and tenure committees, "What a good teacher am I."

Now don't get me wrong. I don't think there's anything wrong with that. In fact, maybe the end justifies the means, because I think this approach might be the only way to get young, reluctant, research-oriented faculty involved in the process of self-evaluation and self-examination about teaching. But once the limited, pragmatic, self-centered, and protective plateau of promotion or tenure has been reached, then what? Is the portfolio to be put on the shelf to be forgotten, only to be dusted off for the next time a promotion or tenure review occurs? In the interim, what happens? Is it business as usual? Are the lecture notes allowed to yellow? Do the cobwebs begin to gather? Does just punching the "time clock" start? What happens to purpose, meaning, and goals? Is there reflective life after promotion, or, especially, after tenure?

"Why," I remember thinking to myself, "if this is the purpose of a portfolio, would I, with tenure and at the top of the promotion ladder, want to waste my time to create something to achieve what I already have?" Yet I have a portfolio. I have been gathering examples of material for the last three years that reflect what I believe about teaching and how I teach. It was only last year that I had created a somewhat formal "teaching portfolio." I am constantly examining it and updating it and fiddling with it each quarter.

I don't think there is any one form of a portfolio that is better than another. It is a very personal statement dictated by individual personality, teaching philosophy, style, and technique. Mine is rather large and extensive. In it, I have enclosed many items. In its opening pages are unsolicited personal letters written to me by students. I do this because I think it is far more important to see what students think and have learned rather than what I think and how I have taught. Then follows: a statement of my educational philosophy; a statement of my teaching principles; a copy of a sample syllabus; copies of "stuff" exercises, those essential bonding and trust things we do in class in an attempt to form a learning community; a sample student journal that a student has given me permission to use; slides of samples of bonding shield projects; videotapes of the class in operation, formed in triads, taking quizzes, engaged in discussion; slides, audio cassettes, and tapes of final exam projects; and, of course, a disc containing the entire collection of Random Thoughts. In the last pages, in the back of the portfolio as a sort of afterthought, is my professional résumé and a sample of a publication or two. I place my résumé last because I don't think research has much relationship to teaching.

I have a portfolio because I think that creating, maintaining, and constantly revising one has a higher purpose. For me, the portfolio is a type of self-imposed evaluation process in which I struggle to consider honestly what I want my professional life to be and what I think my attitudes toward myself and the students ought to be. I think it takes courage to trust this evaluation process in which a teacher discusses his or her character, ability, and activities. When I started gathering material for the portfolio, I found myself beginning protectively, rationalizing any shortcomings or overestimating any strengths; I dreaded being completely honest with myself for fear of finding flaws. It required an enormous amount of time spent in introspection as I took a close inward look at myself and what I did. This isn't instant Lent! It is a very intense and ongoing, but extraordinarily worthwhile, experience. It's an experience that constantly gives me food for thought and material on which I can reflect, and it serves as a catalyst for personal and professional growth. I think maybe this may be the essential meaning of the portfolio: to lay the groundwork for the time ahead and future goals by looking behind and pointing out past deficiencies and inadequacies as well as successes and strengths; to reflect on what you've learned; and then, to point to new experiences and challenges. After all, significant growth follows this cycle of reflection and action.

I have heard smirking and grumbling here on my campus and at conferences over teaching portfolios. Professors have complained about having to "tout myself," of being forced to "lay yourself bare," of being reluctant to "promote myself" and "proclaim myself." "It's like being my own professional agent," I overheard a professor say somewhat disparagingly as she emerged from a conference session on portfolios. Yet, isn't that what we do, promote ourselves, and isn't that what we are, our own agent, when we prepare our own scholarly résumé, when we present conference papers touting the results of our research efforts, when we apply for grants, when we seek promotion or tenure, or when we search for a position? I have been in many conference sessions where many a professor in the audience has unhesitatingly engaged in discussion for the sole purpose of promoting himself or herself. I have read many a review that likewise was seized by the reviewer to proclaim himself or herself at the expense of the author whose book was being reviewed.

In one significant respect, a teaching portfolio is not an oddity. Like my scholarly résumé, it is an acceptably and individually self-centered, introspective celebration of myself, not of the students, the classroom, the campus, or academia in general. It is a time when I turn into myself.

At the same time, a teaching portfolio is an oddity for professors. In a portfolio, professors are asked to reflect on, articulate about, and describe something that they do not do a lot of, have thought relatively little about, and have seldom identified themselves with. In a scholarly résumé, I merely list past accomplishments and rest on those laurels. It's a snapshot in which are frozen past activities. In a teaching portfolio, I do more than list. I describe, explain, evaluate, and offer a vision. The portfolio is more of a motion picture. It has the difficult objective and profound purpose of bringing out the potential ability in each of us rather than merely relating past accomplishments. It is the result of the processes of self-reflection, self-examination, identification, admission, resolution, and application. In one way or another, it addresses some fundamental questions: Who am I? What are the purposes and meaning and goals of what I do? Where do I want to be? Who do I want to be? Am I getting there? Why am I doing what I'm doing? How can I do better? It is a swatch that is taken from the fabric of my classes. It shows the patterns that I have striven to weave between my spirit, my emotion, my intellect and my subject; between me, the students and the subject; and between the students' emotion, intellect, spirit, and the subject.

Preparing a portfolio, then, like preparing a résumé, is an activity in which it's acceptable to be egocentric — but, unlike a scholarly résumé, only if we sincerely approach the portfolio with an air of constructive self-criticism. It forces each of us to go from a non-descriptive, "Oh, you know what I mean" statement about what goes on in our classes to a specific articulated statement, "This is what I mean." It enters the inner sanctum of the class-room and demonstrates, "This is how I have done it," and ends up with a critical, "But it could have been better and this is how I strive to do better."

The higher goal, however, is not to create a portfolio for someone to examine once a year or once every few years. The real purpose is to examine yourself constantly, to emerge from the process of creating or redoing the portfolio as a better, more aware person and teacher than when you started out. It's a form of journaling. It's not an easy process. It is one of those things that is far easier said than done, but it is a powerful thing to do. I think writing and gathering material to exemplify what you have written is different from thinking. When I write, more comes out on paper. Writing somehow forces me to be far more introspective, and it makes me consider my actions and inactions in greater detail. It sure makes me more honest with myself. In some ways, the creation of a teaching portfolio was a victory over fear. I think the troubles we encounter in the confrontation of and conquest of ourselves pale next to anything this process might be compared with. Writing is like asking for reactions and feedback from myself, not to mention from others. It helps me to focus on the truth of my observations and takes me to task on how I may be evading the truth, rationalizing, or making excuses. I find that, as I ponder what I have to put together or alter for my portfolio, I ask myself why I am including this or taking this out or changing this or rethinking that. For me, it was at first a separation process of principles and conviction from ego. Now, it is a constant, self-imposed rethinking of those convictions and their application. Tough as it may be, creating a portfolio is a highly optimistic activity. It certainly is a constructive one. It says that deep down, we believe we can succeed to improve and that we can take the tribulations of self-examination and do something constructive with them. It reflects an attitude that struggles to cast aside the thinking that says, "Of what concern is all this to me?" It promotes the idea that the entire class, campus, and academia are dependent upon each of us; that we are struggling to do our share to make some improvements in our lives and thereby in the lives of those with whom we come into contact; that we are seeking to supply something that is missing; and that we want to leave the world a little better for our stay in it.

A teaching portfolio reminds me that, for all the goodness and success I have experienced during the past year, there is still a heck of a lot of room for improvement. I have not yet attained that elevated position as the perfect teacher that I seek because I do not have the qualities of perfection. And that should not allow me to delude myself into that stagnating type of thinking that there is no room for change and growth.

The introspection that comes with preparing a portfolio or revising it is part of our quest for improvement. It tells us what we are doing in thought and action. In this sense, the mere act of preparing a portfolio is an act of trying to improve; relying on past accomplishments and reputation is not. Doing nothing, sitting on past laurels, is, then, the opposite of striving to be the best teacher you can be. That puts the burden of true reflection on us. We must take the initiative and act on it. We have this responsibility as teachers: of looking within, analyzing what we see, resolving to do better, figuring out how to do it, and then doing it. All these things are within the range of what we can and must do.

True and honest reflection leads to movement. It makes a change from what was to what might be. A sincerely created portfolio is a form of becoming, creating a newer person out of the older one, rearranging the components and producing a newer and improved version — a teacher capable of saying and meaning: "I want to be the best I can be."

Have a good one.

Wednesday, 5 October 1994

WHAT AN EDUCATION
BOILS DOWN TO

It was last Friday. I was sitting with some first-year students from my classes in the Union, sipping a cup of coffee, sucking on a Tootsie Pop, and small talking about the rigors of adjustment during their first few weeks on campus. Somehow, we got around to the seminal questions of why they were in college and why I am a teacher and teach the way I do.

"Aren't we here to get a job?" one student asked.

"Partly, but there's life besides a job," I replied.

"We're here to get information and facts," another student added.

"Maybe, but that's what libraries are for," I parried.

This duel went on for a bit. After a time, one of the students issued me a challenge in mock frustration. "So if you had to get to the point — no rambling, boring bullshit — and had to tell us in one sentence what you think this whole place, every course, every major, every prof — everyone — should be about and how it should help us in everything we do," she posed, "what would you say?"

"Where'd you come up with that one?" I asked. "You a reincarnation of a Chinese emperor?"

They looked at me. I told them about the emperor who commanded his advisors, upon pain of death, to come up with a single sentence that would explain all things and apply to all situations. I told them that I needed a lot of time to think about it.

"We'll be considerate," one of the other students commanded. "Your assignment is due Wednesday! We'll meet you back here. No death sentence, but if you can't do it and don't have an answer, you have to keep us supplied with Tootsie Pops for the rest of the quarter."

Today is Wednesday, and this is what I will tell them. Actually, I've got two variations of the same answer:

    1. Don't copy "what"; ask "why?"

2. This place boils down to acquiring the ability, desire, confidence, and courage to question the answers, not mouth them.

Think I've satisfied their assignment? I hope so. I don't want to keep buying them Tootsie Pops. That could be expensive.

Have a good one.

Monday, 17 October 1994

WHAT BEING A TEACHER BOILS DOWN TO

There's a nip in the air down here in south Georgia. It's delightful. As I went out walking along the dark streets this morning, I didn't have to think about wading through the humidity, inhaling the gnats, or waving off attacking mosquitoes. I probably wouldn't have noticed them anyway, because for the last week I have been struggling with another challenging assignment that those "annoying" and "inquisitive" first-year students gave me.

I had met them in the Union a week ago Friday with my answer to their question about what an education boils down to. I have to say that they were impressed. We talked about it. I have to admit that I was feeling quite pleased with myself. They thought that they had caught me, but I had wiggled out of their trap.

Then, from out of the blue, just as we were getting up from the table to go to our classes, one of the students impishly said, "I'll give you an A on this assignment. But you're not finished. Here's the next one: If that's what you think an education boils down to, then tell us what you think being a teacher boils down to. I'll be kind. You can use TWO sentences this time. No more. It's due in a week, Friday at 10 a.m."

"Damn," I said to them as I froze halfway out of my chair and bit so hard on the stick of the Tootsie Pop I was sucking that I nearly sheared it in half. "Who's the professor at this table?"

With a mischievous smile appearing on her face, she replied, "Today and here, I am."

"Do you all stay up at night plotting these things?" I asked in mock anger.

The only reply was, "One week."

For this past week, I could be seen walking through the halls and on campus muttering, mumbling, and quietly cursing to myself. On occasions that I don't think were accidental, I'd bump into one of the students to whom I was to report. "How's your answer coming?" they'd jokingly ask. Then, like little tormenting gnomes joyfully poking my legs with sharp pitchforks, they'd remind me, "Just four more days" or "Just three days to go." Last Thursday, I seemed to have bumped into all five, who reminded me, "See ya tomorrow morning." At those moments, I think I would have preferred the mosquitoes to those "pests."

Well, last Friday came and I didn't have an answer. I had to beg for an extension. I bribed them each with a Tootsie Pop, an orange Tootsie Pop! "OK," Mary sighed, "you have until Monday morning. But it will cost you a five-point reduction on your grade and a bag of Tootsie Pops."

"And if I can't come up with an answer?" I fearfully asked.

"A quarter's supply of Tootsie Pops for each of us," she replied without missing a beat.

"Thanks for being so understanding," I muttered in simulated annoyance.

I think it was all planned out, and I think they thought they had caught me. So did I.

Well, I could think of little else this weekend. After all, there was a lot at stake. This morning, in the sharp, dark air, I think I've finally got it. This is my answer:

> True teachers cannot be idols because idols only encourage others to act and think like them. True teachers are heroes because heroes give of themselves so that others can be encouraged to become themselves.

Think I passed this assignment? We'll see.
I report this morning to the Union. Say a prayer.

Have a good one.

Monday, 7 November 1994

THE GOOD TEACHER

*W*ell, this is the third part of the assignment my students have given me. Blast them. They are pushing me to think as hard as or maybe even harder than most of my colleagues. I think these three assignments rival, maybe surpass, my doctoral orals. I passed the assignment about what an education boils down to. They gave me an A. I also got an A on the part about what teaching boils down to. I thought I was finished with their course. But they weren't finished. They were still not satisfied. Then they asked me to describe "the good teacher." I looked at them.

"This is your final exam," one of them asserted. "It's worth 40 percent of your grade. Each exam was worth 20 percent. Attitude and effort is worth 20 percent."

I looked at them.

"Why not ask me to define 'love' or 'beauty'?" I replied in an exasperated tone.

"It's due in two weeks" was the answer, as they ignored my statement.

"Can I have more than two sentences?" I begged.

"Yes," was their compassionate reply. And then they added, as smirks began to appear on their faces, "But don't make it too long. After all, we have to read and grade it."

I've been struggling with this assignment for almost two weeks. It has almost become consuming. I've even started to dream dreams about "the good teacher." I think my problem is to weave together what I see as the two distinct, inseparable, and interrelated aspects of defining a good teacher.

There is the artistic aspect of the good teacher who enters the classroom as naturally gifted as a Mozart. This "born" talent is creative and subjective. It cannot be taught or learned. It's almost impossible to measure and it defies definition. It can't be graphed out on a chart, inventoried, piled up and counted, or in any way quantified. It's a "born" feel for the flow of the class, a native ability to recognize issues before they appear, a special rapport with students, an innate talent for knowing when to encourage or to challenge or to speak or to remain silent a bit longer or to accept.

There is also the scientific aspect of being a good teacher; of having both the conceptual and the concrete tools as an artist has brushes, paints, and canvas; of learning all the nuances of those tools. I don't know of any great artists who have come to their art unstudied and untrained and unpracticed. Leonardo da Vinci studied human corpses. Rembrandt drew sketches. Rubenstein played scale drills. Callas rehearsed arias. Astaire practiced his choreography. Benny Goodman took lessons. Good teachers, however innate their ability, do not come to their craft untrained, any more than a great ballet dancer comes on stage without knowing how to perform safely a particular step with both precision and beauty. Good teachers, artists that they are, sweat as they study the basics of their art and convert their raw ability into talent. The good teacher learns that at his or her fingertips, there are so many possibilities of what can be done in the class other than lecture and information presentation. They learn about the processes of learning, and about varied ways to introduce concepts, to involve students in their learning, to assess student progress, to utilize advances in technology, to be sensitive to the changing academic student population, and to assess themselves and their performance. They study to know all the nuances of their tools, no less than the great artists have learned the options offered by their tools — how different brushes make different brush strokes, how using different mediums or different materials creates different effects.

Well, with all that said and done, I've finally been able to put something down on paper and submit it to my "student professors." Here's my essay on my kind of a "good teacher":

In some non-descriptive, intuitive, immeasurable, non-quantitative, inexplicable way, I have begun to sense who is the good teacher and who is the journeyman that merely shows up and makes a presentation. The difference is not so much what each knows, what information each has stored in his or her brain, what knowledge each has available at his or her fingertips, or how each presents the information. It is what each brings or does not bring to the student as a human being. Being human is not an arrangement of flesh and bone. It is a way of thinking, acting, and doing. The teachers are those who rise above the others with something extra. They are competent and know their subject, but they do not identify so strongly with their discipline that they lose their humanity. They go beyond the mechanics of presentation, organizing a class, writing lectures, being prepared, making up quizzes and exams, grading performance, being prompt, and so on. They interplay with the mind, heart, and spirit, for they believe that teaching without love is both shallow and hollow, perhaps wrong and meaningless. They are "wholeness" teachers who realize that learning is not separated from other aspects of human activity. They are concerned with feelings and thoughts. They are concerned with the spirit and emotion of the student as well as the intellect, realizing that they are all interconnected and interacting parts of the same person. They believe that love and caring is good teaching, and they don't let technology or technique substitute for caring. They believe that helping students is more important than how the teacher feels and what is comfortable for him or her. They are more concerned with the learning styles of the students rather than their teaching style. They come as lovers of learning, as classroom stimulants rather than barbituates. They find benefit and the positive in all student efforts and attitudes, and they don't know what a "wrong" or "can't" is. They do not look for "students" in their classes and therefore find only individual human beings. They are more concerned with the question, "Who are you?" than the statement, "I am the professor." They are more concerned with the question, "Are you learning?" rather than the statement, "I am teaching." They are in a relationship with the students rather than with the subject, textbook, and/or class presentations. They do not entice, seduce, or threaten with penalty or reward, by popularity, by grades, or by "feeling good." They earn respect rather than exercise authority and power. They care not only about their subject, but about what goes on in the heart and soul of each student. They listen more than they talk. They proclaim far less their ideas than help students to generate theirs. Their actions are designed to meet the needs of the students, not their own.

These teachers are nurturers. For them, everyone has potential. Everyone belongs in their classes. No one is a loser. No one is poor. No one is worthless. Their classes offer every student the opportunity to succeed. Their classes are filled with the enthusiastic spirit of humility, concern, trust, care, encouragement, community, respect, challenge, growth, and dignity. Their classes are cluttered with creativity, vision, and imagination. Their classes are loving and nurturing worlds of adventure — worlds of growth, transformation, and discovery.

They are never in a comfort zone, never satisfied with themselves. They are demanding of themselves, as they are of their students. They make teaching seem so artful and effortless because they never stop working hard, never stop studying, never stop examining themselves, and never stop carefully reflecting. They struggle to understand why they became teachers and to articulate the purpose and goals of their care, and always ask, "Why do I do what I do?" They care about what goes on inside their own heart and soul and understand that they are not unending fountains of wisdom or sacred caretakers of knowledge. Boredom and routine are not their companions. They get up excited each morning and can't wait to get into the classroom. For them, teaching is a calling. They struggle not to be imprisoned in their own personal and professional ivory towers.

They are humble. For them there are no sacred cows. Change is a welcomed challenge. They leave the classroom convinced a better job could have been done. They assume responsibility when something doesn't work in class. They are sufficiently defined inwardly that they know how to say to students, "I don't know, but let's find the answer together." They are learners who realize that they teach best not what we know but what we want to learn.

They act the way they want the students to live, with a value for themselves and each other, with values greater than the selfish, competitive, material rat race. They somehow understand the spirit of each student and touch that spirit. They come closer to the students, treat them with respect as individuals, and talk about themselves as human beings. They add to the stature of the student as a thinking, feeling, contemplating person. They embark students on an unending voyage of discovering new interests and powers within themselves. They understand that education is a preparation not just for a career, but for a meaningful life. They dream big dreams — dreams not limited to the timely life of the classroom, but expansive, daring, and timeless dreams of life beyond the classroom.

That's my feeling of what a good teacher is. I'll hand in my assignment tomorrow. I hope they like it. I have to maintain my A in this course to keep my scholarship.

Have a good one.

THOUGHTS ON
RANDOM THOUGHTS

"*A*n extraordinary book. … In this volume, Louis Schmier provides us with a transformative and inspirational discussion of what we are REALLY supposed to be doing in the classroom. He leads us on a phenomenological journey into the very heart and soul of a sensitive and reflective teacher."

DALE FITZGIBBONS
Associate Professor of Management, Illinois State University

"*H*is anecdotes draw our attention dramatically to the swirling complex of individual human characteristics and feelings which fill classrooms and establish an environment which will determine whether teaching and learning have a reasonable chance to take root. … In forcing our attention to the humanity of teaching, Schmier challenges us to reconsider what education should be and to reassess our understanding of what constitutes educational success for any one individual and for the entire process.

TOM POWERS
Professor of History, University of South Carolina at Sumter

"*I*nitially, *Random Thoughts* appear to be a charming series of vignettes concerning academic life today. It is that — but much more. It is in fact concerned with renewing a humanistic approach to teaching — and life — and it is concerned with showing the obstacles to that renewal. At its core, *Random Thoughts* resonates with the traditional notion that sincerity is at the heart of every meaningful endeavor. Teaching, then is not the mere accumulation or recitation of facts, nor is it separate from the issue of character. It requires a conversation that is purposeful and compassionate. A conversation where the intellectual, the moral, and the spiritual coincide. It requires a conversation where convictions are at stake, but where compassion informs the narrative.

ARTHUR PONTYNEN
Associate Professor of Art History, University of Wisconsin-Oshkosh

" *A*t a time when so many critics of higher education are blasting the academy for what it is and is not doing, Schmier offers an extraordinarily fresh perspective. ... In the artful, thoughtful and poignant steps his students take, Schmier offers frustrated teachers everywhere a vision of how to follow learning wherever it goes, without having to forever worry about controlling and otherwise leading the pedagogical process. ... If Schmier is not the future of higher education, at least his book reveals a profound reason for suspecting that such a future exists.

DOUGLAS MACKAMAN
Assistant Professor of History, University of Southern Mississippi

" *T*his book is an important and timely addition to the national, and international, discussion of the role of higher education. It challenges us to look up from the bottom line to see the faces and listen to the voices of the students. It is not a prescription for change, but one person's experience from which we can all learn and take heart."

ROBERT CLIFT
Executive Director, Confederation of University Faculty Associations of British Columbia

"If you want to climb mountains, don't practice on mole hills."